The BIG BOOK of LOGOS

Edited by
David E. Carter

Book Design
Suzanna M.W. Brown

Production & Layout
Kristin J. Back

The Big Book of Logos

First published in 1999 in harcover by Hearst Books International
Now published by
HBI, a division of HarperCollins Publishers
10 East 53rd Street
New York, NY 10022-5299
United States of America

Paperback ISBN: 0-06-093802-1

Distributed in the U.S. and Canada by
Watson-Guptill Publications
770 Broadway
8th Floor
New York, NY 10003-9595
Tel: 800.451.1741
            732.363.4511 in NJ, AK, HI
Fax: 732.363.0338

Paperback ISBN: 0-8230-0538-0

Distributed throughout the rest of the world by
HarperCollins International
10 East 53rd Street
New York, NY 10022-5299
Fax: 212.207.7654

Published in Germany by
Nippan
Nippan Shuppan Hanbai
Deutschland GmbH
D-40549 Dusseldorf
Tel: 0211.504.8089
Fax: 0211.504.9326

Paperback ISBN: 3-931884-94-5

Printed in Hong Kong by Everbest Printing Company through Four
Colour Imports, Louisville, Kentucky.

It was a dark and stormy night.

The publisher had said, "How about doing a big book of logos—almost 400 pages, with the book in full color?"

As lightning flashed outside in the woods, casting flickering shadows on the parlor wall, David Carter paced the Persian carpet wondering how to go about gathering materials for such a book.

Suddenly, inspiration came. "We'll call the book LOGO 2000," Carter thought. Soon, designers from all over America were invited to send their best work.

More than 11,000 logos came in to be considered. After a long process of elimination, approximately 2,500 logos were chosen for this book.

And somewhere along the way, the title became **The Big Book of Logos**.

It's an appropriate title, since this is the largest logo book ever published in America.

This big book shows some of the best logo design work in America, as nearly every top design firm in the country submitted work for the book.

This comprehensive book should become a classic reference source, as designers can flip the pages and see a huge variety of styles and techniques for logo creation.

ABBOTT 1.

2.

Amtrak 3.

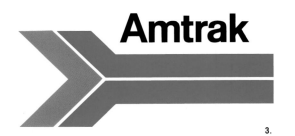
4.

HARRIS BANK 5.

6.

Harvard **Vanguard** 7.

8.

9.

10.

HARTMARX

11.

PRIMERICA

12.

 Kobrick Cendant Funds

13.

 **CALTEX**

14.

Comerica

15.

 **SAMSUNG**

16.

 **The Gillette Company**

17.

FINOVA

18.

 *caliber*

19.

(all)
Design Firm **Lippincott & Margulies**
1.
Client *Abbott*
2.
Client *Allied Corporation*
3.
Client *Amtrak*
Designer J. Gordon Lippincott
4.
Client *Guidant*
5.
Client *Harris Bank*
Designer Kenneth Love
6.
Client *Bank Atlantic*
7.
Client *Harvard Vanguard*
Designers Jerry Kuyper, Brendán Murphy
8.
Client *American Greetings*
Designers Arthur Congdon, Jack Weller

9.
Client *Handok*
Designer Kenneth Love
10.
Client *UNUM*
11.
Client *Hartmarx*
12.
Client *Primerica*
13.
Client *Kobrick Cendant Funds*
Designers Kenneth Love, Brendán Murphy
14.
Client *Caltex*
15.
Client *Comerica*
16.
Client *Samsung*
Designer Constance Birdsall
17.
Client *The Gillette Company*
Designer Constance Birdsall
18.
Client *Finova*
Designer Constance Birdsall
19.
Client *Roadway "caliber"*
Designer Kenneth Love

1.  FMC

2.  Scripps

3.  TELUS

4. SOUTHERN COMPANY

5. Continental

6.  PRAXAIR

7. DOMAIN ENERGY

8. DIMON

9. TENNECO

10. SCANA

11.

12.

13.

14.

15.

16.

17.

19.

TheStPaul

18.

INFINITI

1.

2.

3.

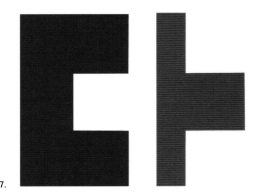

conectiv

4.

5.

THE
FITNESS CENTER
OF
EXCELLENCE

6.

7.

8.

9.

NITROMED

10.

ENRON CORP

11.

The
McGraw·Hill
Companies

12.

Pizza Hut

13.

ALSA

14.

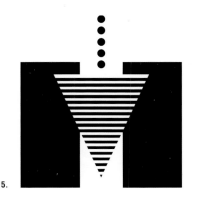

15.

1, 3, 4, 5, 11, 12, 13
Design Firm **Lippincott & Margulies**
2, 7-10, 14, 15
Design Firm **TGD Communications, Inc.**
6
Design Firm **Ted DeCagna Graphic Design**
1.
Client   *Infiniti*
2.
Client   *Borello White Printing*
Designers   Rochelle Gray, Catherine Conley
3.
Client   *Dyneon*
Designer   Rodney Abbot
4.
Client   *Conectiv (Delmarva Power)*
Designer   Constance Birdsall
5.
Client   *PPG*
6.
Client   *American Standard Corporation*
Designer   Ted DeCagna (Choice Signs)

7.
Client   *National Health Strategies*
Designers   Rochelle Gray, Eva Barsin
8.
Client   *Alexandria Chamber of Commerce*
Designers   Rochelle Gray, Leonardo Bentos
9.
Client   *Alexandra Doctor's Network*
Designers   Rochelle Gray, Trish Palasik
10.
Client   *Euromed*
Designer   Chip Griffin
11.
Client   Enron Corporation
12.
Client   The McGraw-Hill Companies
Designer   Constance Birdsall
13.
Client   *Pizza Hut*
14.
Client   *Analytical Life Science Systems Association*
Designers   Chris Harrison, Gloria Vestal
15.
Client   *Minkoff Corporation*
Designer   Rochelle Gray

1.

2.

3.

FraserPapers

4.

experian

5.

HUMANA®

6.

F L A G S T A R

7.

so1o

8.

9.

1, 3 - 7
Design Firm **Lippincott & Margulies**
2.
Design Firm **FRCH Design Worldwide (Cincinnati)**
8
Design Firm **Pentagram Design, Inc.**
9
Design Firm **Bob Rankin Design**
1.
Client *EATON*
2.
Client *Harrah's (Carnaval Court)*
Designers Eric Daniel, Gina Beckerink
3.
Client *Humana*
4.
Client *Fraser Papers*
Designer Jerry Kuyper

5.
Client *Experian (TRW)*
Designer Alex de Jánosi
6.
Client *Humana*
Designers Jerry Kuyper, Brendán Murphy
7.
Client *Flagstar*
Designer Constance Birdsall
8.
Client *Successmaker Solo*
Designers Lowell Williams, Bill Carson
9.
Client *Move It*
Designer Bob Rankin
(opposite)
Client *University Mall*
Design Firm **FRCH Design Worldwide (Cincinnati)**
Designers Juliette Fiehrer, Erik Brown

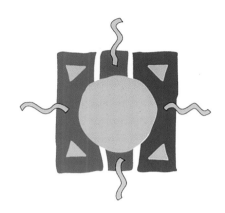

university mall

1.

Van Romer Chiropractic

2.

3.

4.

5.

GENEVA, NY
SENSATIONAL BY NATURE!

6.

7.

8.

12

9.

10.

11.

12.

13.

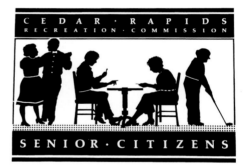

14.

15.

1, 4, 5, 8, 10, 11, 14, 15
Design Firm **Mickelson Design & Assoc.**
2, 3, 6, 7, 12
Design Firm **In House Graphic Design, Inc.**
9, 13
Design Firm **Lightspeed Commercial Arts**

1.
Client *Scheaffer Collection Agency*
Designer Alan Mickelson
2.
Client *Van Romer Chiropractic*
Designer Dennis Angelo
3.
Client *In House Graphic Design, Inc.*
Designer Dennis Angelo
4.
Client *Tunes & Tones*
Designer Alan Mickelson
5.
Client *Harmony Business Machines*
Designer Alan Mickelson
6.
Client *Geneva Area Chamber of Commerce*
Designer Dennis Angelo
7.
Client *Mobilnet Management Services, Inc.*
Designer Dennis Angelo

8.
Client *Story Time*
Designer Alan Mickelson
9.
Client *Challenge International*
Designer Michael J. Hamers
10.
Client *Cedar Rapids Recreation Commission*
Designers Mary Bendgen, Alan Mickelson
11.
Client *Cedar Rapids Recreation Commission*
Designers Mary Bendgen, Alan Mickelson
12.
Client *Morley Financial Services*
Designer Dennis Angelo
13.
Client *Institute for Change Research*
Designer Michael J. Hamers
14.
Client *Cedar Rapids Recreation Commission*
Designers Mary Bendgen, Alan Mickelson
15.
Client *Professional Reclamation Inc.*
Designer Alan Mickelson

1.

2.

3.

4.

5.

6.

7.

1 - 7
Design Firm **Kiku Obata & Company**
1.
Client *St. Louis Public Schools*
Designer Jeanna Stoll
2.
Client *Great Lakes Science Center*
Designer Kathleen Robert
3.
Client *Zaro's Bread Basket*
Designer Joe Floresca
4.
Client *City of Wildwood, MO*
Designer Amy Knopf

5.
Client *Coors Field*
Designer Todd Mayberry
6.
Client *Bluefins*
Designer Kathleen Robert
7.
Client *Simon DeBartolo Group*
Designer Todd Mayberry
(opposite)
Client *Aronoff Center for the Arts*
Design Firm **FRCH Design Worldwide (Cincinnati)**
Designers Michael Beeghly, Martin Treu, Eric Daniel

1.

2.

3.

4.

5.

ErgoCentrics, Inc.

6.

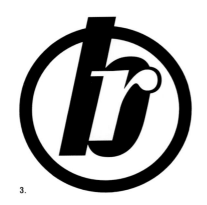

7.

8.

9.

10.

11.

12.

13.

14.

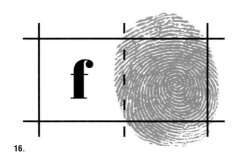

15.

16.

BEAVER COLLEGE

THE
COMMON
THREAD
1.

coaches
vs
cancer
2.

3.

Cricket Hill
4.

Doylestown Presbyterian Church
5.

6.

PERFORMING
ARTS
LEAGUE of PHILADELPHIA
7.

1 - 7
Design Firm **Art 270, Inc.**
1.
Client   *Beaver College*
Designer   John Opet
2.
Client   *Coaches vs. Cancer*
Designer   Dana Sykes
3.
Client   *HResults!*
Designer   Steve Kuttruff
4.
Client   *Cricket Hill Estate*
Designer   Steve Kuttruff

5.
Client   *Doylestown Presbyterian Church*
Designers   Pat Singer, Carl Mill
6.
Client   *Philadelphia Theatre Company*
Designer   Steve Kuttruff
7.
Client   *The Performing Arts League
              of Philadelphia*
Designer   Pat Singer
(opposite)
Client   *Aca Joe*
Design Firm   **FRCH Design Worldwide
              (Cincinnati)**
Designers   Tim Frame, Bob Swank

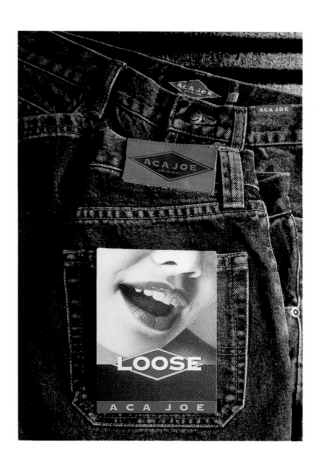

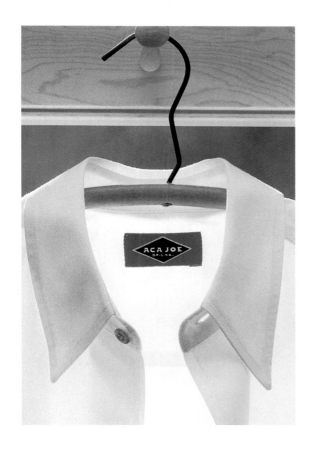

1.

2. **x** a n d **o**

3.

4.

5. O V **I** D

6.

7.

8.

9.

10.

11.

12.

B A S E B A L L

13.

14.

15.

16.

17.

1, 3, 4, 6, 7, 15, 17
  Design Firm **Yoe! Studio**
2, 5, 8, 11, 14
  Design Firm **The Leonhardt Group**
9, 10
  Design Firm **Pentagram Design, Inc.**
12
  Design Firm **Love Packaging Group**
13, 16
  Design Firm **Louis London**
1.
  Client   *Miller Brewing Co.*
  Designer   Craig Yoe
2.
  Client   *Xando*
  Designer   Candace Morgan
3.
  Client   *Jim Henson Productions*
  Designer   Craig Yoe
4.
  Client   *3-D Inc.*
  Designers   Yoe! Studio
5.
  Client   *Ovid Technologies*
  Designers   Ray Ueno, Dennis Clouse
6.
  Client   *Matinee*
  Designers   Yoe! Studio
7.
  Client   *Parachute Press*
  Designers   Yoe! Studio
8.
  Client   *Gargoyles Eyewear*
  Designers   Mark Popich, Greg Morgan

9.
  Client   *Taco Bueno*
  Designers   Lowell Williams, Bill Carson,
              Jeff Williams, Julie Hoyt,
              Marc Stephens
10.
  Client   *Thomas Hayward*
  Designers   Lowell Williams, Bill Carson
11.
  Client   *Experience Music Project*
  Designers   Candace Morgan, Ray Ueno,
              Steve Watson, Renee Sullivan,
              Greg Morgan
12.
  Client   *The Fantastic World of
              Gourmet Chocolate*
  Designers   Chris West, Brian Miller
13.
  Client   *Kirkwood Athletic Assoc.*
  Art Director David Bannecke
14.
  Client   *Lexant*
  Designer   Janee Kreinheder
15.
  Client   *Mickey & Co.*
  Designers   Yoe! Studio
16.
  Client   *Shell Oil Company*
  Art Director Sam Monica
17.
  Client   *Parachute Press*
  Designers   Yoe! Studio

1. **S P G**

2. ADVANCED LASER GRAPHICS

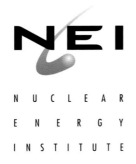

NEI

NUCLEAR
ENERGY
INSTITUTE

3.

*Global*Cable

4.

GCSS ARMY
Global Combat Support System–Army

5.

N I M I

6.

O | D | C

7.

1 - 7
Design Firm **Tim Kenney Design Partners**
1.
    Client   *Solutions Planning Group*
    Designers   Tim Kenney, Tom Snoreck
2.
    Client   *Advanced Laser Graphics*
    Designer   Tim Kenney
3.
    Client   *Nuclear Energy Institute*
    Designers   Tim Kenney, Tom Snoreck
4.
    Client   *Global Cable Consulting Group*
    Designers   Tim Kenney, Monica Banko

5.
    Client   *GRC International, Inc.*
    Designers   Tim Kenney, Moira Ratchford
6.
    Client   *NASDAQ International Market
                Initiatives (NIMI)*
    Designers   Tim Kenney, Moira Ratchford
7.
    Client   *Overseas Development Council*
    Designer   Tim Kenney
(opposite)
    Client   *Chesapeake Bagel—St. Louis*
    Design Firm **Kiku Obata & Company**
    Designer   Jane McNeely

23

 OBJECT SPACE

1.

2.

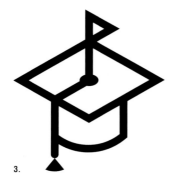

3.

AMC

THE WORLD'S LARGEST
TRADE MART/TRADE SHOW
ORGANIZATION

4.

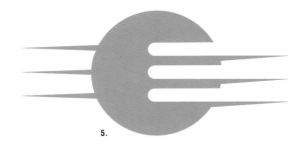

5.

6.

CONCORD
7. MALL

8.

9.

GLOBAL TRADE PARTNERS
AN AMC, INC. INITIATIVE

10.

11.

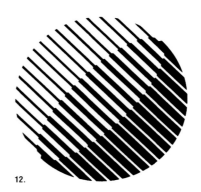

12.

AmeriHealth

14.

13.

15.

1 - 3, 6 - 9, 12, 13, 15
Design Firm **Joseph Rattan Design**
4, 5, 10, 11, 14
Design Firm **Young & Martin Design**

1.
Client *Object Space*
Designer Joseph Rattan

2.
Client *Batrus Hollweg*
Designer Joseph Rattan

3.
Client *Benton Shipp Golf Tournament*
Designer Joseph Rattan

4.
Client *AMC, Inc.*
Designers Steve Martin, Joe Alcober

5.
Client *EPTI*
Designer Steve Martin

6.
Client *Friends of WRR*
Designer Joseph Rattan

7.
Client *Concord Mall*
Designer Diana McKnight

8.
Client *Habitat for Humanity*
Designers Joseph Rattan, Greg Morgan

9.
Client *Hanaco*
Designer Joseph Rattan

10.
Client *Global Trade Partners*
Designers Ed Young, Steve Martin

11.
Client *Wesli Mancini Fabric Design*
Designer Steve Martin

12.
Client *International Broadcast Systems, Inc.*
Designer Joseph Rattan

13.
Client *Cintron Lehner Barrett*
Designer Joseph Rattan

14.
Client *AmeriHealth*
Designer Steve Martin

15.
Client *Group Gallagher*
Designers Joseph Rattan, Greg Morgan

1. S O N G S M I T H

2.

3. version x

4.

G A T E W A Y

5.

Williams Construction **6.**

7.

1, 6
Design Firm **Lauren Smith Design**
2, 4, 5, 7
Design Firm **The Graphic Expression, Inc.**
3
Design Firm **Glyphix Studio**
1.
Client *Songsmith*
Designer Lauren Smith
2.
Client *Aquatic Leisure International*
Designer Kurt Finkbeiner
3.
Client *Version X*
Designer Brad Wilder
4.
Client *Ascent Entertainment Group*
Designer Kurt Finkbeiner

5.
Client *Gateway Insurance Company*
Designer Kurt Finkbeiner
6.
Client *Williams Construction*
Designer Lauren Smith
7.
Client *Young at Art*
Designer Kurt Finkbeiner
(opposite)
Client *Dayton Mall*
Design Firm **FRCH Design Worldwide—(Cincinnati)**
Designer Michael Beeghly, Charles Aenlle, Erik Brown, Lori Seibert

DAYTON MALL

GRAPHIC PIZZA

1.

2. William Morrow and Associates

Avante

3.

ANNUITY BUYERS USA

4.

FARMLAND MORTGAGE

5.

artax

6.

ACME KAZOO CO.

7.

8. American Air Show Network

St. John's Orthopædic Services

9.

UStelcard ®

10.

Crest Graphics, Inc.

11.

Building *B* Creations

12.

EQUIBOND

13.

DANet

14.

ESPRIT

DOMESTIQUE ET INTERNAÇIONALE

15.

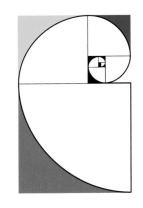

1.

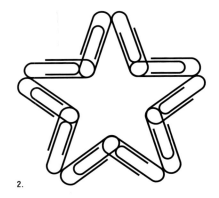

2.

3.

4.

5.

6.

7.

1, 6
　　Design Firm **DesignLab**
2 - 5, 7
　　Design Firm **Michael Lee Advertising & Design, Inc.**
1.
　　Client　　*GSH Design*
　　Designers　Kennah Harcum, Gary Henley
2.
　　Client　　*Texas Office Products*
　　Designer　Michael Lee
3.
　　Client　　*SeaSea Multi-Hulls*
　　Designers　Michael Lee, Debby Stasinopoulou
4.
　　Client　　*St. Elizabeth Hospital's Wilton P. Hebert Health & Wellness Center*
　　Designers　Michael Lee, Debby Stasinopoulou

5.
　　Client　　*Lamar University*
　　Designer　Michael Lee
6.
　　Client　　*DesignLab*
　　Designer　Kennah Harcum
7.
　　Client　　*XL Systems*
　　Designers　Michael Lee, Debby Stasinopoulou
(opposite)
　　Client　　*Harrah's (OnStage)*
　　Design Firm **FRCH Design Worldwide— (Cincinnati)**
　　Designers　Paul Lechleiter, Steve McGowan, Eric Daniel

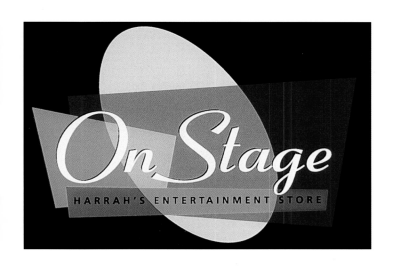

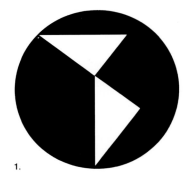

1.

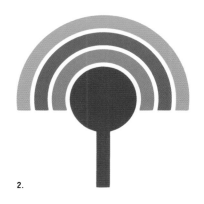

2.

3.

4.

5.

6.

Rutenberg Homes

7.

8.

PEGASUS TRAVEL 9.

 10.

meadowlark

 11.

 12.

13.

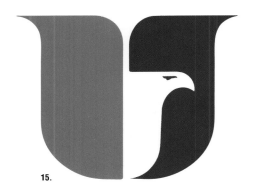 14.

15.

(all)
Design Firm **The Brothers Bogusky**
Designer   Bill Bogusky

1.
   Client   *Pan American Bank*
2.
   Client   *Raintree Homes*
3.
   Client   *Ville La Reine*
4.
   Client   *Diabetes Research Institute*
5.
   Client   *Miacord*
6.
   Client   *Shadow Wood*
7.
   Client   *Rutenberg Homes*

8.
   Client   *Deep 6*
9.
   Client   *Pegasus Travel*
10.
   Client   *Art Center*
11.
   Client   *Meadowlark Estates*
12.
   Client   *TransAmerica*
13.
   Client   *Robinson Racing Products*
14.
   Client   *Hydrotech*
15.
   Client   *University Federal Savings & Loan*

1.

LINDA
CREED
Breast Cancer
2. Foundation

3.

STRATEGIC FOCUS
CONSULTING

4.

5.

6.

BAR FOUNDATION

7. LEGACY SOCIETY

1-8
Design Firm **Art 270, Inc.**
1.
Client   *Abington Hospital*
Designers Pat Singer, Carl Mill
2.
Client   *Linda Creed Breast Cancer
          Foundation*
Designers Steve Kutruff, Sue Ströhm
3.
Client   *Strategic Focus Consulting*
Designers Carl Mill
4.
Client   *State Street Cafe*
Designers Dana Sykes, Carl Mill
5.
Client   *CVB Consultants*
Designer Carl Mill

6.
Client   *Interconnect Systems, Inc.*
Designer Carl Mill
7.
Client   *Philadelphia Bar Foundation
          Legal Society*
Designers Dianne Mill, Pat Singer,
          Sue Ströhm, Dana Breslin
8.
Client   *Asterisk*
Designer Carl Mill
(opposite)
Client   *The Minnesota Zoo*
Design Firm **Rapp Collins Communications**
Designer Bruce Edwards

8.

SOUTHWEST GOURMET
F O O D   S H O W

1.

THE RIVER WALK SAN ANTONIO

2.

alamo.com

3.

4.

5.

6.

splash down™

7.

Central Park Mall

8.

 Universal Advisory Services, Inc.

9.

10.

 SAN ANTONIO SPORTS FOUNDATION

11.

12.

13.

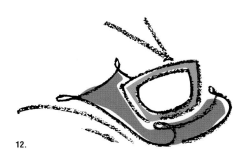

14.

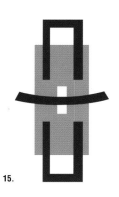

15.

1 - 11
Design Firm **Creative Link Studio, Inc.**
12 - 14
Design Firm **Nestor•Stermole Visual Communication Group**
15
Design Firm **Crimm Design**

1.
Client *Central Park Mall Southwest Gourmet Food Show*
Designers Kyle Derr, Kevin La Rue
2.
Client *Riverwalk San Antonio Video*
Designer Mark Broderick
3.
Client *Alamo.com*
Designers Drew Dela Cruz, Kyle Derr
4.
Client *Pacificare Matters on Maternity*
Designer Mark Broderick
5.
Client *Racquetball and Fitness Clubs Kidzone*
Designers Kevin La Rue, Kyle Derr, Mark Broderick
6.
Client *Origin Software*
Designers Kevin La Rue, Mark Broderick, Kyle Derr

7.
Client *Coca-Cola Southwest— Splash Down*
8.
Client *Central Park Mall*
Designers Kevin La Rue, Cheryl Abts
9.
Client *Universal Advisory Services, Inc.*
Designers Mark Broderick, Kyle Derr, Kevin La Rue
10.
Client *San Antonio Parks & Recreation JazzSalive*
Designer Mark Broderick
11.
Client *San Antonio Sports Foundation*
Designers Kyle Derr, Kevin La Rue
12.
Client *Tapestry International*
Designers Okey Nester, Jeanne Grecco
13.
Client *Millenium Pharmaceuticals*
Designers Okey Nester, Carla Miller
14.
Client *Wolper Sales Agency*
Designer Okey Nestor
15.
Client *Crimm Design*
Designer G.M. Crimm

37

1.

PLS 2.

NTCA

The Voice of Rural Telecommunications

3.

4.

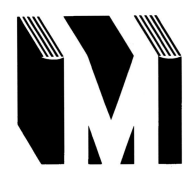

5.

ACCA
SOURCE 6.

OPASTCO

7.

1, 4, 5
Design Firm **Frank D'Astolfo Design**
2, 3, 6, 7
Design Firm **Coleman Design Group, Inc.**
1.
Client   *Alimenterics Inc.*
2.
Client   *Personal Library Software*
Designers   Amanda Grupe, Michael B. Raso
3.
Client   *National Telephone Cooperative Association*
Designers   John Nettleton, Michael B. Raso
4.
Client   *American Association of Spinal Cord Injury Nurses*

5.
Client   *Rutgers University School of Management*
6.
Client   *American Corporate Counsel Association*
Designers   Michael B. Raso, Beth Ready
7.
Client   *OPASTCO*
Designers   Amanda Grupe, Beth Ready
(opposite)
Client   *Fluoroware, Inc.*
Design Firm **Larsen Design + Interactive**
Art Director   Richelle Huff
Designer   Todd Mannes

1.

2.

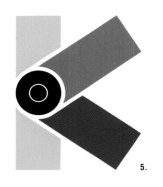

3.

4.

5.

AGRADO™

Feed Ingredient by **Solutia**

6.

7.

AQUASTAR

8.

40

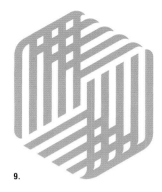

9.

10.

11.

scitex

12.

QUALITY & VALUE

13.

MERIDIAN PARTNERS

INCORPORATED

14.

OLD ORCHARD

15.

1 - 11	
Design Firm	**Stan Gellman Graphic Design**
12	
Design Firm	**Studio Ilan Hagari**
	Tel Aviv, Israel
14	
Design Firm	**Lincoln Design**
13 - 15	
Design Firm	**Berni Design**

1.
Client — *Technology Source*
Designer — Barry Tilson

2.
Client — *Marlo Graphics Inc.*
Designer — Kurt Meinecke

3.
Client — *Michael Fox, Inc.*
Designer — Stan Gellman

4.
Client — *Clipper Cruise LIne*
Designer — Barry Tilson

5.
Client — *Kohler and Sons Printing Company*
Designer — Stan Gellman

6.
Client — *Solutia*
Designer — Barry Tilson

7.
Client — *Moneta Group Inc.*
Designer — Barry Tilson

8.
Client — *Monsanto*
Designer — Barry Tilson

9.
Client — *McMichael Auman Consultants*
Designer — Barry Tilson

10.
Client — *Gellman Growth Partners*
Designer — Stan Gellman

11.
Client — *Liberty Printing Company*
Designer — Barry Tilson

12.
Client — *Scitex Corporation Ltd.*
Designers — Linda Benveniste, Yosh Kahana, Ilan Hagari

13.
Client — *Twin County Grocers, Inc.*
Designer — Jung Kim

14.
Client — *J. P. Harkins*
Designer — Thomas Lincoln

15.
Client — *Apple Valley International, Inc.*
Designer — Mark Eckstein

1.

2.

3.

4.

5.

6.

7.

1, 3, 4
  Design Firm **Sacks Design Group**
2, 5, 7
  Design Firm **Gardner Design**
6
  Design Firm **Lumina Studios**

1.
  Client   *Overland Trading Co.*
  Designers   Jaye H. Sacks, Kathryn Klein
2.
  Client   *Cowley County Community College*
  Designers   Bill Gardner, Brian Miller
3.
  Client   *Feldman Photography*
  Designer   Jaye H. Sacks

4.
  Client   *Keller Photography*
  Designer   Jaye H. Sacks
5.
  Client   *Cat Hospital of Wichita*
  Designer   Bill Gardner
6.
  Client   *Overland Trading Co.*
  Designers   Jaye H. Sacks, Kathryn Klein
7.
  Client   *Anastasia Marie Cosmetics*
  Designer   Brian Miller
(opposite)
  Client   *Hilbert Interactive Group*
  Design Firm **Hal Apple Design**
  Designers   Jason Hashmi, Hal Apple

42

HILBERT
INTERACTIVE
GROUP, LLC

Jeff Hilbert
625 13th Street
Manhattan Beach CA 90266
Phone 310 796-0207
Fax 310 796-0217
jeff.hmm@ix.netcom.com

1.

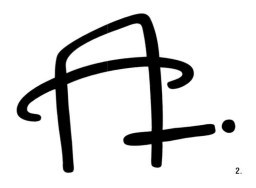

2.

3.

4.

5.

6.

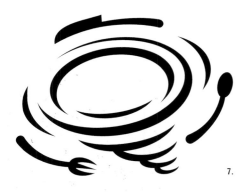

7.

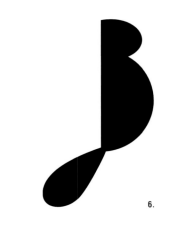

8.

THE CAT

9.

B R A V O ▪ B U S

10.

ARTISAN

11.

RED MOUNTAIN PARK

14.

13.

15.   **THE MERIT SYSTEM**

12.

(all)
Design Firm **DogStar**

1.
| Client | *University of Montevallo Falcons* |
| Designers | Jeff Martin, Rodney Davidson |

2.
| Client | *Cigar Aficionado Magazine* |
| Designer | Rodney Davidson |

3.
| Client | *Billy's* |
| Designers | Vicki Schenck-Atha, Rodney Davidson |

4.
| Client | *AIGA— (jacket icon for) Ecology of Design* |
| Designers | Brian Collins, Rodney Davidson |

5.
| Client | *Birmingham Ecoplex* |
| Designers | Charles Black, Stefanie Becker— Gillis Adv.; Rodney Davidson— DogStar |

6.
| Client | *Beaver Construction* |
| Designers | Terry Slaughter—Slaughter Hanson; Rodney Davidson |

7.
| Client | *Typhoon* |
| Designers | Barbara Lee—Suka & Friends; Rodney Davidson |

8.
| Client | *DogStar* |
| Designer | Rodney Davidson |

9.
| Client | *The Cat/Northumberland* |
| Designers | Bruce Hamilton—Target Marketing; Rodney Davidson |

10.
| Client | *Birmingham Metropolitan Arts Council* |
| Designer | Rodney Davidson |

11.
| Client | *Artisan Films* |
| Designers | Laura Marince, Karen Hostetter, Rodney Davidson |

12.
| Client | *Kirk Alford* |
| Designer | Rodney Davidson |

13.
| Client | *Supon Design Group/ Intnl logos & TM 3* |
| Designer | Rodney Davidson |

14.
| Client | *Red Mountain Park* |
| Designers | Gregory Hodges—Hodges & Associates; Rodney Davidson |

15.
| Client | *Ther Merit System/ Jefferson Co. Personnel Board* |
| Designers | Gregory Hodges—Hodges & Associates; Rodney Davidson— DogStar |

45

1.

2.

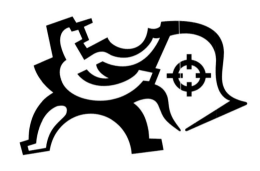

3.

4.

6.

5.

7. *G L O R Y*

1, 4, 5
Design Firm **Pat Jenkins Design**
2, 3, 6, 7
Design Firm **Gardner Design**
1.
 Client   ATDC
 Designer   Pat Jenkins
2.
 Client   *Wichita State Uniersity Men's Crew Team*
 Designer   Brian Miller
3.
 Client   *International Association of Printing House Craftsmen*
 Designers   Brian Miller, Bill Gardner
4.
 Designer   Pat Jenkins

5.
 Client   *Making America Work*
 Designer   Pat Jenkins
6.
 Client   *Wichita State University Shocker Crew Team*
 Designer   Brian Miller
7.
 Client   *GLORY*
 Designers   Bill Gardner, Karen Hogn
(opposite)
 Client   *Old Capitol Mall*
 Design Firm   **FRCH Design Worldwide (Cincinnati)**
 Designers   Michael Beeghly, Erik Brown

1.

2.

3.

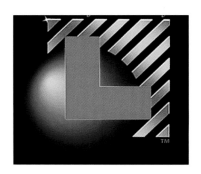

4.

5.

1ST NATIONWIDE BANK

A FEDERAL SAVINGS BANK

6.

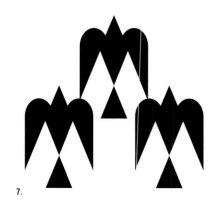

7.

LOOSE

Levi's

8.

9.

10.

11.

12.

13.

JAZZ

14.

15.

1, 4, 5, 8, 10, 11, 14, 15
Design Firm **SBG Enterprise**
2, 3, 6, 7, 9, 12, 13
Design Firm **Gardner Design**
1.
Client *Cheskin+Masten/ImageNet*
Designer Jessie McAnulty
2.
Client *Gardner Design*
Designer Bill Gardner
3.
Client *Auto Craft*
Designer Bill Gardner
4.
Client *California State Lottery*
Designer Mark Bergman
5.
Client *1st National Bank*
Designers Nicolas Sidjakov, Lester Ng
6.
Client *RVP (Recreational Vehicle Products)*
Designer Bill Gardner
7.
Client *Kansas Health Foundation/*
Leadership Seminar
Designer Bill Gardner

8.
Client *FCB/Honig*
Designer Paul Woods
9.
Client *Business Bank of America*
Designer Bill Gardner
10.
Client *Berkly System*
Designer Courtney Reeser
11.
Client *Eureka Bank*
Designer Amy Knapp
12.
Client *Oris Technologies*
Designer Bill Gardner
13.
Client *The Independent School*
Designer Bill Gardner
14.
Designer Jim Nevins
15.
Client *Hewlett Packard*
Designer Thomas Bond

1.

CONNECT

A NORSTAN COMPANY

2.

3.

ƆEAF

4.

INFORMATION ADVANTAGE®

5.

6.

7.

8.

1 - 5
Design Firm **Larsen Design + Interactive**
6, 7
Design Firm **Hershey Associates**
8
Design Firm **Jack Nadel, Inc.**

1.
Client *Opus Corporation*
Creative Director
Tim Larsen
Art Director Gayle Jorgens
Designer Todd Mannes

2.
Client *Connect Computer*
Art Director Tim Larsen
Designer Marc Kundmann

3.
Client *Imation Corporation*
Creative Director
Nancy Whittlese
Designers Sascha Boecker, Todd Nesser

4.
Client *DEAF*
Creative Director
Richelle Huff
Designer Kevin Ylitalo

5.
Client *Information Advantage*
Creative Director
Richelle Huff
Designer Sascha Boecker

6.
Client *Hamilton Court*
Designers R. Christine Hershey, Lisa Joss

7.
Client *Keith-Beer Medical Group*
Designer R. Christine Hershey

8.
Client *LifeScan*
Designer Miguel Rosa
(opposite)
Client *HOC Industries*
Design Firm **Gardner Design**
Designer Brian Miller

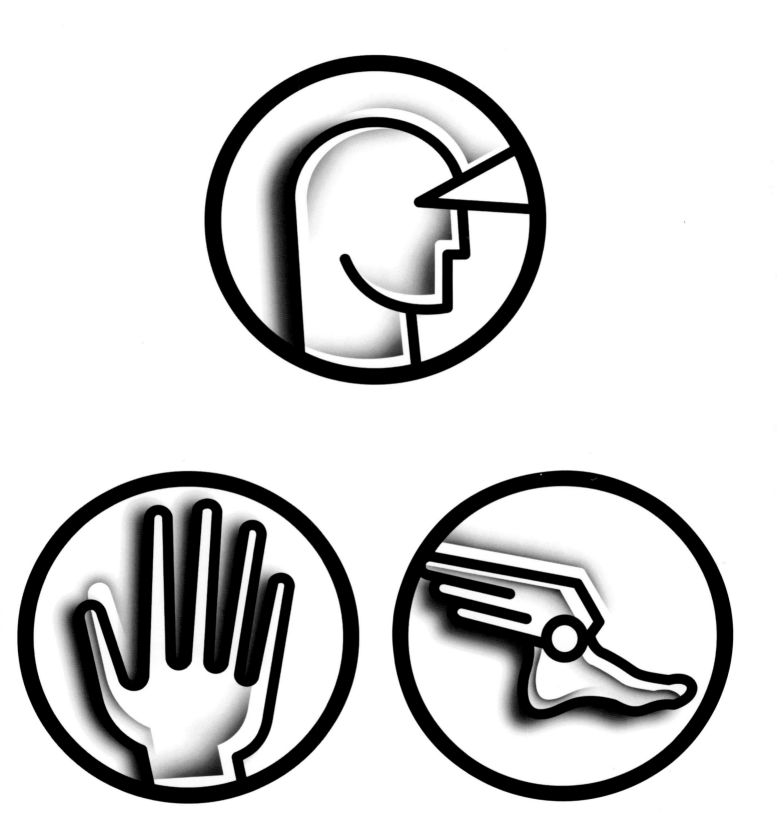

1.

2.

3.

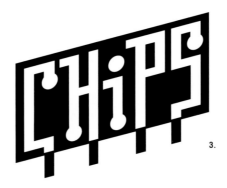

4.

SAN FRANCISCO
SYMPHONY

5.

7.

6.

8.

9.

10.

11.

12.

13.

14.

1, 4, 5, 8, 10, 11, 14, 15
Design Firm **Gardner Design**
2, 3, 6, 7, 9, 12, 13
Design Firm **SBG Enterprise**
1.
Client   *Fat Chance*
Designer   Bill Gardner
2.
Client   *3M*
Designer   Mary Brucken
4.
Client   *CHiPS*
Designer   Bill Gardner
5.
Client   *DeCotiis Erhard Strategic Consulting Group*
Designer   Bill Gardner
6.
Client   *SF Symphony*
Designer   Paul Wood
7.
Client   *SF Giants*
Designer   Kate Greene

8.
Client   *Grider and Company P.A.*
Designer   Bill Gardner
9.
Client   *Samaritan*
Designer   Jackie Foshaug
10.
Client   *Cramer Calligraphy*
Designer   Brian Miller
11.
Client   *Catholic Diocese of Wichita*
Designer   Bill Gardner
12.
Client   *Transamerica*
Designer   Thomas Bond
13.
Client   *US Air*
Designer   Jackie Foshaug
14.
Client   *TumbleDrum*
Designer   Bill Gardner
15.
Client   *The Independent School— 3 Level Private School*
Designer   Bill Gardner

vantive

1.

2.

3.

PRESIDIO
S Y S T E M S

4.

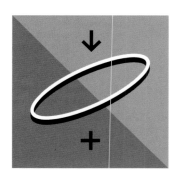

Wavepath

5.

6.

7.

1 - 7
Design Firm **Beggs Design**
Designer Lee Beggs
1.
Client *Vantive*
2.
Client *Southern Florida Bank/ Wilson Communications*
3.
Client *University Chiropractic Clinic*
4.
Client *Presidio Systems*
5.
Client *WavePath/Information Arts Inc.*
6.
Client *Cromenco, Inc.*
7.
Client *Diane Strongwater*

(opposite)
Client *Borders (Cafe Espresso)*
Design Firm **FRCH Design Worldwide (Cincinnati)**
Designer Tim Frame

1.

2.

3.

4.

5.

6.

Netfinity

7.

8.

9.

10.

11.

FRONTLINE

12.

```
S R T E C E   F T F S U
N O R T O N   T F S U F
( S E C R E T   S T U F F )
E R S C E T   F U F T S
T E R E C S   U F T S F
```

13.

14.

15.

MᴄLᴇᴀɴ Cᴏᴜɴᴛʏ Pʀᴇɴᴀᴛᴀʟ Cʟɪɴɪᴄ

1.

2.

3.

TRANSFORMING
OUR ENERGY 4.

C C A N

P R I S M
S Y S T E M

5.

6.

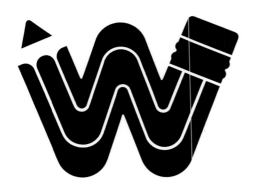

7.

1
  Design Firm **John Walker Graphic Design**
2 - 6
  Design Firm **Michael Orr + Associates, Inc.**
7
  Design Firm **J. Robert Faulkner**

1.
  Client   *McLean County Prenatal Clinic*
  Designer John Walker
2.
  Client   *NYSAIR/NYSEG*
  Designer Michael R. Orr
3.
  Client   *Corning Incorporated*
  Designer Michael R. Orr

4.
  Client   *NYSEG*
  Designers Michael R. Orr, Gregory Duell
5.
  Client   *The Gunlocke Company*
  Designers Michael R. Orr, Gregory Duell
6.
  Client   *CCAN*
  Designers Michael R. Orr, Gregory Duell
7.
  Client   *World Education Center*
  Designer J. Robert Faulkner
(opposite)
  Client   *Post Tools*
  Design Firm **SBG Enterprise**
  Designer Thomas Bond

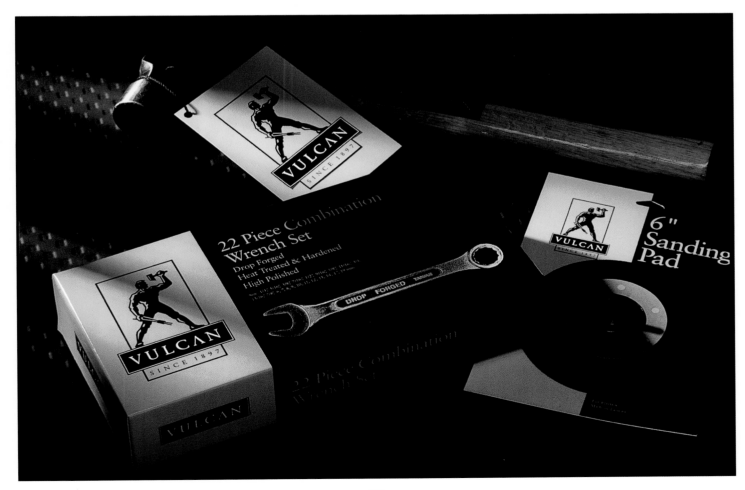

1.

2.

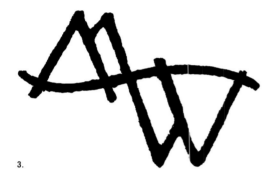

3.

4.

5.

6.

7.

8.

9.

AVEO 10.

11. INVENTA

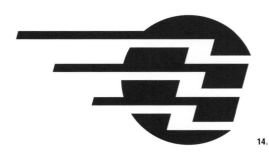

BOLT

12.

PROTIX

13.

14.

15.

1.

2.

SALISBURY STUDIOS

3.

4.

5.

BERBEE

6.

7.

1 - 3, 6
Design Firm **Planet Design Company**
4, 5
Design Firm **CWA, Inc.**
7
Design Firm **Heather Brook Graef**

1.
Client   *Adams Outdoor Advertising*
Designers   Martha Graettinger, Kevin Wade
2.
Client   *Natural Nylon*
Designer   Kevin Wade
3.
Client   *Salisbury Studios*
Designers   Raelene Mercer, Kevin Wade

4.
Client   *Navatek Ships*
Designers   Susan Merritt, Calvin Woo
5.
Client   *Pasternak*
Designers   Susan Merritt, Calvin Woo
6.
Client   *Berbee Information Networks Corp.*
Designers   James Karlin, Kevin Wade
7.
Client   *John Wilmer Studioworkshop*
           Antique Restoration & Upholstery
Designer   Heather Brook Graef
(opposite)
Client   *Embassy Suites*
Design Firm **SBG Enterprise**
Designer   Paul Woods

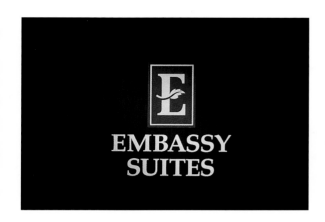

1.

2.

ARABIAN MOCHA SANANI STARBUCKS COFFEE ™

3.

Starbucks

4.

5.

KENYA ™

6.

STARBUCKS COFFEE
KENYA
™

7.

8.

9.

10.

11.

12.

TELANOPHY

13.

14.

15.

(all)		
Design Firm	**David Lemley Design**	
Designer	David Lemley	

1.
Client   *Starbucks Coffee—Lyre*

2.
Client   *Starbucks Coffee— Ethiopia Yergacheffe*

3.
Client   *Starbucks Coffee*

4.
Client   *Starbucks Coffee— Ship According to Timothy Leary*

5.
Client   *Starbucks Coffee—La Sirena*

6.
Client   *Starbucks Coffee—Kenya Decaf*

7.
Client   *Starbucks Coffee—Kenya*

8.
Client   *Starbucks Coffee—Yukon Blend*

9.
Client   *O'Brien International*

10.
Client   *B-WILD*

11.
Client   *Dark Horse Clothing*

12.
Client   *Microsoft*

13.
Client   *Active Voice*

14.
Client   *Muzak*

15.
Client   *Microsoft*

I O 7
Ocean Bistro
DISTINCTIVE GLOBAL SEAFOOD

1.

Eli's ROAD HOUSE
It's Time To Eat!

2.

3.

Lemongrass
Asian Inspired Contemporary Cuisine

4.

BAJA TORTILLA GRILL
• MADE FRESH •

5.

CAFE CP PARAGON

6.

7.

8.

THE
ART
STUDIO

9.

10.

11.

G I R O

12.

Weiler
CORPORATION

13.

14.

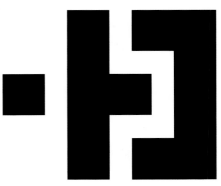

15.

1 -6, 9
Design Firm **Adkins/Balchunas**
7
Design Firm **Sibley/Peteet Design**
8, 10
Design Firm **CWA, Inc.**
11, 12
Design Firm **Gauger & Silva**
13-14
Design Firm **Kollberg/Johnson Associates**
15
Design Firm **Olver Dunlop Associates**

1.
Client *107 Ocean Bistro*
Designers Jerry Balchunas, Matt Fernberger
2.
Client *Eli's Roadhouse*
Designer Jerry Balchunas
3.
Client *Hyland Printing*
Designers Jerry Balchunas, Dan Stebbings
4.
Client *Lemongrass*
Designers Jerry Balchunas, Matt Fernberger
5.
Client *Tortilla Ventures*
Designers Jerry Balchunas, Dan Stebbings

6.
Client *Cafe Paragon*
Designers Jerry Balchunas, Micheline Bouju,
Michelle Phaneuf
7.
Client *ChoiceCom*
Designer Mark Brinkman
8.
Client *Crest International*
Designers Susan Merritt, Calvin Woo
9.
Client *The Art Studio*
Designer Jerry Balchunas
10.
Client *Solectek*
Designers Calvin Woo, Christy Vandeman,
Leah Hewitt
11.
Client *Dividend*
Designers David Gauger, Lori Murphy
12.
Client *Giro*
Designers Bob Ankers, David Gauger
13.
Client *Weiler Brush Company*
Designer Gary Kollberg
14.
Client *Kollberg/Johnson Associates*
Designer Michael Carr
15.
Client *Beecken Petty & Company*
Designer Courtney O'Shea

1.

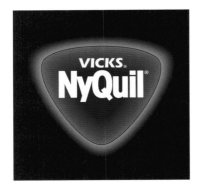

2.

POND'S®

3.

4.

5.

6.

7.

cosmetic associates

8.

STRIDEX ®

9.

FABERGÉ
POWER STICK ®

10.

Hofbauer VIENNA

11.

Only OREO
1912 · 85th ANNIVERSARY EDITION · 1997

12.

LEVER 2000 ®

13.

SCIMAT

14.

ALEVE ®

15.

(all)
Design Firm **Hans Flink Design Inc.**

1.
Client   Colgate Palmolive
Designers   Mark Krukowis, Susan Kunschaft,
Chang Mei Lin, Mike Troian

2.
Client   Procter & Gamble
Designers   Hans D. Flink, Stephen Hooper

3.
Client   Chesebrough-Pond's
Designers   Hans D. Flink, Chang Mei Lin,
Mark Krukowis

4.
Client   Alberto Culver
Designers   Hans D. Flink, Mark Krukowis,
Chang Mei Lin

5.
Client   Chesebrough-Pond's
Designers   Susan Kunschaft, Mark Krukowis

6.
Client   Alberto Culver
Designers   Mark Krukowis

7.
Client   Nestlé
Designers   Hans D. Flink, Stephen Hooper,
Chang Mei Lin

8.
Client   Cosmetic Associates
Designer   Hans D. Flink

9.
Client   Bayer Corp.
Designers   Hans D. Flink, Stephen Hooper,
Suzanne Clark

10.
Client   Fabergé
Designers   Hans D. Flink, Chang Mei Lin,
Stephen Hooper

11.
Client   Hofbauer Vienna Ltd.
Designers   Hans D. Flink, Jane Parasczak

12.
Client   Nabisco
Designers   Susan Kunschaft, Mike Troian

13.
Client   Unilever HPC, USA
Designers   Mark Krukowis, Susan Kunschaft,
Mike Troian, Chang Mei Lin

14.
Client   SCIMAT Scientific Machinery, Inc.
Designer   Hans D. Flink

15.
Client   Procter & Gamble
Designers   Hans D. Flink, Chris Dane,
Stephen Hooper

Telecel

1.

2.

3.

4 3 3 5

4.

Mentadent®

5.

Merrill Lynch

6.

7.

Ameritrust

8.

9.

United States
Post Office

10.

Z O Ë

Pan-Asian Caf
and catering company

11.

Z O Ë

Pan-Asian Caf
and catering company

12.

KING·CASEY

BRAND·RETAIL INNOVATORS

13.

CHRYSALIS

14.

15.

1, 2, 6, 8, 9, 10, 13
Design Firm **King Casey Inc.**
3, 7, 15
Design Firm **Lotas Minard Patton McIver**
11, 12
Design Firm **The Puckett Group**
4
Design Firm **Fairly Painless Advertising**
5
Design Firm **Hans Flink Design Inc.**
14
Design Firm **Augusta Design Group**
1.
Client *Telecel*
Designer John Chrzanowski
2.
Client *Norelco*
Designer King Casey
3.
Client *Lotas Minard Patton McIver*
Designers Lotus Minard Patton McIver
4.
Client *Miller SQA*
Designers Steve Frykholm, Brian Hauch
5.
Client *Unilever HPC, USA*
Designers Hans D. Flink, Chang Mei Lin, Harry
Bentschmann

6.
Client *Merrill Lynch*
Designer King Casey
7.
Client *Renaissance Cosmetics Inc.*
Designer Lotas Minard Patton McIver
8.
Client *Ameritrust*
Designer King Casey
9.
Client *United States Postal Service*
Designers Gene Casey, John Chrzanowski
10.
Client *United States Postal Service*
Designers John Chrzanowski, Steve Brent
11.
Client *Zoë Pan-Asian Café*
Designer Candy Freund
12.
Client *Zoë Pan-Asian Café*
Designer Candy Freund
13.
Client *King Casey Inc.*
Designers John Chrzanowski, Steve Brent
14.
Client *Chrysalis*
Designer Megan Ploska
15.
Client *Renaissance Cosmetics Inc.*
Designer Lotas Minard Patton McIver

2.

1.

7.

4.

3.

5.

6.

8.

9.

10.

11.

SABAN

12.

DIRECTV

13.

14.

IMPROVED
PACKAGING

15.

1
    Design Firm **LMPM**
2, 10
    Design Firm **Back Yard Design**
3, 4, 8
    Design Firm **Lorna Stovall Design**
5
    Design Firm **Musikar Design**
6, 11
    Design Firm **Berry Design, inc**
7, 14
    Design Firm **Nassar Design**
9, 15
    Design Firm **Nealy Wilson Nealy, Inc.**
12, 13
    Design Firm **Pittard Sullivan**
1.
    Client   *Max Factor*
    Designers   Lotas Minard Patton McIver
2.
    Client   *Back Yard Design*
    Designer   Lorna Stovall
3.
    Client   *Generator Digital Post*
    Designer   Lorna Stovall
4.
    Client   *Warner Bros. Records*
    Designer   Lorna Stovall

5.
    Client   *American Federation of*
                 Government Employees
    Designer   Sharon R. Musikar
6.
    Client   *Popeyes Chicken & Biscuits*
    Designer   Bob Berry
7.
    Client   *Coastal Leasing*
    Designer   Nelida Nassar
8.
    Client   *Evolution Film & Tape*
    Designer   Lorna Stovall
9.
    Client   *Simco*
    Designer   Steve Nealy
10.
    Client   *Nestea*
    Designer   Lorna Stovall
11.
    Client   *Branded Restaurant Group*
    Designer   Bob Berry
12.
    Client   *Saban*
13.
    Client   *DirecTV*
14.
    Client   *Elizabeth Gibb Architect*
    Designers   Nelida Nassar, Chris Parks
15.
    Client   *Inland Paperboard & Packaging, Inc.*
    Designer   Michael J. Garber

AFTER HOURS
DESIGN▸ADVERTISING

1.

2.

ASPEN
HOME SYSTEMS

3.

4.

5.

DATA ARCHITECHS

6.

TRANSWORLD
LUBRICANTS, INC.

7.

1
Design Firm **After Hours Design & Advertising**
2, 3, 6, 7
Design Firm **Imtech Communications**
4
Design Firm **Phillips Design**
5
Design Firm **Arthur Andersen, LLP**
1.
  Client   *After Hours Design & Advertising*
  Designer Elizabeth Shott
2.
  Client   *Treasures of China*
  Designer Robert Keng
3.
  Client   *Aspen Home Systems*
  Designer Robert Keng

4.
  Client   *Phillips Design*
  Designer Michael V. Phillips
5.
  Client   *Andersen Consulting*
  Designer Ilia M. Wood
6.
  Client   *Data Architects*
  Designer Robert Keng
7.
  Client   *Transworld Lubricants, Inc.*
  Designer Robert Keng
(opposite)
  Client   *TNT*
  Design Firm **Pittard Sullivan**

1.

Corrin

3.

5.

Machado & Associates

ADVERTISING

7.

2.

4.

ORIGINALIS

6.

BB-INTERACTIVE

8.

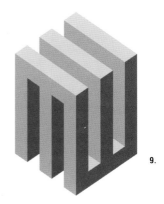

9.

10.

11.

12. *Maitri*

FLEA • FOR • ALL
FLEA MARKET OF BRIGHT IDEAS

13.

ColorAd Printers 14.

15.

1, 5, 10, 11, 15
Design Firm **Michael Doret Graphic Design**
3, 7, 9, 14
Design Firm **Takigawa Design**
4, 12
Design Firm **Becca Smidt**
6, 8
Design Firm **Cawrse + Effect**
2
Design Firm **Studio Archetype**
13
Design Firm **Hallmark Cards**

1.
Client *Fuddruckers*
Designer Michael Doret
2.
Client *Avenue Skin Care*
Designer Andrew Cawrse
3.
Client *Corrin Produce*
Designer Jerry Takigawa
4.
Client *Palo Alto Utilities*
Designer Becca Smidt
5.
Client *NBA Properties*
Designer Michael Doret

6.
Client *Originalis*
Designer Andrew Cawrse
7.
Client *Machado & Associates*
Designers Jerry Takigawa, Jay Galster
8.
Client *BB - Interactive*
Designer Andrew Cawrse
9.
Client *Mark Watson Building & Renovation*
Designer Glenn Johnson
10.
Client *Chic-A-Boom*
Designer Michael Doret
11.
Client *Graphic Artists Guild*
Designer Michael Doret
12.
Client *Maitri Aids Hospice*
Designer Becca Smidt
13.
Client *Flea•For•All Idea Group*
Designers James Caputo, Jim Ramirez
14.
Client *ColorAd Printers*
Designers Jay Galster, Jerry Takigawa
15.
Client *Coolsville Records*
Designer Michael Doret

77

1.

DESIGN
RANCH

2.

3.

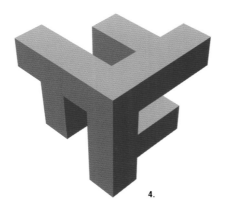

4.

EVERGREEN
WOODWORKS

5.

**BLOOMING
PRAIRIE**

6.

PERSONAL COMMUNICATIONS INTERACTIVE

7.

1
  Design Firm **Ford & Earl Associates**
2, 5, 6
  Design Firm **Design Ranch**
3
  Design Firm **LMImage**
4, 7
  Design Firm **Forward Design**
1.
  Client   *Formula 5 International Inc.*
  Designer   Todd Malhoit
2.
  Client   *Design Ranch*
  Designers   Gary Gnade, Chris Gnade
3.
  Client   *MedChem*
  Designer   Chip Griffin

4.
  Client   Forward Design
  Designer   W. James Forward
5.
  Client   *Evergreen Woodworking*
  Designer   Gary Gnade
6.
  Client   *Blooming Prairie Natural Foods*
  Designers   Gary Gnade, Danette Anqerer
7.
  Client   *Personal Communications
              Interactive*
  Designer   Daphne Stofer
(opposite)
  Client   *Kabel 1*
  Design Firm **Pittard Sullivan**

78

1.

2.

3.

NATIONAL POLICY AND
RESOURCE CENTER ON
WOMEN & AGING

4.

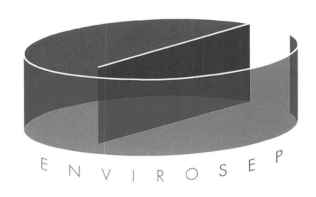

E N V I R O S E P

5.

6.

7.

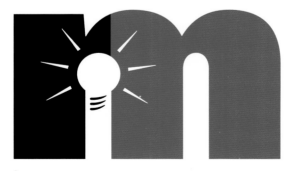

8.

80

9.

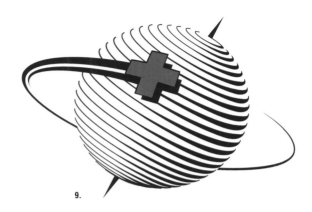

10.

WESTERN

11.

12.

13.

14.

15. **avstar**

1, 2, 9, 15
Design Firm **Perceive, LLC**
3, 8, 11, 12
Design Firm **Blevins Design**
6,7,10,13,14
Design Firm **Dean Corbitt Studio**
4
Design Firm **Susan Bercu Design Studio**
5
Design Firm **Sorrell Co.**

1.
Client   *Aerotech*
Designer   John White

2.
Client   *Edison Source*
Designers   Dave Matea, Scott Littlejohn

3.
Client   *Security Associates International*
Designers   Brian Blevins, Chris Blevins

4.
Client   *National Policy & Resource Center on Women & Aging*
Designer   Susan Bercu

5.
Client   *Envirosep*
Designer   Angela Berlingeri

6.
Client   *Ovarian Cancer Detection & Prevention Center (Hawaii)*
Designer   Dean Corbitt

7.
Client   *SmartShield Sunscreens, LTD.*
Designer   Dean Corbitt

8.
Client   *Robinson Marketing*
Designer   Brian Blevins

9.
Client   *National Physicians Network*
Designer   John White

10.
Client   *Phoenix Ventures*
Designer   Dean Corbitt

11.
Client   *Western Humidor*
Designers   Brian Blevins, Chris Blevins

12.
Client   *Anderson Shumaker*
Designer   Brian Blevins

13.
Client   *Title Nine Sports*
Designer   Dean Corbitt

14.
Client   *Communication Concepts, Inc./ Service Strategies International, Inc.*
Designer   Dean Corbitt

15.
Client   *IVS*
Designers   Jamie Graupner, Dave Matea, Scott Littlejohn, Nora Singer

bailey design group inc

1.

GOLDEN GLOVES

2.

3.

T<small>RANS</small>C<small>ORE</small>

4.

Fresh Mark

5.

Environmental Accounting Project

6.

7.

1, 4, 5
Design Firm **Bailey Design Group, Inc.**
2, 6
Design Firm **Levine and Associates**
3, 7
Design Firm **1-earth GRAPHICS**

1.
Client — *Bailey Design Group, Inc.*
Art Directors — Ken Cahill, David Fiedler
Designer — Gary LaCroix

2.
Client — *United Brotherhood of Carpenters*
Designer — Lena Markley

3.
Client — *Miami County Recovery Council*
Designer — Lisa Harris

4.
Client — Transcore
Art Director — David Fiedler
Designer — Laura Markley

5.
Client — *Fresh Mark Inc.*
Designer — Bailey Design Group, Inc.

6.
Client — *Environmental Protection Agency*
Designer — Andrew Criss

7.
Client — *Cornerstone Natural Foods*
Designer — Lisa Harris
(opposite)
Client — *DNA Plant Technologies*
Design Firm — **Bailey Design Group, Inc.**
Art Director — David Fiedler
Designer — Stephen R. Perry

82

PLAYERS INC

1.

2.

3.

4.

5.

SMITHSONIAN
6. STUDY TOURS

7.

8.

9.

IAMS COMPANY

10.

CINCRON
AUTOMATED PALLET CELL

11.

ALEXANDER
CONSTRUCTION INC.

12.

WESTLAKE
SURGICAL
C E N T E R

13.

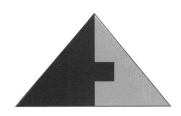

NEW YORK UNIVERSITY

School of Continuing and
Professional Studies

14.

MLSPA™

15.

1, 3, 6, 15
Design Firm **Grafik Communications, Ltd.**
2, 8
Design Firm **The Rittenhouse Group**
4, 5, 10, 11
Design Firm **Pavone Fite Fulwiler**
7
Design Firm **UniWorld Group, Inc.**
9
Design Firm **Yvonne Fitzner Design**
12
Design Firm **LaFond Design**
13
Design Firm **Belyea Design Alliance**
14
Design Firm **O & J Design, Inc.**

1.
Client — *Player's Inc.*
Designers — David Collins, Judy Kirpich
2.
Client — *CAFFE A go go*
Designer — Shelby Keefe
3.
Client — *American Zoo & Aquarium Association*
Designers — David Collins, Susan English, Judy Kirpich
4.
Client — *Clermont Nursing & Convalescent Center*
Designer — Jeff D. Fulwiler
5.
Client — *Paradigm Communication Group*
Designer — Jeff D. Fulwiler

6.
Client — *Smithsonian Institution*
Designers — Lynn Umemoto, Judy Kirpich
7.
Client — *Acapulco Black Film Festival*
Designer — Vincent St. Vincent
8.
Client — *Impact Engineering Solutions, Inc.*
Designer — Jason Evans
9.
Client — *La Cabana*
Designer — Yvonne Fitzner
10.
Client — *The Iams Company*
Designer — Jeff D. Fulwiler
11.
Client — *Cincinnati Milacron*
Designer — Jeff D. Fulwiler
12.
Client — *J. L. Alexander Group*
Designer — Lori LaFond LaMore
13.
Client — *Westlake Surgical Center*
Designer — Samantha Hunt
14.
Client — *New York University School of Continuing and Professional Studies*
Designers — Andrzej J. Olejniczak, Leslie M. Nayman, Christina Mueller
15.
Client — *Major League Soccer Players Association*
Designers — David Collins, Judy Kirpich

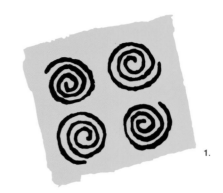

1.

2.

3.

4.

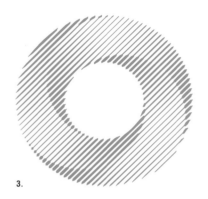

5.

M A R K E T
S C I E N C E S

6.

7.

8.

BRIDGE

9.

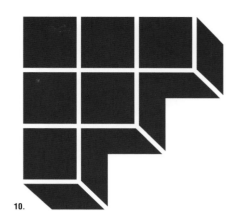

10.

11.

12.

13.

14.

15.

1, 11
Design Firm **A-Hill Design**
2, 3, 5, 7, 9, 12
Design Firm **Point Zero Design**
4, 14
Design Firm **Skeggs Design**
6, 8
Design Firm **The Focus Group**
10, 13
Design Firm **Richard Danne & Associates**
15
Design Firm **Steel Wool Design**

1.
Client *Kitchen Dimensions*
Designers Sandy Hill, Tom Antreasian
2.
Client *Viacare, Inc.*
Designer Point Zero Design
3.
Client *Corvel Corporation*
4.
Client *Bill Ballenberg*
Designer Gary Skeggs
5.
Client *Crown Zellerbach*
Designer Point Zero Design

6.
Client *Market Sciences*
Designer John Rutkowski
7.
Client *Oak Valley Resort*
Designer Point Zero Design
8.
Client *Fontaine's*
Designer John Rutkowski
9.
Client *Bridge Medical*
Designer Point Zero Design
10.
Client *Financial Security Assurance*
Designer Gary Skeggs
11.
Client *Robert Reck Photography*
Designers Emma Roberts, Sandy Hill
12.
Client *Earth Tech*
Designer Point Zero Design
13.
Client *Norfleet Press*
Designer Gary Skeggs
14.
Client *The Praedium Group*
Designer Gary Skeggs
15.
Client *Hallmark Cards, Inc.*
Designer Kristy D. Lewis

1.

Species Survival Plan

2.

3.

A C C U R A T E
T Y P I N G
S E R V I C E S
I N C.

4.

5.

6.

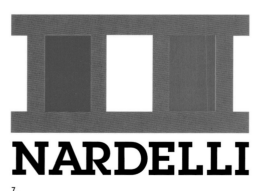

7.

1
Design Firm **IE Design**
2, 5
Design Firm **Brookfield Zoo Design Department**
3, 4, 6, 7
Design Firm **Fleury Design**
1.
Client   *American Isuzu Motors Inc.*
Designer   Marcie Carson
2.
Client   *American Zoo and Aquarium Association*
Designer   Hannah Jennings
3.
Client   *Fleury Design*
Designer   Ellen Fleury
4.
Client   *Accurate Typing Service, Inc.*
Designer   Ellen Fleury

5.
Client   *Brookfield Zoo*
Designer   Hannah Jennings
Illustrator Edie Emmenegger
6.
Client   *Bagel Heaven*
Designer   Ellen Fleury
7.
Client   *Nardelli Associates*
Designer   Ellen Fleury
(opposite)
Client   *Brookfield Zoo*
Design Firm **Brookfield Zoo Design Department**
Designer   Hannah Jennings
Illustrator Steve Stratakos

1.

Franchini

3.

V I V O

2.

4.

S C H O O N O V E R

5.

Shawmut Capital

6.

7.

8.

9.

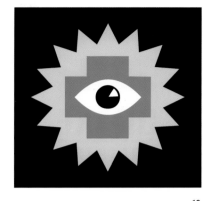

10.

11.

12.

13.

14.

15.

DRAKE DUNN

1.

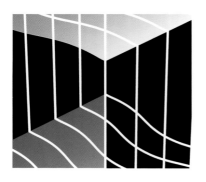

2.

3.

4.

I C T V

5.

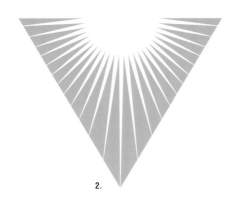

N E T W O R K
POWER & LIGHT

6.

GR 95 W

7.

V I A N T

8.

9.

INKTOMI
CORPORATION

10.

11.

WILLOWS
S O F T W A R E

12.

13.

14.

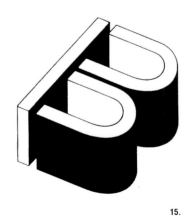

15.

1, 3
Design Firm **ID, Incorporated**
2, 7, 13
Design Firm **Drive Communications**
4, 9
Design Firm **Ronald Emmerling Design, Inc.**
5, 6, 8, 10, 11, 12, 14
Design Firm **California Design International**
15
Design Firm **Julie Johnson Design**

1.
Client *Drake Construction Company*
Designer Jonathan Mulcare
2.
Client *Vuepoint, Inc.*
Designer Michael Graziolo
3.
Client *West Linn Paper Company*
Designers Steve Smith
4.
Client *Altec Lansing Technologies*
Designer Ronald Emmerling
5.
Client *Interactive Cable Television*
Designers Chris Ardito, Suzy Leung
6.
Client *Network Power & Light*
Designers Chris Ardito, Suzy Leung, Dan Liew

7.
Client *KPMG*
Designer Michael Graziolo
8.
Client *Viant*
Designers Linda Kelley, Brian Sasville
9.
Client *Ronald Emmerling Design, Inc.*
Designer Ronald Emmerling
10.
Client *Inktomi*
Designers Linda Kelley, Tom Lamar
11.
Client *Mostel*
Designer Chris Ardito, Christine Benjamin
12.
Client *Willows Software*
Designers Chris Ardito, Suzy Leung
13.
Client *BMW Manufacturing Inc.*
Designer Michael Graziolo
14.
Client *Niehaus Ryan Group*
Designers Chris Ardito, Suzy Leung
15.
Client *The Baughman Group*
Designer Julie Johnson

1.

2.

3.

4.

5.

6.

7.

(all)
Design Firm **Dixon & Parcels Associates, Inc.**
1.
Client   *R.J.R. Foods, Inc.*
Designers   Dixon & Parcels Associates
2.
Client   *Mars, Inc.*
Designers   Dixon & Parcels Associates
3.
Client   *La Choy Food Products, Inc.*
Designers   Dixon & Parcels Associates
4.
Client   *Borden Inc.*
Designers   Dixon & Parcels Associates

5.
Client   *Crest International*
Designers   Dixon & Parcels Associates
6.
Client   *Superior Brands, Inc.*
Designers   Dixon & Parcels Associates
7.
Client   *Lighthouse for the Blind*
Designers   Dixon & Parcels Associates
(opposite)
Client   *Quaker State Corporation*
Design Firm   **Dixon & Parcels Associates, Inc.**

1.

2.

3.

4.

5.

6.

7.

8.

9.

Animated
Resolutions

10.

11.

© PENN STATE MCMLXXXIII

12.

13.

GEORGIA
SOUTHERN
UNIVERSITY

14.

MATSURI™

15.

1.

2.

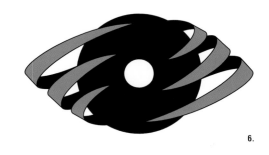

3.

4.

5.

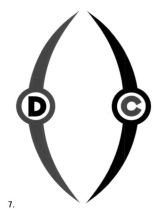

6.

7.

8.

OCEAN SPORTS CLUB

9.

MTW

10.

IN TOUCH

11.

OCEAN FOX DIVE SHOP

HARBOUR ISLAND, BAHAMAS

12.

13.

THE GEGENHEIMER GROUP LTD.

14.

15.

1 - 8
Design Firm **Swieter Design U.S.**
9 - 15
Design Firm **Tom Fowler, Inc.**
1.
Client *Converse Basketball*
Designers John Swieter, Kevin Flatt
2.
Client *Pierce Contracting*
Designer Mark Ford
3.
Client *Carman Engineering*
Designers John Swieter, Mark Ford
4.
Client *Royal Rack*
Designer Mark Ford
5.
Client *Converse Basketball*
Designers John Swieter, Kevin Flatt
6.
Client *Ominidia, Inc.*
Designers John Swieter, Jim Vogel
7.
Client *Dallas Cowboys Football*
Designers John Swieter, Mark Ford

8.
Client *Activerse*
Designers John Swieter, Mark Ford
9.
Client *Four Seeds Corporation*
Designer Thomas G. Fowler
10.
Client *Ocean Fox Dive Shop*
Designer Thomas G. Fowler
11.
Client *NYNEX*
Designer Karl S. Maruyama
12.
Client *M-Two*
Designer Karl S. Maruyama
13.
Client *Bull's Head Animal Hospital*
Designer Samuel Toh
14.
Client *Gegenheimer Group Ltd.*
Designer Elizabeth P. Ball
15.
Client *TIAA CREF*
Designers Elizabeth P. Ball, Thomas G. Fowler

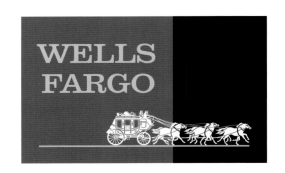

1.

2.

3.

4.

5.

6.

7.

8.

9.

10.

11.

Official Brand

12.

13.

14.

SAN FRANCISCO CLOTHING

975 Lexington Avenue   New York, N.Y. 10021   (212) 472-8740

15.

1, 2		
Design Firm	**Yuguchi Group, inc.**	
3 - 14		
Design Firm	**David Lemley Design**	
15		
Design Firm	**George Tscherny, Inc.**	
1.		
Client	*Wells Fargo Bank*	
Designers	Clifford Yuguchi, Koji Takei, David Brewster	
2.		
Client	*SurLuster*	
Designer	Clifford Yuguchi	
3.		
Client	*E. Alexander Hair Studio*	
Designer	David Lemley	
4.		
Client	*The Bon Marché via Leslie Phinney*	
Designer	David Lemley	
5.		
Client	*Overlake Press*	
Designer	David Lemley	
6.		
Client	*Barry Fishler Direct Response Copywriting*	

Designer	David Lemley
7.	
Client	*Active Voice*
Designer	David Lemley
8.	
Client	*Nike Boyswear*
Designer	David Lemley
9.	
Client	*David Lemley*
Designer	David Lemley
10.	
Client	*One Reel*
Designer	David Lemley
11.	
Client	*Garden Botanika*
Designer	David Lemley
12.	
Client	*Nike—Official Brand*
Designer	David Lemley
13.	
Client	*Muzak*
Designer	David Lemley
14.	
Client	*Aldus*
Designer	David Lemley
15.	
Client	*San Francisco Clothing*
Designer	George Tscherny

1.

LensBuff ™

2.

DIGITAL
IMAGING
TECHNOLOGY
CENTER

3.

A
ALTEON
N E T W O R K S

4.

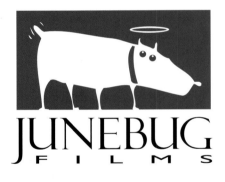

JUNEBUG
F I L M S

5.

R E S O N A T E

6.

7.

1, 2
Design Firm **icon Graphics, Inc.**
3 - 7
Design Firm **Scott Brown Design**
1.
Client   *Eastman Kodak Company*
2.
Client   *Eye Openers*
3.
Client   *Xerox Corp.*
Designer   Scott Brown
4.
Client   *Alteon Networks*
Designer   Scott Brown
5.
Client   *Junebug Films*
Designer   Scott Brown

6.
Client   *Resonate*
Designer   Scott Brown
7.
Client   *Scott Brown Design*
Designer   Scott Brown
(opposite)
Client   *AVASTOR*
     (Digital Equipment Corporation)
Design Firm **Larsen Design + Interactive**
Creative Director
     Tim Larsen
Art Director   Gayle Jorgens
Designers   Larsen Design Staff

TIAN TAN CARPETS
BEIJING

1.

ADENAK

2.

AFS INTERCULTURAL PROGRAMS

3.

E. LEON JIMENES, C. POR A.

4.

UNITED BRANDS

5.

DAINANA
SECURITIES

6.

PUERTO RICO

7.

GANNETT

8.

I F T

9.

ZOËTICS

10.

11.

MERCURY

12.

Drackett

13.

CHICOPEE

14.

BANCO DE PONCE

15.

(all)
Design Firm **Yasumura Assoc./**
 Muts & Joy & Design
Designers Muts
1.
 Client *Tian-Tan Carpets*
 Designers Muts
2.
 Client *Adenak*
 Designers Muts
3.
 Client *AFS*
 Designer Joy Greene
4.
 Client *E. Leon Jimenes, C. Por A.*
 Designers Hitomi, Muts
5.
 Client *United Brands Inc.*
 Designers Muts
6.
 Client *Dainana Security*
 Designers Muts

7.
 Client *Puerto Rico Tourism & Commerce*
 Designers Muts
8.
 Client *Gannett Co.*
 Designers Muts Yasumura
9.
 Client *IFT*
 Designer Gisele Sangiovanni
10.
 Client *Zoetics Inc.*
 Designer Gisele Sangiovanni
11.
 Client *Merrill Lynch Realty*
 Designers Muts
12.
 Client *Mercury*
 Designer Richard H. Muts
13.
 Client *Drackett*
 Designer Andy L. Muts
14.
 Client *Chicopee*
 Designer Richard H. Muts
15.
 Client *Banco De Ponce*
 Designers Muts Yasumura

1.

Knowledge
Action
Performance

2.

3.

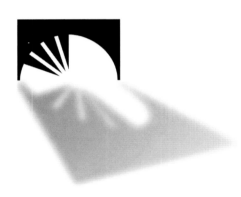

4.

5.

6.

7.

1, 2
Design Firm **McKenzie & Associates**
3 - 7
Design Firm **aire design company**
1.
Client   *S.M.A.R.T.*
2.
Client   *Ernst & Young—Stanford Project*
3.
Client   *Tucson Electric Power Co.*
Designer   Matthew Rivera
4.
Client   *Arizona International Campus*
Designer   Shari Rykowski

5.
Client   *aire design company*
          (formerly C-Kim Design)
Designer   David Kolb
6.
Client   *Loews Ventana Flying V Bar & Grill*
Designers   Kerry Martyr, Catharine M. Kim
7.
Client   *Avikan International Academies*
Creative Director, Designer, Illustrator
          Catharine M. Kim
Contributors   Matthew Rivera, Shari Rykowski
(opposite)
Client   *Minneapolis Planetarium*
Design Firm **Larsen Design + Interactive**
Creative Director
          Tim Larsen
Designer   Marc Kundmann

MINNEAPOLIS PLANETARIUM

1.

2.

3.

4.

5.

6.

HALOGEN

7.

8.

9.

10.

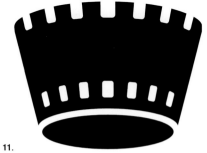

11.

12.

13.

14.

15.

1 - 7, 9 - 13 - 15
Design Firm **Sibley/Peteet Design**
8
Design Firm **The Invisions Group**

1.
Client   *EnerShop*
Designer   Derek Welch
2.
Client   *Vignette*
Designer   Mark Brinkman
3.
Client   *Boundless Technologies*
Designer   Mark Brinkman
4.
Client   *Mercury Messenger Service*
Designer   Tom Hough
5.
Client   *The Container Store*
Designer   David Beck
6.
Client   *Dal Tile*
Designer   Rex Peteet
7.
Client   *Halogen Systems*
Designer   Mark Brinkman

8.
Client   *The Buffalo Club*
Designers   Leo Mullen, Michael Kraine
9.
Client   *Scotland Yards*
Designer   Rex Peteet
10.
Client   *Televentures*
Designer   Rex Peteet
11.
Client   *Mike King Photography*
Designers   Rex Peteet, Tom Kirsch
12.
Client   *Haggar Apparel Company*
Designer   David Beck
13.
Client   *American Campus Communities*
Designers   Mark Brinkman, Rex Peteet
14.
Client   *C-Core*
Designer   Brent McMahan
15.
Client   *Energy Central*
Designer   Mark Brinkman

1.

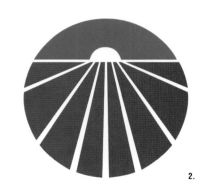

2.

PUMP
R E C O R D S

3.

S K I R B A L L   C U L T U R A L   C E N T E R

M E R R I T T

4.

5.

M.A. Weatherbie & Co., Inc.

T O S C A N A

6.

T H E
INVISIONS
G R O U P

7.

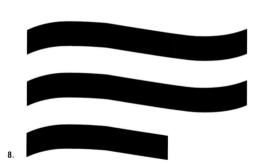

8.

1, 3, 4, 6		
Design Firm	**Kim Baer Design**	
2, 5		
Design Firm	**Inc 3**	
7		
Design Firm	**The Invisions Group**	
8		
Design Firm	**Gams Chicago, Inc.**	
1.		
Client	*Pump Records*	
Designer	Liz Roberts	
2.		
Client	*Fairhaven Partners*	
	Investment Group	
Designers	Harvey Appelbaum,	
	Nick Guarracino	
3.		
Client	*Skirball Cultural Center*	
Designer	Jennifer Miller	
Illustrator	Benjamin Cziller	

4.		
Client	*The Merritt Co.*	
Designer	Maxine Mueller	
5.		
Client	*Matthew A. Weatherbie & Co., Inc.*	
Designers	Harvey Appelbaum, Nick Guarracino	
6.		
Client	*Toscana Restaurant*	
Designer	Barbara Cooper	
7.		
Client	*The Invisions Group*	
Designers	Roo Johnson, The Invisions Group	
8.		
Client	*Follett Library Resources*	
Designers	John V. Anderson	
(opposite)		
Client	*Novellus Systems*	
Design Firm	**Larsen Design + Interactive**	
Creative Director		
	Tim Larsen	
Art Director	Donna Root	
Designer	Sascha Boecker	

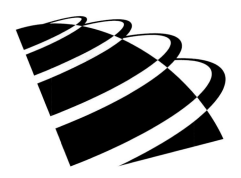

S P E E D

1.

2.

TROPICAL DISCOVERY

3.

4.

BAIGLOBAL

5.

the
Sausalito
Art Festival

6.

COMPLETE CONTACT LENS CARE

7.

8.

9.

CDA

Copper Development Association

10.

11.

CAPITOL RISK CONCEPTS

12.

C A M B I U M

13.

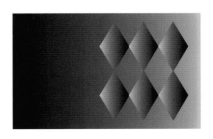

Argyle Associates

14.

MONTEREY BAY
AQUARIUM

15.

1, 2, 4, 5, 7, 9 - 14
Design Firm **Lee Communications, Inc.**
3, 6, 15
Design Firm **Ace Design**
1.
Client   *Tocqueville Asset Mgmt*
Designers   Bob Lee, Dennis DeFrancesco
2.
Client   *Adgis, Inc.*
Designer   Bob Lee
3.
Client   *Denver Zoo*
Art Director Richard Graef
Designer   Bonnie Russell
4.
Client   *The Fairchild Corporation*
Designer   Bob Lee
5.
Client   *BAIGlobal Inc.*
Designer   Bob Lee
6.
Designer   Richard Graef
7.
Client   *PuriLens, Inc.*
Designer   Bob Lee

8.
Client   *US Employment Service,*
            Dept. of Labor
Designer   Arthur Congdon
9.
Client   *Darwin Asset Management*
Designers   Bob Lee, Dennis DeFrancesco
10.
Client   *Copper Development Assn.*
Designer   Bob Lee
11.
Client   *Com.plete/GlobeWave, Inc.*
Designer   Bob Lee
12.
Client   *Capitol Risk Concepts, Ltd.*
Designers   Bob Lee, Dennis DeFrancesco
13.
Client   *Cambium House, Ltd.*
Designer   Bob Lee
14.
Client   *Argyle Associates, Inc.*
Designer   Bob lee
15.
Client   *Monterey Bay Aquarium*
Designer   Richard Graef

1.

2.

Van Lines

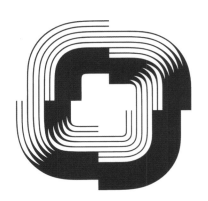

3.

4.

5.

6.

7.

1 - 3, 6
Design Firm **Lippincott & Margulies, Inc.**
4, 5, 7
Design Firm **Congdon Macdonald Inc.**
1.
  Client   *Fleetwood Enterprises Inc.*
  Designer   Arthur Congdon
2.
  Client   *United Van Lines*
  Designers   Arthur Congdon, Michael Toomey
3.
  Client   *First Union National Bank*
  Designer   Arthur Congdon
4.
  Client   *Sports Metaskills*
  Designer   Arthur Congdon

5.
  Client   *The Investment Properties Group*
  Designer   Arthur Congdon
6.
  Client   *The Great Atlantic and*
              Pacific Tea Company
  Designer   Arthur Congdon
7.
  Client   *Hackney (Freeway Oil)*
  Designer   Arthur Congdon
(opposite)
  Client   *Coca Cola Co.*
  Design Firm **SBG Enterprise**
  Designers   Vicki Cero, Mary Brucken

1.

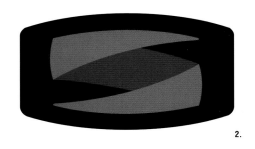

2.

3.

4.

5.

6.

7.

8.

SPARK HOLDINGS

9.

10.

T·H·QUEST

11.

12.

13.

14.

15.

(all)
Design Firm **Swieter Design U.S.**

1.
Client — *Young Presidents' Organization*
Designers — John Swieter, Mark Ford

2.
Client — *Serrano Interiors*
Designers — John Swieter, Mark Ford

3.
Client — *Mercury Messenger*
Designer — Mark Ford

4.
Client — *Sports Lab*
Designer — John Swieter

5.
Client — *Young Presidents' Organization*
Designers — John Swieter, Mark Ford

6.
Client — *Street Savage*
Designers — John Swieter, Mark Ford

7.
Client — *Backdoor Delivery*
Designers — John Swieter, Mark Ford

8.
Client — *Young Presidents' Organization*
Designers — John Swieter, Mark Ford

9.
Client — *Spark Holdings*
Designer — John Swieter

10.
Client — *Uptown Jazz Festival*
Designer — Mark Ford

11.
Client — *T.H. Quest*
Designer — Mark Ford

12.
Client — *Shears*
Designer — Mark Ford

13.
Client — *Shower Head*
Designers — John Swieter, Paul Munsterman

14.
Client — *Vellum Point*
Designer — Mark Ford

15.
Client — *Connectware*
Designer — John Swieter

117

1.

2.

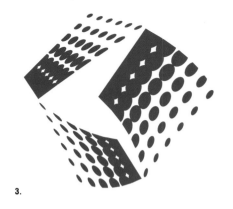

3.

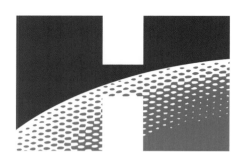

4.

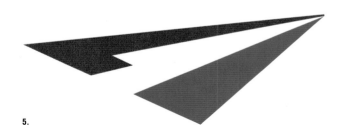

5.

6.

7.

✳ MetLife

1.

CAPITOLTOWER

2.

ASSASSINS

3.

L·I·F·E

MANAGER

4.

CIRCLE MARKETING

5.

6.

7.

8.

120

9.

10.

11.

12.

O R I E N T

A I R L I N E S

A S S O C I A T I O N

13.

14.

Seattle Symphony

15.

1		
Design Firm	**Gams Chicago, Inc.**	
2 - 10		
Design Firm	**Rickabaugh Graphics**	
11		
Design Firm	**Rick Eiber Design (RED), RVT Inc.**	
12 - 15		
Design Firm	**Rick Eiber Design (RED)**	
1.		
Client	*Health & Fitness Center of Oak Brook Hills*	
Designer	John V. Anderson	
2.		
Client	*The Galbreath Comany*	
Designer	Eric Rickabaugh	
3.		
Client	*Players Theatre*	
Designer	Eric Rickabaugh	
4.		
Client	*Nationwide Insurance*	
Designer	Eric Rickabaugh	
5.		
Client	*Circle Marketing*	
Designer	Eric Rickabaugh	
6.		
Client	*Port Columbus Executive Park*	
Designer	Eric Rickabaugh	

7.		
Client	*The Ohio State University*	
Designers	Michael Tennyson Smith, Eric Rickabaugh	
8.		
Client	*NBA Properties*	
Designers	NBA Properties, Tom O'Grady, Eric Rickabaugh	
9.		
Client	*Run for Christ*	
Designer	Eric Rickabaugh	
10.		
Client	*Nationwide Insurance*	
Designer	Eric Rickabaugh	
11.		
Client	*UNR Inc.*	
Designer	Rick Eiber	
12.		
Client	*Ardco, Inc.*	
Designer	Rick Eiber, John Fortune	
13.		
Client	*Orient Airlines Assn.*	
Designer	Rick Eiber	
14.		
Client	*Woodland Investment Co.*	
Designer	Rick Eiber	
15.		
Client	*Seattle Symphony*	
Designer	Rick Eiber	

1.

2.

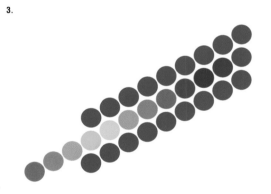

GOLFDOME

3.

JENNY WOODS DANCE

4.

5.

6.

7.

1, 2
Design Firm **Segura Inc**
3, 4
Design Firm **The Majestic Group, Inc.**
5, 6
Design Firm **Allan Miller & Associates**
7
Design Firm **Donaldson, Lufkin & Jenrette**

1.
Client   *Q101 Radio*
Designers Carlos Segura, Brent Riley
2.
Client   *Sun + Moon*
Designers Susana Detembleque, Carlos Segura
3.
Client   *Golfdome*
Designer Stephen E. Nagy

4.
Client   *Jenny Woods Dance*
Designer Stephen E. Nagy
5.
Client   *Birm*
Designer Allan Miller
6.
Client   *Acacia Landscape*
Designer Allan Miller
7.
Client   *Sprout Group*
Designers DLJ Graphics
(opposite)
Client   *PCEQ*
Design Firm **Yasumura Assoc.,
Muts & Joy & Design**
Designer Emi Yasumura

1.

LAKEMARY
CENTER

POWELL
GARDENS

2.

3.

4.

5.

6.

7.

8.

CUTS
PLUS

124

9.

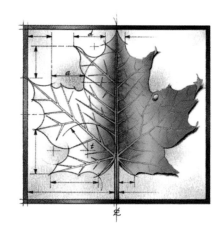

10.

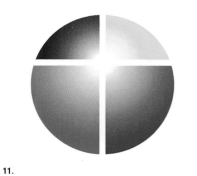

11.

12.

13.

14.

AQUARIAN BICYCLES

15.

Chicago Pneumatic

1.

Skaneateles Country Club

2.

3.

Linkon

4.

GERBER

5.

APS

6.

PMA

PERFORMANCE MANAGEMENT ASSOCIATES

7.

UNITED STATES POSTAL SERVICE

8.

Medical Transcriptions

9.

MARK
INDUSTRIES
SINCE 1964

10.

11. PRIME COMPANIES, INC.

12.

13.

MOWTOWN
COMMERCIAL & RESIDENTIAL LAWN SERVICE

14.

15.

kenya's
GOURMET BAKERY

1 - 2			**6.**		
	Design Firm	**Cleminshaw Design Group**		Client	*Applied Professional Systems*
3 - 7				Designer	Virginia Bilodeau
	Design Firm	**Donaldson Makoski Inc**	**7.**		
8				Client	*Performance Management*
	Design Firm	**Yasumura Assoc.,**			*Associates*
		Muts & Joy & Design		Designer	Jane Heft
9, 10, 12, 14			**8.**		
	Design Firm	**Howard Blonder & Associates**		Client	*United States Postal Service*
11, 13				Designers	Joy Greene, Katherine Hames,
	Design Firm	**Debra Lamfers Design**			Muts Yasumura, Fuji
	Designers	Melissa Nery, Debra Lamfers	**9.**		
15				Client	*Mullikin Medical Transcriptions*
	Design Firm	**Creative Dynamics Inc.**		Designer	Sue Sandoval
1.			**10.**		
	Client	*Chicago Pneumatic Tool Co.*		Client	*Mark Industries*
	Designers	Linda Cleminshaw,		Designer	Sue Sandoval
		Doug Cleminshaw	**11.**		
2.				Client	*Prime Companies, Inc.*
	Client	*Skaneateles Country Club*	**12.**		
	Designers	Linda Cleminshaw,		Client	*RPM Investment*
		Doug Cleminshaw		Designer	Sue Sandoval
3.			**13.**		
	Client	*The Butcher Company*		Client	*Broudy Printing, Inc.*
	Designer	Virginia Bilodeau	**14.**		
4.				Client	*Mowtown*
	Client	*Linkon Corporation*		Designer	Alan Blonder
	Designer	Virginia Bilodeau	**15.**		
5.				Client	*Kenya's Gourmet Bakery*
	Client	*Gerber Scientific, Inc.*		Designer	Gerald Moscato
	Designer	Debby Ryan			

Advertising Club
of Greater St. Louis

1.

2.

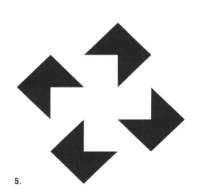

3.

4.

5.

6.

7.

8.

9.

Washington's
L A N D I N G

10.

11.

12.

Summit Strategies, Inc.

13.

14.

15.

1, 8, 13
Design Firm **McDermott Design**
2 - 7, 9 - 12, 14, 15
Design Firm **Agnew Moyer Smith**

1.
Client *Advertising Club of St. Louis*
Designer Bill McDermott

2.
Client *Pittsburgh Dance Council*
Designer John Sotirakis

3.
Client *Pittsburgh Zoo*
Designer Reed Agnew

4.
Client *Pittsburgh Department of City Planning/ Pittsburgh Downtown Plan*
Designer John Sotirakis

5.
Client *Kane Regional Center*
Designer Don Moyer

6.
Client *Lincoln Elementary School PTA, Aileen Owens*
Designer Randy Ziegler

7.
Client *California University of Pennsylvania*
Designer John Sotirakis

8.
Client *St. Louis Blues, NHL*
Designer Bill McDermott

9.
Client *Pittsburgh Light Rail Transit System*
Designer Don Moyer

10.
Client *Washington's Landing*
Designer Jim Curl

11.
Client *The Benedum Center for the Performing Arts*
Designer John Sotirakis

12.
Client *Three Rivers Stadium*
Designer John Sotirakis

13.
Client *Summit Strategies, Inc.*
Designer Bill McDermott

14.
Client *Port of Pittsburgh*
Designer Gina Datres

15.
Client *The San Damiano Players*
Designer John Sotirakis

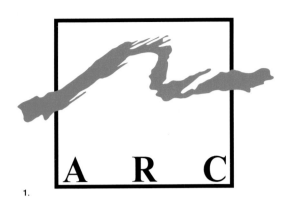

A R C

1.

Rock Creek
TECHNOLOGIES

2.

HOTEL VINTAGE PARK

3.

WORKING

4.

KIMPTON GROUP™

5.

WARRIOR

6.

7.

VISTA CLARA RANCH
resort and spa

8.

130

9.

ARTS

10.

VISTA

CONTROL SYSTEMS 11.

HOTEL VINTAGE COURT

12.

14.

M I R A G E

THE HOTEL JULIANA

13.

15.

1, 6, 9
Design Firm **The Robin Shepherd Group**
2
Design Firm **Axis Communications**
3, 5, 12, 14
Design Firm **Hunt Weber Clark Associates**
4, 10
Design Firm **E. Christopher Klumb Associates, Inc.**
7, 11, 13, 15
Design Firm **Cisneros Design**
8
Design Firm **Griego Design**

1.
Client   *Arc International Inc.*
Designers   Tom Schifanella, Robin Shepherd

2.
Client   *Rock Creek Technology*
Designers   Craig Byers, Chris Paul

3.
Client   *Kimpton Hotel Group/ Vintage Park Hotel*
Designers   Nancy Hunt-Weber, Gary Williams

4.
Client   *E. Christopher Klumb Associates, Inc.*
Designer   Christopher Klumb

5.
Client   *Kimpton Hotel Group*
Designers   Nancy Hunt-Weber, Deborah Dickson

6.
Client   *Working Warrior*
Designer   Justin Lee

7.
Client   *Pasta Pomodoro*
Designer   Eric Griego

8.
Client   *Vista Clara Ranch*
Designer   Eric Griego

9.
Client   *Juice n' Java Caffé and Restaurant*
Designer   Mike Earnhart

10.
Client   *Darien Arts Center*
Designer   Christopher Klumb

11.
Client   *Vista Control Systems*
Designer   Fred Cisneros

12.
Client   *Vintage Court Hotel/ Kimpton Hotel Group*
Designers   Nancy Hunt-Weber, Christopher Clark

13.
Client   *Route 66/Mirage*
Designer   Harry Forehand III

14.
Client   *The Hotel Juliana/ Kimpton Hotel Group*
Designers   Nancy Hunt-Weber, Gary Williams

15.
Client   *Pizzaz Sports Bar*
Designer   Fred Cisneros

KEHRS MILL
FAMILY DENTAL CARE

1.

The
LEGACY
Group, Inc.

Estate Planning & Asset Protection

2.

BROUGHTON
International

3.

NOVA

4.

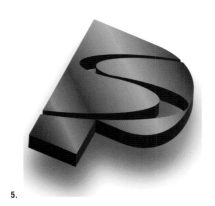

5.

TICKETS
now
MEDIA SERVICES

6.

7.

1, 2, 4 - 7				**5.**	
	Design Firm	**AKA Design, Inc.**		Client	*The Printing Source*
3				Designer	Richie Murphy
	Design Firm	**FMG Design**		**6.**	
1.				Client	*Tickets Now, Inc.*
	Client	*Kehrs Mill Family Dental Care*		Designer	Richie Murphy
	Designer	Richie Murphy		**7.**	
2.				Client	*Anheuser-Busch Companies*
	Client	*The Legacy Group (Estate Planners)*		Designer	Stacy Lanier
	Designers	Craig Simon, Stacy Lanier		**(opposite)**	
3.				Client	*United States Postal Service*
	Client	*Broughton International*		Design Firm	**Yasumura Assoc., and**
	Designer	Ferdinand Meyer, Mary R. Grems			**Muts & Joy & Design**
4.				Designers	Katherine Hames, R.L.,
	Client	*Nova Marketing Company*			Muts Yasumura
	Designer	Richie Murphy			

UNITED STATES
POSTAL SERVICE

1.

CatheyAssociates,Inc.

Graphic Design & Identity Development

2.

ELECTRONIC GRAPHIC ARTISTS OF DALLAS

3.

4.

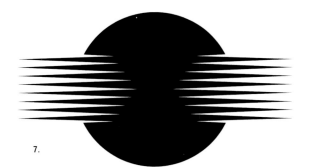

Tele*cellular, Inc.*

5.

AccuSight

6.

7.

SANDFORD COLOR CORPORATION

8.

134

Procurement & Logistics

9.

MONTGOMERY RIDGE
PERMIT No 12
18 72

10.

The Kinsey Institute For Research
in Sex, Gender and Reproduction

11.

12.

START

13.

NAqcess℠

14.

Second Opinion
INTERIORS

15.

1, 10
Design Firm   **Seasonal Specialties In House Design Group**

2, 3, 5, 8, 15
Design Firm   **Cathey Associates, Inc.**

4, 6, 7, 9, 13
Design Firm   **Julia Tam Design**

11, 12, 14
Design Firm   **Enock**

1.
Client   *Menards*
Designer   Jennifer Sheeler

2.
Client   *Cathey Associates, Inc.*
Designer   Gordon Cathey

3.
Client   *Electronic Graphic Artists of Dallas*
Designer   Gordon Cathey

4.
Client   *Telesis Health Care*
Designer   Julia Chong Tam

5.
Client   *Telecellular, Inc.*
Designer   Matt Westapher

6.
Client   *Accusight*
Designer   Julia Chong Tam

7.
Client   *Electronic Melody*
Designer   Julia Chong Tam

8.
Client   *Sandford Color Corporation*
Designer   Gordon Cathey

9.
Client   *Procurement & Logistics Dept./ Southern California Gas Company*
Designer   Julia Chong Tam

10.
Client   *Montgomery Wards*
Designer   Jennifer Sheeler

11.
Client   *The Kinsey Institute*
Designer   David Enock

12.
Client   *The Nasdaq Stock Market*
Designer   Matthew Enock

13.
Client   *Los Angeles Times/ Starbucks Coffee START Program*
Designer   Julia Chong Tam

14.
Client   *The Nasdaq Stock Market*
Designer   Chris Enock

15.
Client   *Second Opinion Interiors*
Designers   Matt Westapher, Gordon Cathey

1.

2.

3.

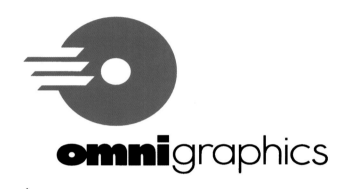

4.

5.

6.

7.

8.

9.

DAVOL

10.

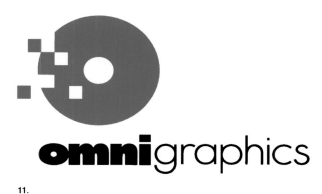

omni graphics

11.

12.

13.

14.

15.

1, 3, 4, 7, 11, 14, 15
Design Firm   **Dever Designs**
2, 9
Design Firm   **Halleck Design Group**
5, 10
Design Firm   **Cole Design Group**
6, 8, 12, 13
Design Firm   **Toni Showalter Design**

1.
Client   *Telcom Insurance Group*
Designer   Jeffrey L. Dever
2.
Client   *Integral Training Systems*
Designer   Ellen Rudy
3.
Client   *Total Life Creations*
Designer   Jeffrey L. Dever
4.
Client   *Omnigraphics*
          (printing & finishing division)
Designer   Jeffrey L. Dever
5.
Client   *Sonics & Materials Inc*
Designer   Jason Berry
6.
Client   *Morse Diesel*
Designer   Toni Schowalter

7.
Client   *Center for Population, Health and*
          Nutrition (USAID)
Designer   Jeffrey L. Dever
8.
Client   *Manes Space*
Designer   Toni Schowalter
9.
Client   *Parrot Tree Plantation*
Designers   Wayne Wright, Ellen Rudy
10.
Client   *Davol Communications*
Designer   Laura Dechaine
11.
Client   *Omnigraphics*
          (digital studio division)
Designer   Jeffrey L. Dever
12.
Client   *Beacon Hill Club*
Designer   Toni Schowalter
13.
Client   *American Institute of Wine & Food*
Designer   Toni Schowalter
14.
Client   *MCI/Vnet Card*
Designers   Jeffrey L. Dever, Douglas Dunbebin
15.
Client   *International Religious*
          Liberty Association
Designer   Jeffrey L. Dever

1.

2.

MOSS CAIRNS

Raising meetings to new heights

3.

PALE ALE

4.

5.

6.

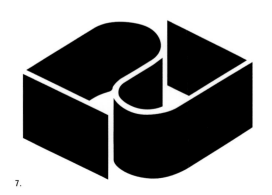

7.

8.

BONDI

9.

10.

11.

> > >
Scott
Braman
photography

12.

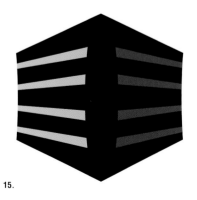

13.

iMAGEMAKER

14.

15.

1, 11			**6.**	
Design Firm	**Oakley Design Studios**		Client	*Cascade Bike Club*
2			Designer	Tim Celeski
Design Firm	**Tyler School of Art Graduate Graphic Design Program**		**7.**	
			Client	*Professional Practice Environments*
3			Designer	Tim Celeski
Design Firm	**Foley Sackett**		**8.**	
4, 8, 9			Client	*S. Asimakopoulas Cafe*
Design Firm	**Lance Anderson Design**		Designer	Lance Anderson
5, 6, 7, 10, 13, 14, 15			**9.**	
Design Firm	**Tim Celeski Studios**		Client	*Michael Bondi Metal Design*
12			Designer	Lance Anderson
Design Firm	**McGaughy Design**		**10.**	
1.			Client	*Interactive Design*
Client	*Doug Baldwin • Writer*		Designer	Tim Celeski
Designer	Tim Oakley		**11.**	
2.			Client	*Meyer Projection Systems*
Client	*Temple University*		Designer	Tim Oakley
Designer	Kristine F. Herrick		**12.**	
3.			Client	*Scott Braman Photography*
Client	*Moss Cairns*		Designer	Malcolm McGaughy
Designer	Chris Cortilet		**13.**	
4.			Client	*Washington Hand Surgery Center*
Client	*California Cafe*		Designer	Tim Celeski
Designers	Lance Anderson, Richard Escasany	**14.**		
5.			Client	*Imagemaker Salon*
Client	*Kathryn Buffum, DDS*		Designer	Tim Celeski
Designer	Tim Celeski		**15.**	
			Client	*Innovation, Inc.*
			Designer	Tim Celeski

1.

2.

3.

4.

5.

6.

7.

8.

P R E M I S E
9. COMMUNICATION SYSTEMS

10.

INTEGRATED
NETWORK
CONCEPTS

11.

SALEM STATE COLLEGE
PROGREDI
1854

12.

KOMAR®

13.

a family of sleepwear

DIAMOND EXCHANGE ◆X

14.

VIACOM NEWMEDIA™

15.

1, 2, 3, 7, 10, 12
Design Firm **Selbert Perkins Design Collaborative**

4, 6, 8, 13, 14, 15
Design Firm **Doublespace**

5, 9, 11
Design Firm **Stein & Company**

1.
Client   *The Jerde Partnership*
Designers Robin Perkins, Heather Watson, Tony Dowers

2.
Client   *Los Angeles International Airports*
Designers Clifford Selbert, Gemma Lawson, Jamie Diersing, Rick Simner

3.
Client   *The Jerde Partnership*
Designers Robin Perkins, Greg Welsh

4.
Client   *Diamond Technology Partners*
Creative Director
          Jane Kosstrin
Designer Mark Maltais

5.
Client   *Digital Navigation*
Designer Susan Lesko

6.
Client   *Crunch*
Creative Director
          Jane Kosstrin
Designer Robert Wong

7.
Client   *Open Market, Inc.*
Designers Mike Balint, Clifford Selbert

8.
Client   *The Kitchen*
Creative Director
          Jane Kosstrin
Designer David Buddenhagen

9.
Client   *Premise Communication System*
Designer Randall Herrera

10.
Client   *The Jerde Partnership*
Designers Robin Perkins, John Lutz, Mike Balint, Greg Welsh

11.
Client   *Integrated Network Concepts*
Designers Susan Lesko, Randall Herrera

12.
Client   *Salem State College*
Designers Clifford Selbert, Robert Merk

13.
Client   *Komar*
Creative Director
          Jane Kosstrin
Designer David Lee

14.
Client   *Diamond Technology Partners*
Creative Director
          Jane Kosstrin
Designer Mark Maltais

15.
Client   *Viacom, New Media*
Creative Director
          Jane Kosstrin
Designer Reinhard Knolebelspies

1.

Duluth Playhouse

2.

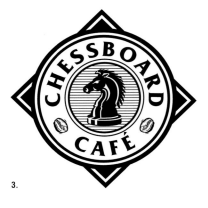

CHESSBOARD CAFÉ

3.

4.

PICCARI PRESS INC.

5.

6.

7.

8.

142

The PRINT Company

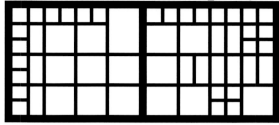

established 1971

9.

ClickCom

10.

11.

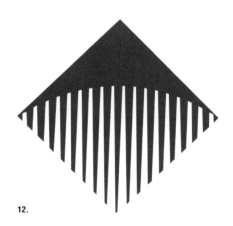

12.

BARR Pictures

13.

Bullseye

14.

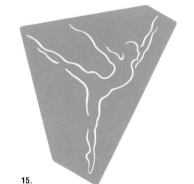

15.

PRIMETECH

1.

2.

3.

4.

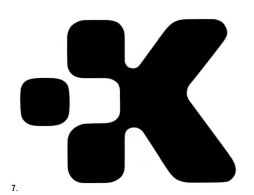

5.

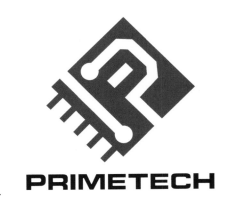

6.

7.

8.

9.

10.

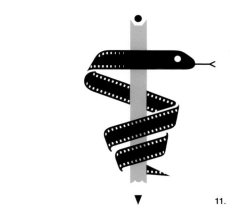

11.

12.

13.

14.

15.

1, 2, 4, 5, 6, 8, 9, 10, 13, 14
Design Firm **The Visual Group**
3, 7, 11, 12, 15
Design Firm **Eskil Ohlsson Associates Inc.**

1.
Client *Primetech, Inc.*
Designers Ark Stein, Bill Mifsud

2.
Client *Andrew Hunt Photography*
Designer Ark Stein

3.
Client *F.T. & M. Inc.*
Designer Eskil Ohlsson

4.
Client *Taxi Service Co.*
Designer Ark Stein

5.
Client *Microtech Co. Inc.*
Designer Ark Stein

6.
Client *The Visual Group*
Designers Ark Stein, Vadim Goretsky

7.
Client *Kroma Lithographers, Inc.*
Designer Eskil Ohlsson

8.
Client *Cabaña Hotel*
Designer Ark Stein

9.
Client *Zero G Software*
Designers Ark Stein, Bill Mifsud

10.
Client *To The Point*
Designer Ark Stein

11.
Client *Cline, Davis & Mann Inc. (Proworx)*
Designers Andy Moore, Eskil Ohlsson

12.
Client *Mercantile Leasing Corp.*
Designer Eskil Ohlsson

13.
Client *Evotech Co. Inc.*
Designer Ark Stein

14.
Client *Sentius Corporation*
Designers Bill Mifsud, Ark Stein

15.
Client *T. Rowe Price*
Designer Eskil Ohlsson

1.

SaraLee®

2.

Memorex®

3.

COMFORTS
SAN ANSELMO, CALIFORNIA

4.

5.

6.

7.

c o n

1.

2.

3.

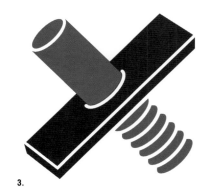

TROY SYSTEMS

4.

SYNETICS

5.

6.

TechnologyChambers

7.

8.

9.

10.

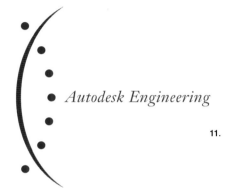

Autodesk Engineering

11.

12.

STACKS'

13.

METASYS

14.

FRANZIA

15.

1		
Design Firm	**R. Morris Design**	
2, 6, 7, 14		
Design Firm	**Steve Thomas Marketing Communications**	
3, 8, 9, 11-13		
Design Firm	**Bruce Yelaska Design**	
4, 5		
Design Firm	**Grafik Communications, Ltd**	
10		
Design Firm	**Heckler Associates**	
15		
Design Firm	**Axion Design Inc.**	
1.		
Client	*Icon Design*	
Designer	Rock Morris	
2.		
Client	*Loftin & Company*	
Designer	Steve Thomas	
3.		
Client	*Autodesk Engineering*	
Designers	Bruce Yelaska, John Seminario	
4.		
Client	*Troy Systems*	
Designers	David Collins, Judy Kirpich	
5.		
Client	*Synetics*	
Designers	Kristin Moore, Judy Kirpich	

6.	
Client	*Fred Wilkerson*
Designer	Steve Thomas
7.	
Client	*Technology Chambers*
Designer	Steve Thomas
8.	
Client	*La Pinata*
Designer	Bruce Yelaska
9.	
Client	*Cafe Toma*
Designers	Bruce Yelaska
10.	
Client	*Starbucks Coffee Co.*
Designer	Terry Heckler
11.	
Client	*Autodesk Engineering*
Designer	Bruce Yelaska
12.	
Client	*The University of California*
Designer	Bruce Yelaska
13.	
Client	*Stacks'*
Designer	Bruce Yelaska
14.	
Client	*Metasys*
Designers	Steve Thomas
15.	
Client	*Franzia*

Inland Entertainment
C O R P O R A T I O N

1.

FIRSTWORLD™
C O M M U N I C A T I O N S

2.

3.

AIRTOUCH
PREMIER
PROGRAM

4.

ANIKA
THERAPEUTICS

5.

BIG DEAHL

6.

WILD▷LIFE

7.

1-4, 6, 7
Design Firm **Mires Design, Inc.**

5
Design Firm **Ellis Pratt Design**

1.
Client   *Inland Entertainment Corporation*
Designers   José Serrano, John Ball,
Miguel Perez
Illustrator   Miguel Perez

2.
Client   *First World Communications*
Designers   John Ball, Miguel Perez,
Kathy Carpentier-Moore

3.
Client   *Nike Inc.*
Designers   John Ball, Miguel Perez
Illustrator   Tracy Sabin

4.
Client   *Airtouch Cellular*
Designers   Scott Mires, Deborah Hom

5.
Client   *Anika Therapeutics*
Designers   Elaine Pratt, Vernon Ellis

6.
Client   *Big Deahl*
Designers   José Serrano, Miguel Perez

7.
Client   *California Center for the Arts*
Designers   John Ball, Gale Spitzley
(opposite)
Client   *Green Field Paper Company*
Design Firm   **Mires Design, Inc.**
Designers   José Serrano, Miguel Perez
Illustrator   Dan Thoner

1.

2.

3.

4.

NOVACOR

5.

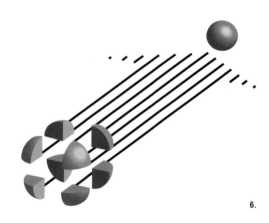

6.

Midland Mall

7.

8.

9.

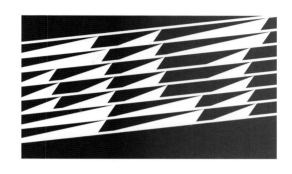

10.

11.

12.

13.

14.

15.

1, 4, 6, 10, 13, 14
  Design Firm **Joe Miller's Company**
2, 3, 7-9, 11, 12, 15
  Design Firm **Herip Design Associates**
5
  Design Firm **Burson Marstellar/
  Joe Miller's Company**

1.
  Client   *Quantum*
  Designers   Joe Miller, Mai Nguyen
2.
  Client   *The Richard E. Jacobs Group*
  Designer   John R. Menter
3.
  Client   *Indian Creek Farm*
  Designer   Walter M. Herip
4.
  Client   *Grand/Abacus Business Forms*
  Designer   Joe Miller
5.
  Client   *Novacor*
  Designer   Joe Miller
6.
  Client   *Tandem*
  Designers   Joe Miller, Michael Lauretano

7.
  Client   *The Richard E. Jacobs Group*
  Designer   John R. Menter
8.
  Client   *Ronald H. Rasmussen Assoc.*
  Designer   Walter M. Herip
9.
  Client   *Herip Design Associates*
  Designer   Walter M. Herip
10.
  Client   *Quantum*
  Designers   Joe Miller, Mai Nguyen
11.
  Client   *Illes Construction Company*
  Designers   Walter M. Herip, John R. Menter
12.
  Client   *John D. May, Jr., Inc.*
  Designer   Walter M. Herip
13.
  Client   *Rocket Productions*
  Designer   Joe Miller
14.
  Client   *Shade*
  Designer   Joe Miller
15.
  Client   *The Richard E. Jacobs Group*
  Designer   Walter M. Herip, John R. Menter

153

DENVER BUFFALO COMPANY

1.

Kootenai
Medical
Center

2.

3.

4.

Hanifen, Imhoff
Clearing Corp.

5.

FISERV CORRESPONDENT SERVICES, INC.

6.

THE ISLAND CLUB
Great Exuma · Bahamas

7.

Commercial Federal

8.

Medical Centers

9.

10.

Golf Lodging™

11.

12.

13.

14.

A VISION OF THE FUTURE

15.

(all)
Design Firm **Matrix International Assoc., Ltd.**

1.
Client — Denver Buffalo Co.
Designers — Duane Wiens, Dan Funk

2.
Client — Kootenai Medical Center
Designers — Duane Wiens, Matt Scharf

3.
Client — Daniels & Associates, Inc.
Designers — Duane Wiens, Carl Baden

4.
Client — Anthem Homes, Inc.
Designers — Duane Wiens, Dan Funk

5.
Client — Hanifen Imhoff, Inc.
Designers — Duane Wiens, Carl Baden

6.
Client — Fiserv Correspondent Services, Inc.
Designers — Duane Wiens, Carl Baden

7.
Client — The Bahama Club
Designers — Duane Wiens, Dan Funk

8.
Client — Commercial Federal Bank, Inc.
Designers — Duane Wiens, Carl Baden

9.
Client — Concentra Medical Centers
Designers — Duane Wiens, Dan Funk

10.
Client — FirsTier Financial Corp.
Designers — Duane Wiens, Carl Baden

11.
Client — Golf Lodging LLC
Designers — Duane Wiens, Dan Funk, Margo Newman

12.
Client — Amquest Financial Corp.
Designers — Duane Wiens, Carl Baden

13.
Client — Vanguard Airlines
Designers — Duane Wiens, Carl Baden

14.
Client — Yale New Haven Health
Designers — Duane Wiens, Margo Newman

15.
Client — Daniels & Associates
Designers — Duane Wiens, Dan Funk

1.

BARCLAY TOWERS

2.

3.

CME

4.

5.

The Children's Hospital

**THE KOSSOW
CORPORATION**

6.

7.

8.

9.

Vail Associates, Inc.

10.

plan west

11.

12.

13.

14.

YMCA OF THE ROCKIES

THE BAHAMA CLUB

15.

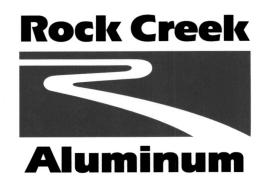

Rock Creek Aluminum

1.

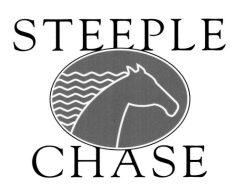

STEEPLE CHASE

2.

SUMMIT CONSULTING GROUP

3.

ULTRA FAB

4.

SUMMIT PARTNERS

5.

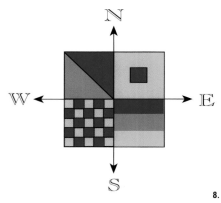

Global Cinema
NETWORK

6.

VIKING

7.

8.

158

9.

10.

11.

12.

13.

JOHNSTON
METAL INDUSTRIES

14.

15.

LINDSAY OLIVE COMPANY · EST 1916

CALIF.   RIPE

Pitted

OLIVES

LARGE

1.

2.

3.

SAN FRANCISCO FOOD BANK

Feeding the programs that feed the people

4.

T|C **The** Learning Company

For Greater Knowledge

5.

6.

VSP

AMERICA'S FIRST CHOICE FOR EYECARE ℠

7.

8.

consensus
H E A L T H

9.

preview

travel SM

10.

LASER & SKIN AESTHETICS CENTER

11.

REEL CITY
P R O D U C T I O N S

12.

pandesic ™

13.

OIL CHANGERS 3000

14.

HOLLAND
BROTHERS ™
HANDMADE IN AMERICA

15.

1, 3-10, 12-15
Design Firm **Addis Group**
2, 11
Design Firm **Pink Coyote Design, Inc.**

1.
Client — *Lindsay Olives Co.*
Designers — Debbie Smith Read, Robert Evans

2.
Client — *Space Age Advertising, Inc.*
Designer — Joel Ponzan

3.
Client — *Bell • Carter Foods*
Designers — Debbie Smith Read, Robert Evans

4.
Client — *San Francisco Food Bank*
Designer — Joanne Hom

5.
Client — *The Learning Company*
Designer — Rick Atwood

6.
Client — *Critical Path*
Designers — James Eli, Bob Hullinger, Jimmy Yeung

7.
Client — *Vision Service Plan*
Designer — Peggy Ng

8.
Client — *Solaris Group*
Designers — David Leong, Justin Oberbauer, Paul Dorian, Hamagami Carrol, Robin MacLean

9.
Client — *Consensus Health*
Designer — Michelle Shibata Schwartz

10.
Client — *Preview Travel*
Designer — Joanne Hom

11.
Client — *Laser & Skin Aesthetics Center*
Designer — Joel Ponzan

12.
Client — *Reel City Productions*
Designer — Joanne Hom

13.
Client — *Pandesic*
Designers — Rick Atwood, James Eli

14.
Client — *Oil Changers*
Designers — James Eli, Rick Atwood

15.
Client — *Holland Brothers*
Designers — Debbie Smith Read, David Leong

1.

2.

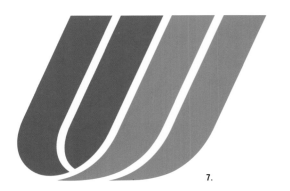

CLOTHES THE DEAL

3.

4. WCBF

5.

6.

7.

(all)
Design Firm **Shimokochi/Reeves**
1.
Client *United Way of America*
Art Director Saul Bass
Designers Saul Bass, Mamoru Shimokochi
Artists Art Goodman, Mamoru Shimokochi
Agency Saul Bass & Assoc.
2.
Client *Intellisystems*
Designers Mamoru Shimokochi, Anne Reeves
3.
Client *Clothes The Deal*
Designers Mamoru Shimokochi, Anne Reeves
4.
Client *WCBF—World Children's Baseball Fair*
Designers Mamoru Shimokochi, Anne Reeves

5.
Client *X-Century*
Designers Mamoru Shimokochi, Anne Reeves
6.
Client *Warp, Inc.*
Designers Mamoru Shimokochi, Anne Reeves
7.
Client *United Airlines*
Art Directors Saul Bass, Art Goodman
Designers Saul Bass, Art Goodman, Mamoru Shimokochi, Vince Carra
Agency Saul Bass & Assoc.
(opposite)
Client *TBS—Tokyo Broadcasting System*
Design Firm **Shimokochi/Reeves**
Designers Mamoru Shimokochi, Anne Reeves

Tokyo Broadcasting System

1.

SHARKFIRE

2.

MINGTAI

3.

ANDON
UNLIMITED

4.

Eltron ®

5.

6.

PACIFIC
WORLD

™

7.

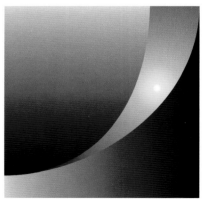

8.

rks

9.

10.

**General
Contractors**

11.

MERCURY *Systems*

12.

Occupational
HealthSource

14.

13.

**ARTUR O
DESIGNS**
distinctive furniture

15.

1, 10
Design Firm **MediaConcepts Corporation**
2, 12, 14, 15
Design Firm **DiBaggio Design**
3, 7
Design Firm **Shimokochi/Reeves**
4, 6, 13
Design Firm **Gable Design Group**
5, 8, 9, 11
Design Firm **RKS Design, Inc.**
1.
Client *Oasis Club/Gatehouse Companies*
Designer Christopher O'Toole
2.
Client *Lopresti Bros. Aircraft, Inc.*
Designer Brad DiBaggio
3.
Client *Mingtai Insurance*
Designers Mamoru Shimokochi, Anne Reeves
4.
Client *Wizards of the Coast*
Designers Tony Gable, Steffanie Lorig
5.
Client *Eltron*
Designer Jonathan Dyer
6.
Client *Kenny G/Artista Records*
Designer Tony Gable

7.
Client *Pacific World Corporation*
Designers Mamoru Shimokochi, Anne Reeves
8.
Client *JM Financial*
Designer Grace Guy
9.
Client *RKS Design, Inc.*
Designer Kristin Allen
10.
Client *Springbrook Commons/*
Gatehouse Cos.
Designers Paul Beaulieu, Tim Coletti
11.
Client *EPI General Contractors*
Designer Jonathan Dyer
12.
Client *Mercury Systems*
Designer Brad DiBaggio
13.
Client *Bronn Journey*
Designers Tony Gable, Jana Nishi
14.
Client *Nix Health Care System*
Designer Brad DiBaggio
15.
Client *Arturo Designs*
Designer Brad DiBaggio

1.

2.

3.

4.

5.

6.

7.

8.

Women for Women 9.

10.

DULLES TECH CENTER 11.

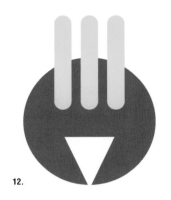

12.

ONE
FAIR
OAKS

13.

TIMEBRIDGE ™
TECHNOLOGIES

14.

15.

1.

TM

3.

SYLVESTRE
FRANC
SALON

4.

5.

7.

2.

6.

8.

9.

10.

PINNACLE

11.

13.

15.

14.

1.

APPLIED
GLOBAL
UNIVERSITY

2.

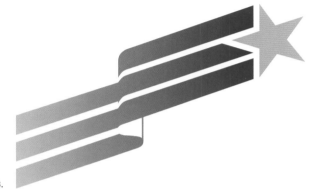

3.

4. SOLUTIONS FOR EMBEDDED SYSTEMS INTEGRATION

5.

6. A S K S

7. PRODUCTION SERVICES INC.

8.

170

Wireless Financial Services

9.

STRUCT-A-LITE 10.

ATCC 11.

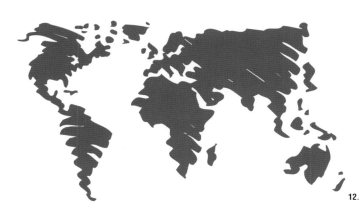

12.

Anergen

13.

ecomat

14.

McCAULEY™

15.

1
Design Firm **Bruce Yelaska Design**
2, 6, 13
Design Firm **Howry Design Associates**
3, 12
Design Firm **MediaConcept Corporation**
4, 7, 8, 10, 15
Design Firm **Nova Creative Group, Inc.**
5
Design Firm **Stephanie Cunningham**
9, 11, 14
Design Firm **Stephen Loges Graphic Design**

1.
Client   *The Gauntlett Group*
Designer   Bruce Yelaska
2.
Client   *Applied Global University*
Art Director Jill Howry
Designer   Todd Richards
3.
Client   *The Boston Plan for Excellence in the Public Schools*
Designer   Chris O'Toole
4.
Client   *ITCN*
Designer   Tim O'Hare
5.
Client   *Arachnid Design*
Designer   Stephanie Cunningham

6.
Client   *Applied Strategic Knowledge Solutions*
Art Director Jill Howry
Designer   Todd Richards
7.
Client   *MainSail Production Services*
Designer   Tim O'Hare
8.
Client   *Elliott Tool Technologies*
Designer   Greg Vennerholm
9.
Client   *Wireless Financial Services, Inc.*
Designer   Stephen Loges
10.
Client   *Struct-A-Lite*
Designer   Tim O'Hare
11.
Client   *ATCC (American Type Culture Collection)*
Designer   Stephen Loges
12.
Client   *Schmid*
Designer   Paul Beaulieu
13.
Client   *Anergen, Inc.*
Art Director Jill Howry
Designer   Gayle Steinbeigle
14.
Client   *Ecofranchising, Inc.*
Designer   Stephen Loges
15.
Client   *McCauley Propellers*
Designer   Dwayne Swormstedt

1.

2.

WOR**LDES**IGN

3.

MACDONALD CONSTRUCTION

4.

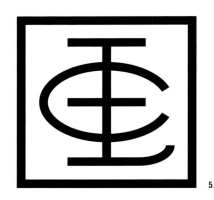

5.

|m|a|h|a|r|a|m|

6.

7.

1, 2
Design Firm **Ross West Design**
3, 5-7
Design Firm **Matsumoto Incorporated**
4
Design Firm **Icon Imagery**
1.
Client   *Universal Bar*
Designer Ross West
2.
Client   *Victory Coffee*
Designer Ross West
3.
Client   *Worldesign Foundation*
Designer Takaaki Matsumoto
4.
Client   *MacDonald Construction*
Designer Ross West

5.
Client   *Sazaby, Inc.*
Designer Takaaki Matsumoto
6.
Client   *Maharam*
Designer Takaaki Matsumoto
7.
Client   *Greenwich Village*
            Chamber of Commerce
Designer Takaaki Matsumoto
(opposite)
Client   *Okinawa Aquarium*
Design Firm **Matsumoto Incorporated**
Designer Takaaki Matsumoto

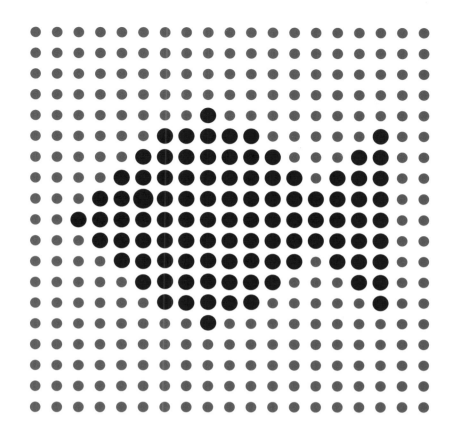

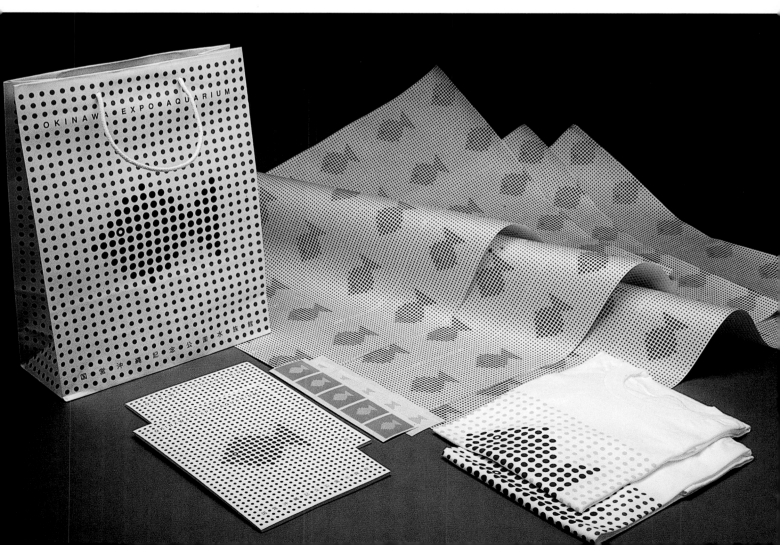

1.

2.

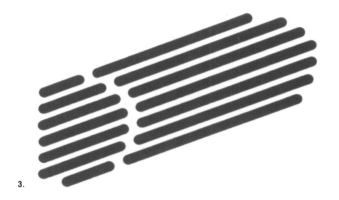

3.

4.

5.

6.

7.

8.

174

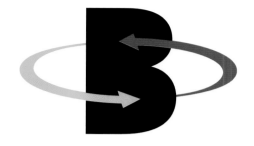

B TREE

9.

10.

11.

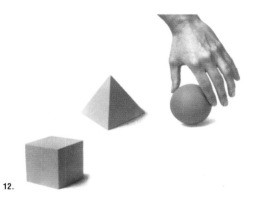

12.

AgriSolutions

13.

14.

15.

175

1-5, 7, 11, 12, 14, 15
Design Firm **Laura Kay Design**
6, 9, 13
Design Firm **Little & Company**
8
Design Firm **David Brodsky Graphic Design**
10
Design Firm **Price Learman Associates**

1.
Client   Tepper Innovations
Designers   Laura Kay, Donald Kay
2.
Client   Southern Oregon Appraisal Services
Designers   Laura Kay, Donald Kay
3.
Client   Draney Telemarketing
Designers   Laura Kay, Donald Kay
4.
Client   Brill Metalworks
Designers   Laura Kay, Donald Kay
5.
Client   Lithia Automotive
Designers   Laura Kay, Donald Kay
6.
Client   D'Amicao, Metropolitan
Design Director
       Jim Jackson
Designers   Tom Riddle, Garin Ipsen

7.
Client   Thomas Register
Designers   Laura Kay, Donald Kay
8.
Client   St. John's Hospital
Designer   David Brodsky
9.
Client   B-Tree
Design Director
       Jim Jackson
Designer   Scott Sorenson
10.
Client   Jim Dickinson
Designer   Ross West
11.
Client   R & R Transportation Services
Designers   Laura Kay, Donald Kay
12.
Client   Southern Oregon Hand
       Rehabilitation
Designers   Laura Kay, Donald Kay
13.
Client   AgriSolutions
Design Director
       Paul Wharton
Designer   Tom Riddle
14.
Client   Tara Labs
Designers   Laura Kay, Donald Kay
15.
Client   Thomas Register
Designers   Laura Kay, Donald Kay

ProduceOne

1.

MIAMI VALLEY
WOMEN'S
CENTER

3.

5.

VINEYARD
CHRISTIAN FELLOWSHIP

7.

Strategic Accounts

2.

T R E A S U R E D

M O M E N T S

P H O T O G R A P H Y

4.

CHEROKEE
COMMUNICATIONS, INC.

6.

1-3, 5, 7
Design Firm **Graphica, Inc.**
4, 6
Design Firm **Zoe Graphics**
1.
Client *Produce One*
Designer Michael England
2.
Client *Square D*
Designers Al Hidalgo, Mike England
3.
Client *Miami Valley Women's Center*
Designer Michael England
4.
Client *Treasured Moments*
Designers Kim Waters, Kelly Dodds
5.
Client *Kim Cooper*
Designer Jeff Stapleton

6.
Client *Cherokee Communications*
Designers Kathy Pagano, Kim Waters
7.
Client *Dayton Vineyard Christian Fellowship*
Designer Michael England
(opposite)
Client *Crown Equipment Corp.*
Design Firm **Graphica, Inc.**
Designer Drew Cronenwett

176

THE CROWN STORE

1.

2.

3.

ACME

4.

5.

IVY *Technologies*™

6.

7.

8.

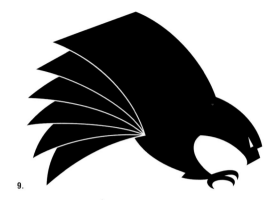

9.

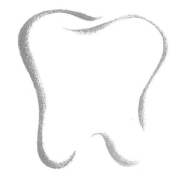

10.

11.

12.

ONE WORLD MUSIC

13.

INTELLIGENT BIOCIDES

14.

15.

1, 5, 9, 10
   Design Firm **Lambert Design Studio**
2, 3, 7, 12, 14, 15
   Design Firm **Little & Company**
4, 6
   Design Firm **Eisenkramer Associates**
8
   Design Firm **Kiku Obata & Company**
11, 13
   Design Firm **Ed Mantels-Seeker**

1.
   Client   *Mary Kay Cosmetics—Career Essentials*
   Designers   Christie Lambert, Dona Smith
2.
   Client   *Venture Stores*
   Designer   Ed Mantels-Seeker
3.
   Client   *Synteni*
   Designers   Ed Mantels-Seeker, Dari Shalon
4.
   Client   *Acme Premium Supply*
   Designer   Ed Mantels-Seeker
5.
   Client   *International Music Network*
   Designers   Christie Lambert, Joy Cathey-Price
6.
   Client   *Ivy Technologies*
   Designer   Ed Mantels-Seeker

7.
   Client   *Ham On Rye Technologies*
   Designer   Deborah Finkelstein
   Illustrator   Bryan Haynes
8.
   Client   *Barnes West County Hospital - Cosmetic Surgery Center*
   Designer   Ed Mantels-Seeker
9.
   Client   *Harrington Elementary Hawk's Nest Publishing*
   Designers   Christie Lambert, Joy Cathey-Price
10.
   Client   *Anita Paulus, DDS*
   Designer   Christie Lambert
11.
   Client   *Metaphase/ NCR Consulting Design Group*
   Designer   Ed Mantels-Seeker
12.
   Client   *Deep Cool*
   Designer   Steve Wienke
13.
   Client   *One World Music*
   Designer   Ed Mantels-Seeker
14.
   Client   *Intelligent Biocides*
   Designer   Ed Mantels-Seeker
15.
   Client   *Tangerine*
   Designer   Deborah Finkelstein

1.

2.

3.

4.

5.

COSMED

6.

7.

1, 5-7
Design Firm **Phoenix Creative, St. Louis**

2
Design Firm **Ed Mantels-Seeker**

3, 4
Design Firm **Kiku Obata & Company**

1.
Client *Shandwick USA/ Jewish Federation of St. Louis*
Designers Ed Mantels-Seeker, Eric Thoelke

2.
Client *The Sambistas*
Designer Ed Mantels-Seeker

3.
Client *Barnes West County Hospital - Sports Medicine Center*
Designer Ed Mantels-Seeker

4.
Client *The Vein Center*
Designer Ed Mantels-Seeker

5.
Client *Net Effects*
Designer Deborah Finkelstein

6.
Client *CosMed*
Designer Ed Mantels-Seeker

7.
Client *Venture Stores*
Designers Ed Mantels-Seeker, Kathy Wilkinson
(opposite)
Client *Kaldi's Coffee Roasting*
Design Firm **Phoenix Creative, St. Louis**
Designer Deborah Finkelstein

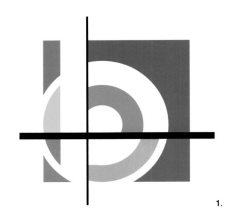

1.

2.

3.

4. **CYPRESS BEND**

PATIO CAFE

5.

6.

cbk:milieu

7.

THE MENTORING INSTITUTE

8.

The Hernia
Institute :

9.

Lil' Britches

10.

11.

COOL BEANS
CAFE

12.

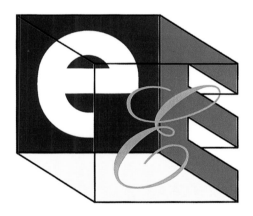

13.

LIGHTHOUSE

14.

SPA SENSE

15.

1, 4, 10 , 11, 15
Design Firm **Sibley/Peteet Design**
2
Design Firm **Ed Mantels-Seeker**
3, 7, 8, 12, 13
Design Firm **Phoenix Creative, St. Louis**
5
Design Firm **CSUS Foundation,
Marketing Services**
6
Design Firm **Angela Jackson**
9
Design Firm **Kiku Obata & Company**
14
Design Firm **Lighthouse Advertising &
Design, Inc.**

1.
Client *Buchanan Printing*
Designer Howard Weliver
2.
Client *Ziezo Modern Clothes*
Designer Ed Mantels-Seeker
3.
Client *Alpine Shop*
Designer Deborah Finkelstein
4.
Client *Cypress Bend*
Designer Donna Aldridge
5.
Client *CSUS Foundation, Food Services*
Designer Angela Jackson

6.
Client *American Portfolio Services*
Designer Angela Jackson
7.
Client *cbk:milieu*
Designer Deborah Finkelstein
8.
Client *The Mentoring Institute*
Designer Steve Wienke
9.
Client *The Hernia Institute*
Designers Ed Mantels-Seeker, Rich Nelson
10.
Client *Lil' Britches*
Designer Howard Weliver
11.
Client *Colorscan Dallas*
Designer Donna Aldridge
12.
Client *Cool Beans Cafe*
Designer Kathy Wilkinson
13.
Client *Studio E / Hok Architects*
Designer Deborah Finkelstein
14.
Client *Lighthouse Advertising*
Creative Director
Katherine Price
Designer/Art Director
Elaine Wilson
15.
Client *CBI Packaging*
Designer Joy Cathey Price

HAMILTON

KENNEDY

1.

SUNHOUSE

2.

Mississippi Museum of Art

3.

WetZone
WAVEGAMES

4.

SHORE SCORES

5.

D4 Creative Group

6.

7.

8.

184

FiberComm L.L.C. 9.

FIRE ANT
FESTIVAL 10.

JUNIOR
LEAGUE
OF JACKSON

11.

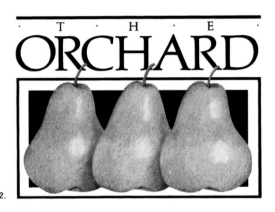

THE
ORCHARD

12.

13.

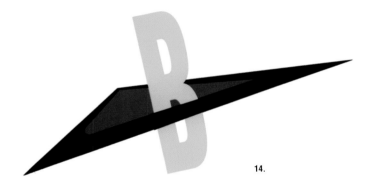

14.

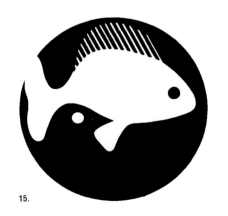

15.

1-3, 8, 10-13, 15
   Design Firm **Communication Arts Company**
4, 14
   Design Firm **Visual Marketing Associates**
5-7, 9
   Design Firm **D4 Creative Group**

1.
   Client   *Hamilton Kennedy*
   Designer Hilda Stauss Owen
2.
   Client   *Sunhouse*
   Designer Hilda Sauss Owen
3.
   Client   *Mississippi Museum of Art*
   Designer Hap Owen
4.
   Client   *InGear*
   Designer Greg Vennerholm
5.
   Client   *Shore Scores*
   Designer Wicky W. Lee
6.
   Client   *D4 Creative Group*
   Designer Wicky W. Lee

7.
   Client   *PrimeStar Satellite TV*
   Designer Wicky W. Lee
8.
   Client   *Junk Jewels*
   Designer Ashley Barron
9.
   Client   *FIberComm L.L.C.*
   Designer Wicky W. Lee
10.
   Client   *Homebrew Productions*
   Designer Hilda Stauss Owen
11.
   Client   *Junior League of Jackson*
   Designer Hap Owen
12.
   Client   *The Orchard*
   Designer Rebecca Olack
13.
   Client   *Phoenix Consulting Corporation*
   Designer Anne-Marie Otvos Cain
14.
   Client   *InGear (Bermuda Triangle)*
   Designer Jason Selke
15.
   Client   *White Cypress Lakes*
   Designer Hap Owen

1.

2.

3.

4.

5.

6.

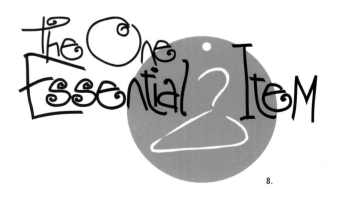

7.

8.

9.

10.

11.

12.

13.

14.

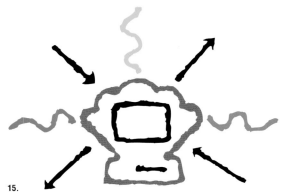

15.

1.

2.

F er E xport
MANAGEMENT INC
3.

HEINEN CONSTRUCTION
4.

5.

K V K   C O M P U T E R S
6.

COMPANY
ANALYST
7.

SHEERLUND FORESTS
CHRISTMAS TREE FARM
EST. 1901
8.

COURTYARD
C A F E

9.

HANNIBAL'S
COFFEE COMPANY

10.

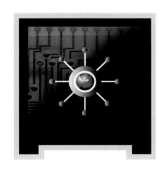

11. D A T A B O X

12.

INFO STAR
I N C O R P O R A T E D

13.

ANALYST TOOL™
A PRODUCT OF DISCLOSURE INCORPORATED

Water Spirits Music

14.

15.

1, 4, 5, 14
Design Firm **Jefrey Gunion Illustration & Design**
2
Design Firm **Design Moves, Ltd.**
3, 6-13, 15
Design Firm **Lomangino Studio, Inc.**

1.
Client *Silicon Graphics*
Designers Frank Doyle, Jefrey Gunion

2.
Client *Association of Home Appliance Manufacturers*
Designers Laurie Medeiros Freed, Laura Munro

3.
Client *Fer Export Management, Inc.*
Designer Lomangino Studio

4.
Client *Heinen Construction*
Designer Jefrey Gunion

5.
Client *Shear Edge*
Designer Jefrey Gunion

6.
Client *KVK Computers*
Designer Arthur Hsu

7.
Client *Disclosure, Inc.*
Designer Kimberly Pollock

8.
Client *Sheerlund Forests*
Designer Alain Blunt

9.
Client *Sheraton Washington Hotel*
Designer Al Berces

10.
Client *Hannibal's Coffee Company*
Designer Alain Blunt

11.
Client *Graphtel*
Designer Enrique Domenech

12.
Client *Infostar, Inc.*
Designer Alan Blunt

13.
Client *Disclosure, Inc.*
Designer Alain Blunt

14.
Client *Water Spirits Music*
Designer Jefrey Gunion

15.
Client *Axiom Training, Inc.*
Designer Kimberly Pollock

CAYMAN ISLANDS

1.

BROWN DEER PRESS

2.

3.

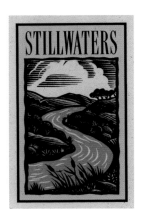

STILLWATERS

4.

5.

BAYONA

6.

THE RIDGE

7.

1, 4
Design Firms **Mires Design, Simple Green**
2
Design Firm **Miriello Grafico**
3
Design Firm **Stoorza, Zeigas & Metzger**
5
Design Firm **Crouch & Naegli**
6
Design Firm **Mires Design**
7
Design Firm **The Flowers Group**
1.
  Client   *The Masters Group*
  Designers Mike Brower, Tracy Sabin
  Illustrator Tracy Sabin
2.
  Client   *Harcourt Brace & Co.*
  Designers Ron Miriello, Tracy Sabin
  Illustrator Tracy Sabin
3.
  Client   *San Diego Gas & Electric*
               (Coyote Division)
  Art Director Craig Fuller
  Designer, Illustrator
               Tracy Sabin

4.
  Client   *Total Quality Apparel*
  Designer   Mike Brower
  Illustrator Tracy Sabin
5.
  Client   *University of California, San Diego*
  Art Directors Jim Crouch, Jim Naegli
  Designer, Illustrator
               Tracy Sabin
6.
  Client   *McMillin Homes*
  Art Director José Serrano
  Designer, Illustrator
               Tracy Sabin
7.
  Client   *The Ridge*
  Designers Cory Sheehan, Tracy Sabin
  Illustrator Tracy Sabin
(opposite)
  Client   *McMillin Homes*
  Design Firm **Mires Design**
  Art Director José Serrano
  Designer, Illustrator
               Tracy Sabin

At Cadiz, we've recreated the look of a traditional Spanish country cottage, right down to the wooden garden gates and the red tile roofs. And, more important, we've recaptured the feel with cozy front gardens, enchanting patios, ...book balconies. ...all the ...ter-

CADIZ

1.

2.

3.

4.

MONKEY  STUDIOS

5.

Bridgewater

6.

7.

CURRENT COMMUNICATIONS

8.

ODYSSEY

9.

10.

BRIDLEWOOD

11.

12.

13.

TRACY SABIN
GRAPHIC DESIGN

14.

15.

1, 6, 11
Design Firm **Knoth & Meads**
2-5, 7-10, 12-15
Design Firm **Tracy Sabin Graphic Design**
1-10, 12-15
Designer, Illustrator
        Tracy Sabin

1.
  Client   *McMillin Homes*
  Art Director José Serrano
2.
  Client   *The Miller Band*
  Art Director Jim Welsh
3.
  Client   *Consolite Corporation*
  Art Director Robert Stetzel
4.
  Client   *Chief Executive Magazine*
  Art Director Michael Carpenter
5.
  Client   *Monkey Studios*
  Art Director Russell Sabin
6.
  Client   *McMillin Homes*
  Art Director José Serrano

7.
  Client   *California Beach Co.*
  Art Director Richard Sawyer
8.
  Client   *Current Communications*
  Art Director Alison Hill
9.
  Client   *Harcourt Brace & Co.*
  Art Director Lisa Peters
10.
  Client   *Taylor Guitars*
  Art Director Rita Hoffman
11.
  Client   *McMillin Homes*
  Designer   John Vitro
  Illustrator Tracy Sabin
12.
  Client   *Turner Entertainment*
  Art Director Alison Hill
13.
  Client   *Turner Entertainment*
  Art Director Lisa Peters
14.
  Client   *Tracy Sabin Graphic Design*
15.
  Client   *Uptown Car Wash*
  Art Director Van Oliver

BRIDGING *the* PACIFIC

1.

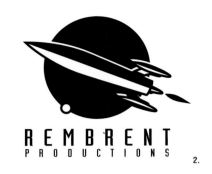

REMBRENT
PRODUCTIONS

2.

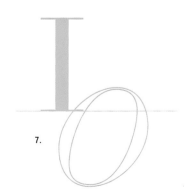

3.

GREATER MINNEAPOLIS
CHAMBER OF COMMERCE

4.

KeyWare™

5.

6.

7.

STERNER™

8.

PENTAMERICA PICTURES

9.

LUTHERAN BROTHERHOOD

10.

DigitalMedia*L.L.P.*

11.

12.

BARLOW RESEARCH ASSOCIATES, INC.

13.

14.

THE VENETIAN
Resort·Hotel·Casino ~ Las Vegas

15.

1, 4, 5, 8, 10 - 14
Design Firm **Yamamoto Moss**
2, 3, 6, 9
Design Firm **B.D. Fox & Friends, Advertising**
7, 15
Design Firm **Maddocks & Company**
1.
  Client   *Northwest Airlines*
  Designer Brian Adducci
2.
  Client   *Rembrent Productions*
  Designer Garrett Burke
3.
  Client   *Interplay*
  Designer Garrett Burke
4.
  Client   *Greater Minneapolis*
            Chamber of Commerce
  Designer Keiko Takahashi
5.
  Client   *Racotek*
  Designers Alan Tse, Chris Cortilet
6.
  Client   *The Sci-Fi Channel*
  Designer Rob Biro
7.
  Client   *CBI Laboratories, Inc.*
  Creative Director, Designer
            Julia Precht

8.
  Client   *Sterner Lighting System Inc.*
  Designer Kasey Worrell
9.
  Client   *Pentamerica Pictures*
  Designer Rob Biro
10.
  Client   *Lutheran Brotherhood*
  Designer Hideki Yamamoto
11.
  Client   *Digital Media*
  Designer Alan Tse
12.
  Client   *Barlow Research Associates*
  Designer Keiko Takahashi
13.
  Designer Amee Husek
14.
  Client   *CNS*
  Designers Joan McCarrell, Alan Tse
15.
  Client   *The Venetian Hotel & Resort*
  Creative Director
            Mary Scott
  Designer Dave Chapple, Amy Hershman
  Illustrator Martin Ledvard

1.

2.

3.

4.

5.

6.

7.

1, 2
Design Firm **Inklings Design**
3, 6
Design Firm **Karen Skunta & Company**
4, 5, 7
Design Firm **Cadmus Com**
1.
Client — *Inklings Design*
Designer — John Gruber
2.
Client — *Plaza Builders Inc.*
Designer — John Gruber
3.
Client — *Signal Bank*
Designers — Karen L. Hauser, Christopher Oldham, Christopher Suster, Karen A. Skunta

4.
Client — *Azalea Films*
Designer — Brian Thomson
5.
Client — *CFW Communications*
Designer — Brian Thomson
6.
Client — *Whole Health Management Inc.*
Designers — Christopher Suster, Karen A. Skunta
7.
Client — *Gabbert Hood Photography*
Designer — Jess Schaich
(opposite)
Client — *The Freedom Forum*
Design Firm **Yasumura Assoc., Muts & Joy & Design**
Designer — Gisele Sangiovanni

1.

MTM FAMILY NETWORK

2.

3.

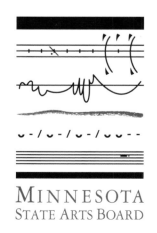

Gillette Children's *Specialty Healthcare*

4.

Guthrie Theater

5.

The **Fisher's** Net

6.

MINNESOTA STATE ARTS BOARD

7.

Discovery begins here

8.

9.

10.

11.

12.

13.

14.

15.

1 - 3, 10 -13		
Design Firm	**B.D. Fox & Friends, Advertising**	
4 - 9, 14, 15		
Design Firm	**Yamamoto Moss**	
1.		
Client	*Warner Bros.*	
Designers	Bill Garland, Lee MacLeod	
2.		
Client	*MTM Television Distribution*	
Designer	Cindy Luck	
3.		
Client	*Big Entertainment*	
Designer	Garrett Burke	
4.		
Client	*Gillette Children's Hospital*	
Designer	Kasey Worrell	
5.		
Designer	Brian Adducci	
6.		
Client	*Lutheran Brotherhood*	
Designer	Alan Tse	

7.	
Client	*Minnesota State Arts Board*
Designer	Julie Szamocki
8.	
Designer	Brain Adducci
9.	
Client	*TARGET Greatland*
Designer	Brian Adducci
10.	
Client	*Sega of America*
Designer	Garrett Burke
11.	
Client	*Republic Pictures*
Designer	Cindy Luck
12.	
Client	*Big Entertainment*
Designers	Rob Biro, Mike Bryan
13.	
Client	*Summit Entertainment*
14.	
Client	*Green Mountain Energy Partners*
Designers	Kasey Worrell, Keiko Takahashi
15.	
Client	*Concordia College*
Designer	Brian Adducci

1.

2.

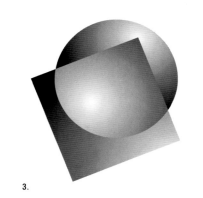

3.

NOVALIS™

4.

SUSQUEHANNA
ADDICTIONS CENTER

5.

6.

7.

1
  Design Firm **McDermott Design**
2 - 7
  Design Firm **Albert•Bögner Design
                Communications**
1.
  Client   *Leisuremaster, Inc.*
  Designer   Bill McDermott
2.
  Client   *ISMS*
  Designer   Kelly Albert
3.
  Client   *Eastern Technology Council*
  Designer   Susan Blakely

4.
  Client   *Novalis International Limited*
  Designer   Marie-Elaina Miller
5.
  Client   *Susquehanna Addiction Center*
  Designer   Marie-Elaina Miller
6.
  Client   *JAS Technology*
  Designer   Kelly Albert
7.
  Client   *Shinkosky Remodeling & Design*
  Designer   Susan Blakely
(**opposite**)
  Client   *MGM/UA Home Video*
  Design Firm **B.D. Fox & Friends, Advertising**
  Designer   Garrett Burke

DR. NO

YOU ONLY LIVE TWICE

GOLDFINGER

LIVE and LET DIE

THUNDERBALL

THE MAN with THE GOLDEN GUN

MOONRAKER

Octopussy

LICENCE TO KILL

THE JAMES BOND **007** COLLECTION

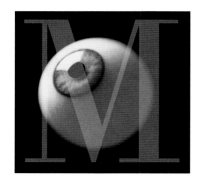

1.

2.

3.

4.

Stillwaters™

5.

MUNICIPAL·FLOW
—PROMOTIONS—

6.

7.

NOMADS

8.

9.

10.

11.

GREENING
EARTH
SOCIETY

12.

MB339·LOCKHEED·AERMACCHI·HUGHES

13.

14.

LOCK
ON
TECHNOLOGY ™

15.

1, 7 - 10, 12
Design Firm **Signal Communications**
2 - 6
Design Firm **Simple Green Design**
11
Design Firm **Pirman Communications**
13 - 15
Design Firm **B.D. Fox & Friends, Advertising**
1.
  Client   *Picture Factory*
  Designer Scott Severson
2.
  Client   *Department of Power*
  Designer Mike Brower
3.
  Client   *Department of Power*
  Designers Mike Brower, Russ Acol-Scott
4.
  Client   *Total Quality Apparel*
  Designer Mike Brower
5.
  Client   *Total Quality Apparel*
  Designer Mike Brower
6.
  Client   *Municipal Flow Promotions*
  Designer Russ Acol-Scott

7.
  Client   *Dan Mullen Photography*
  Designer Scott Severson
8.
  Client   *Nomads*
  Designer JJ Chrystal
9.
  Client   *Photo Effects*
  Designer Scott Severson
10.
  Client   *Starland Cafe*
  Designer Scott Severson
11.
  Client   *Pirman Communications*
  Designer Brian Pirman
12.
  Client   *Greening Earth Society*
  Designer Scott Severson
13.
  Client   *Lockheed*
  Designer Rob Biro
14.
  Client   *Warner Bros.*
  Designers Tom Nikosey, Garrett Burke
15.
  Client   *Sega of America*
  Designer Cindy Luck

1.

CHARLOTTE

2.

3.

PILCH

4.

5.

UNCCHARLOTTE

6.

SEQUOIA
TECHNOLOGY

7.

1, 7
Design Firm **Via Design Inc.**
2 - 6
Design Firm **Design/Joe Sonderman**
1.
  Client   *Biodynamics, Inc.*
  Designer   Lee Perrault
2.
  Client   *City of Charlotte*
  Designers   Yasu Taguchi, Mary Head,
              Joe Sonderman
3.
  Client   *The Hilton Head Co.*
  Designer   Joe Sonderman
4.
  Client   *Pilch, Inc.*
  Designers   Joe Sonderman, Tim Gilland

5.
  Client   *Charlotte Motor Speedway*
  Designer   Joe Sonderman
6.
  Client   *UNC Charlotte*
  Designers   Tim Gilland, Joe Sonderman,
              Andy Crews
7.
  Client   *Sequoia Technology*
  Designers   Lee Perrault, George Holt
(opposite)
  Client   *Steuben Child Care Project*
  Design Firm **Michael Orr + Associates, Inc.**
  Designers   Michael R. Orr + Associates

1.

2.

3.

4.

5.

6.

7.

8.

PEAPOD PROPERTIES LTD.

9.

10.

ERNST & YOUNG LLP

entyron

11.

12.

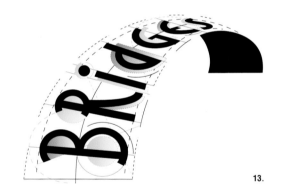

13.

14.

15.

1 - 3, 6 - 8
Design Firm **Graphica, Inc.**
4, 5, 9 - 15
Design Firm **Hansen Design Company**

1.
Client   *Michael Bonilla Illustration*
Designer Drew Cronenwett

2.
Client   *Square D*
Designer Drew Cronenwett

3.
Client   *Leeds Inc.*
Designer Michael England

4.
Client   *Polaris Venture Partners*
Designers Pat Hansen, Carrie Adams

5.
Client   *MariCulture Systems*
Designers Pat Hansen, Kate Dodd

6.
Client   *Lexis-Nexis*
Designer Drew Cronenwett

7.
Client   *Fitzpatrik Masonry*
Designer Jeff Stapleton

8.
Client   *Mead Products*
Designer Drew Cronenwett

9.
Client   *Peapod Properties Ltd.*
Designers Pat Hansen, Kate Dodd
Illustrator Jonathon Combs

10.
Client   *The Tai Ping Yang—
Westin Shanghai*
Designers Pat Hansen, Sheila Schimpf

11.
Client   *Entyron*
Designers Pat Hansen, Carrie Adams

12.
Client   *The Loop Corporation*
Designer Pat Hansen

13.
Client   *Bridges International
Repertory Theatre*
Designers Pat Hansen, Carrie Adams

14.
Client   *The Tai Ping Yang Westin—
Shanghai*
Designers Pat Hansen, Sheila Schimpf

15.
Client   *Long Shot*
Designers Pat Hansen, Jeff Berend

1.

2.

3.

4.

5.

6.

7.

(all)
Design Firm **DSI/LA**

1.
Client   *Louisiana Electric Cooperatives, Inc.*
Designers Hoa Van Vu, Rod Parker

2.
Client   *Brocato International*
Designers Todd Palisi, Rod Parker

3.
Client   *DSI/LA*
Designers Pat Vining, Carol Caulfield,
         Todd Palisi

4.
Client   *Reily Electrical*
Designer Bryan Murphy

5.
Client   *Walsh Cinematography*
Designers Rod Parker, Tim Hope

6.
Client   *Louisiana Health Services, LLC*
Designer Todd Palisi

7.
Client   *Premier Bank*
Designers Tim Hope, Bryan Murphy

(opposite)
Client   *Leshner Inc.*
Design Firm **Muts & Joy & Design**
Designers Katherine Hames,
         Gisele Sangiovanni

THE CITY OF
SPOKANE

1.

Riverfront Park™

2.

JOHN SCHERER & ASSOCIATES
Transforming the world at work

3.

SPOKANE
VALLEY
CHAMBER
OF COMMERCE

4.

L A N D
EXPRESSIONS LLC

5.

AMERICAN INDIAN
COMMUNITY
CENTER

6.

[cyberjava]
internet services

7.

8.

EAGLE RIDGE

9.

Spokane Airport System

10.

11.

12.

TIGERS ®

SUCCESS SERIES

13.

14.

PARAGON
CAPITAL

15.

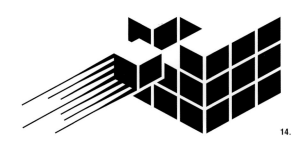

1 - 7, 9, 10, 13, 14
Design Firm **Klundt + Hosmer Design Assoc.**
8, 11, 12, 15
Design Firm **Crocker Inc.**

1.
Client *City of Spokane*
Designers Darin Klundt, Rick Hosmer,
Brian Gage

2.
Client *Riverfront Park*
Designers Darin Klundt, Rick Hosmer,

3.
Client *John Scherer & Associates*
Designers Darin Klundt, Rick Hosmer,
Brian Gage

4.
Client *Spokane Valley
Chamber of Commerce*
Designers Darin Klundt, Amy Gunter,
Rick Hosmer

5.
Client *Land Expressions*
Designers Darin Klundt, Brian Gage

6.
Client *American Indian Community Center*
Designers Darin Klundt, Rick Hosmer,
Brian Gage

7.
Designer Brian Gage

8.
Client *Mt. Sinai Children's Center*
Designer Bruce Crocker

9.
Client *Genstar*
Designers Darin Klundt, Brian Gage

10.
Client *Spokane Airport System*
Designers Darin Klundt, Rick Hosmer,
Brian Gage

11.
Client *Steve Marsel Studio*
Designer Bruce Crocker

12.
Client *National Sports Center for Disabled*
Designer Bruce Crocker

13.
Client *Tigers Success Series*
Designers Darin Klundt, Rick Hosmer,
Brian Gage

14.
Client *Personnel Unlimited*
Designers Darin Klundt, Rick Hosmer

15.
Client *Paragon Capital*
Designer Bruce Crocker

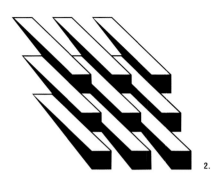

1.

2.

7.

10.

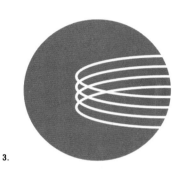

4.

3.

5. B O D Y S C A P E S

Fulcrum

6.

TOPTIX

8.

9.

picnic works

212

11.

12.

13.

14.

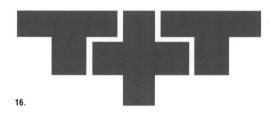

16.

15.

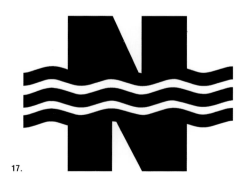

17.

1, 3, 4, 7, 12, 15
Design Firm **Vance Wright Adams & Associates**
2, 5, 6, 8, 9, 11, 13, 14, 17
Design Firm **Essex Two / Chicago**
10
Design Firm **arismendi KNOX, Ltd.**
16
Design Firm **T+T Design**

1.
Client — Pittsburgh Penguins
Designers — Gary Adams, Karen Burns

2.
Client — Paslode, Inc
Designers — Joseph Michael Essex, Nancy Denney Essex

3.
Client — Coury Financial Services, Inc.
Designers — Gary Adams, Susan Borach

4.
Client — Pittsburgh Civic Arena
Designer — Karen Burns

5.
Client — Bodyscapes, Inc.
Designer — Nancy Denney Essex

6.
Client — The Fulcrum Network, Inc.
Designers — Nataile Mills Bontumasi, Joseph Michael Essex

7.
Client — Pace Entertainment Group
Designers — Susan Borach, Karen Burns

8.
Client — Spiegel, Inc.
Designers — Joseph Michael Essex, Nancy Denney Essex

9.
Client — Motorola, Inc.
Designers — Joseph Michael Essex, Nancy Denney Essex

10.
Client — Picnic Works
Designers — Rafael A. Holguin, Susan K. Hodges

11.
Client — National Surgery Centers, Inc.
Designers — Joseph Michael Essex, Nancy Denney Essex

12.
Client — Pittsburgh Sports Festival
Designer — Paul Schifino

13.
Client — Johnson Products, Inc. and the Dr. Martin Luther King Foundation
Designers — Joseph Michael Essex, Nancy Denney Essex

14.
Client — The Weaving Workshop, Inc.
Designers — Joseph Michael Essex, Nancy Denney Essex

15.
Client — Mountaineer Race Track & Resort
Designer — Gary Adams

16.
Client — T+T Design
Designers — Theodore C. Alexander, Jr., Therese Alexander

17.
Client — River North Association
Designers — Joseph Michael Essex, Nancy Denney Essex

 DISCOUNT CLEANERS ™

1.

 PRISM

2.

InterLan  Networks ™

3.

 RED TOMATO

4.

 CLINICAL INFORMATION CONSULTANTS, INC.

5.

 HIGH SIERRA ® PASSPORT TO ADVENTURE

6.

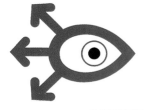 Air Quality Laboratory

7.

 R I C E P A P E R

8.

INTERNETsource

9.

CAP Solutions Compounded

10.

11. Keller Groves, Inc.

12.

13.

14.

Xⁿ **exponential**

15.

SHANGHAI 1930
RESTAURANT

16.

TRIANGLE MLS
MULTIPLE LISTING SERVICES

17.

1, 3, 5, 7, 17
Design Firm **Polloni Design**
Designer Alberto Polloni
2, 4, 6, 11, 12, 13, 14
Design Firm **JOED Design Inc.**
Designer Edward Rebek
8, 10, 15, 16
Design Firm **Russell Leong Design**
Designer Russell Leong
9
Design Firm **Maddocks & Company**
1.
Client *Discount Cleaners*
2.
Client *Prism Systems*
3.
Client *Interlan Networks*
4.
Client *Red Tomato Inc.*
5.
Client *Clinical Information Consultants, Inc.*

6.
Client *H.Bernbaum Import Export Co.*
7.
Client *Air Quality Laboratory*
8.
Client *Rice Paper, Inc.*
9.
Client *Internet Source*
Creative Director
Mary Scott
Designers Winnie Li, Paul Farris
10.
Client *Central Avenue Pharmacy*
11.
Client *Keller Groves Inc.*
12.
Client *Candle Corporation of America*
13.
Client *American Heart Association*
14.
Client *TradeLink America, Inc.*
15.
Client *Exponential Technologies, Inc.*
16.
Client *GQC Holdings, Inc.*
17.
Client *Triangle MLS*

1.

2.

3.

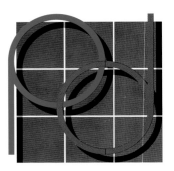

POLLONI DESIGN 4.

5.

6.

7.

8.

9.

10.

THE JOURNEY

TO TEAMS

™

11.

12.

13.

4.

15.

1-3, 5-10, 12-14
Design Firm **Mires Design, Inc.**
4, 11, 15
Design Firm **Polloni Design**

1.
Client — *Taylor Guitars*
Designers — Scott Mires, Miguel Perez
Illustrator — Michael Schwab
Calligrapher — Judythe Sieck

2.
Client — *Taylor Guitars*
Designers — Scott Mires, Miguel Perez
Illustrator — Michael Schwab
Calligrapher — Judythe Sieck

3.
Client — *Nike Inc.*
Designer — José Serrano
Illustrator — Tracy Sabin

4.
Client — *Polloni Design*
Designer — Alberto Polloni

5.
Client — *Donnelley Enterprise Solutions*
Designers — José Serrano, Miguel Perez

6.
Client — *Tee Shirt Company*
Designer — José Serrano
Illustrator — Dan Thoner

7.
Client — *McGraw Hill Home-Interactive*
Designers — John Ball, Miguel Perez

8.
Client — *M.G. Swing Company*
Designer — Mike Brower
Illustrator — Tracy Sabin

9.
Client — *Taylor Guitars*
Designers — Scott Mires, Miguel Perez
Illustrator — Michael Schwab
Calligrapher — Judythe Sieck

10.
Client — *Taylor Guitars*
Designers — Scott Mires, Miguel Perez
Illustrator — Michael Schwab
Calligrapher — Judythe Sieck

11.
Client — *The Journey to Teams*
Designers — Alberto Polloni,
Clina Polloni-Köstner

12.
Client — *Miller Brewing Company*

13.
Client — *Ektelon*
Designer — José Serrano
Illustrator — Dan Thoner

14.
Client — *Taco Pronto*
Designers — John Ball, Scott Mires, Miguel Perez

15.
Client — *Bankers International Trust*
Designer — Alberto Polloni

2.

1.

3.

8.

4.

JABRA

6.

5.

7.

8.

9.

10.

11.

12.

ANACOMP

13.

BAY 2 BAY
USA

14.

15.

(all)
Design Firm **Mires Design, Inc.**
1.
Client Chaos Lures
Designer José Serrano
Illustrator Tracy Sabin
2.
Client Mitsubishi Foods
Designers Scott Mires, Miguel Perez
3.
Client IVAC Corporation
Designer Scott Mires
Illustrator Tracy Sabin
4.
Client Miller Brewing Company
Designer Scott Mires
5.
Client Upper Deck
Designer José Serrano
Illustrator Gerald Bustamante
6.
Client Jabra Corporation
Designers Scott Mires, Miguel Perez
7.
Client Fusion Media
Designers John Ball, Deborah Hom

8.
Client Davidson Communities
Designers Scott Mires, Catherine Sachs
9.
Client Woodstock Idea Factory
Designer John Ball
Illustrator Nadeem Zzidi
10.
Client Hot Rod Hell
Designer José Serrano
Illustrator Tracy Sabin
11.
Client Davidson Communities
Designer José Serrano
Illustrator Dan Thoner
12.
Client Tee Shirt Company
Designer José Serrano
Illustrator Dan Thoner
13.
Client Anacomp
Designers John Ball, Miguel Perez
14.
Client YMCA
Designer José Serrano
15.
Client Industry Pictures
Designers José Serrano, Deborah Hom
Illustrator Tracy Sabin

1.

2.

MAGIC
CARPET

BOOKS

3.

■ PHOTOGRAPHY ■
1242 BARFORD AVE.
HACIENDA HEIGHTS
CALIFORNIA 91745
TEL. (818) 333-7754
■ ANTONIO   MERCADO ■■■■■■■■■

4.

FUSION

6.

THE BIG ISLAND

Be First With Heart

5.

Moore and Associates

7.

8.

(all)
Design Firm **Mires Design, Inc.**
1.
Client   *Chaos Lures*
Designer   José Serrano
Illustrator Tracy Sabin
2.
Client   *Cranford Street*
Designer   José Serrano
Illustrator Tracy Sabin
3.
Client   *Harcourt Brace & Co.*
Designer   José Serrano
Illustrator Tracy Sabin
4.
Client   *Antonio Mercado*
Designer   José Serrano
5.
Client   *Fusion Sports*
Designer   José Serrano

6.
Client   *Masters Group*
Designers   Scott Mires, Mike Brower
Illustrator Tracy Sabin
7.
Client   *The Masters Group*
Designer   José Serrano
Illustrator Tracy Sabin
8.
Client   *Moore & Associates*
Designers   Scott Mires, Deborah Hom
(opposite)
Client   *Avenue One*
Design Firm **Sibley/Peteet Design**
Designer   Rex Peteet

JUMPSTART™

1.

DEEP ELLUM 2.

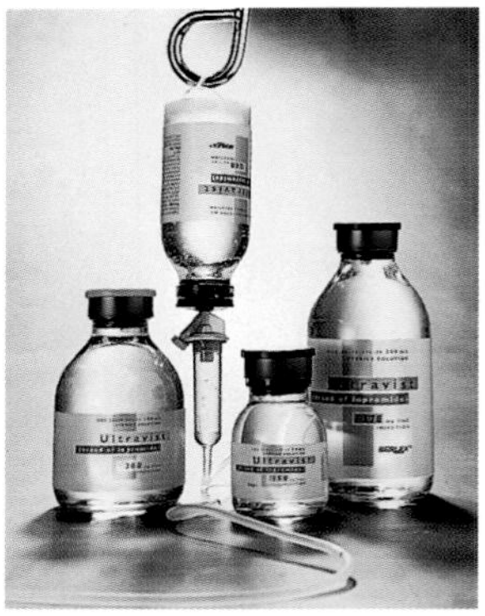

3.

NICKTOONS™

4.

BAKES &
FRESCHETTA
RISES ™

5.

6.

Green Giant®

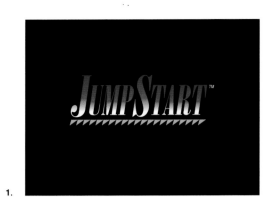

7.

8.

9. **EverLink**™

10.

11.

12.

13.

COMBAT

14.

15.

1
  Design Firm **Wynn Art Direction**
2, 9
  Design Firm **Squires & Company**
3, 12
  Design Firm **Smart Design Inc.**
4
  Design Firms **J.J. Sedelmaier Productions, Inc.,**
  Yoe! Studio
5, 7, 11, 14, 15
  Design Firm **Pedersen Gesk**
6
  Design Firm **ID8 (RTKL Associates Inc.)**
8, 13
  Design Firm **Mires Design, Inc.**
10
  Design Firm **Conflux Design**

1.
  Client   *VLSI Technology, Inc.*
  Designer   Christopher Wynn
2.
  Client   *Deep Ellum Association*
  Designer   Paul Black
3.
  Client   *Berlex*
  Designers Tom Dair, Tam Thomsen,
             Evelyn Teploff
4.
  Client   *MTV Networks/Nickelodeon*
  Designers J.J. Sedelmaier, Craig Yoe
5.
  Client   *Schwan's Sales Ent.*
  Designer   Rony Zibara

6.
  Client   *Turnberry Associates*
  Designer   Charlie Greenawalt
7.
  Client   *Grand Metropolitan*
8.
  Client   *Nike, Inc.*
  Designers John Ball, Miguel Perez
9.
  Client   *Anyware Technologies*
  Creative Director
             Paul Black
  Designer   Anna Magruder
10.
  Client   *Digital Textures*
  Designer   Greg Fedorev
11.
  Client   *Pepsi-Co Company*
  Designer   Rony Zibara, Pepsi-Co
12.
  Client   *OXO International*
  Designers Davin Stowell, Rie Norregaard
13.
  Client   *Nike Inc.*
  Designers Scott Mires, Mike Brower
14.
  Client   *The Clorox Company*
  Designers Rony Zibara, Morgan Brig, Julie So
15.
  Client   *Jim Beam Brands*
  Designers Rony Zibara, Andrea Williams

IMPERIAL BANCORP

1.

Merry Mary Fabrics, Inc.

2.

THE
KEYSTONE
SOCIETY

3.

WOMEN'S
HEALTH
CONNECTION

4.

BONNEVILLE PRODUCTIONS

5.

KAWabunga!

6.

7.

1, 2, 5-7
Design Firm **Yuguchi Group, Inc.**
3, 4
Design Firm **Emphasis Seven Communications, Inc.**

1.
Client — *Imperial Bank*
Designer — Clifford Yuguchi

2.
Client — *Merry Mary Fabric*
Designer — Clifford Yuguchi

3.
Client — *Resurrection Health Care (The Keystone Society)*
Designers — E7ci Staff Designers

4.
Client — *Resurrection Health Care (Women's Health Connection)*
Designer — Debra Nemeth

5.
Client — *Bonneville Productions*
Designer — Clifford Yuguchi

6.
Client — *Kawasaki*
Designer — Clifford Yuguchi

7.
Client — *Pizza Hut*
Designer — Clifford Yuguchi

(opposite)
Client — *Monrovia*
Design Firm — **Maureen Erbe Design**
Designers — Maureen Erbe, Efi Latief, Rita Sowins

1.

Advantagekbs

2.

The Linus Pauling Institute

3.

4.

corporate**computing** e x p o

5.

OpenCon Systems, Inc.
WORLDWIDE COMMUNICATIONS SOLUTIONS

6.

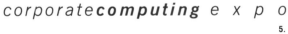

7.

CHRISTINA FIELDS
CIBTAC. A.o.R. Pract. Assoc. MAR.
Clinical Reflexolgist

8.

Pasadena Civic Ballet

9.

10.

11.

12.

13.

14.

15.

227

1, 4, 7, 10, 11, 14, 15
Design Firm **Zunda Design Group**
2, 5, 6, 12, 13
Design Firm **David Morris Creative, Inc.**
3, 8, 9
Design Firm **Corporate Visuals**

1.
Client   *Hershey Chocolate U.S.A.*
Designer   Charles Zunda
2.
Client   *Advantagekbs*
Designer   Glenn Gontha
3.
Client   *Linus Pauling Institute*
Designer   Ronald Rampley
4.
Client   *Zunda Design Group*
Designers   Charles Zunda, Jon Voss
5.
Client   *JKW*
Designer   Glenn Gontha
6.
Client   *OpenCon Systems, Inc.*
Designer   Matt Gilbert

7.
Client   *Best Foods Baking*
Designer   Charles Zunda
8.
Designer   Ronald Rampley
9.
Client   *Pasadena Civic Ballet*
Designer   Ronald Rampley
10.
Client   *Personal Care Group*
Designers   Charles Zunda, Greg Martin
11.
Client   *Ben & Jerry's Homemade, Inc.*
Designer   Charles Zunda
12.
Client   *Firewheel Automotive*
Designer   Tim O'Donnell
13.
Client   *DMS*
Designer   Matt Gilbert
14.
Client   *Hershey Chocolate U.S.A.*
Designer   Charles Zunda
15.
Client   *Hershey Chocolate U.S.A.*
Designers   Charles Zunda, Maija Riekstins

1.

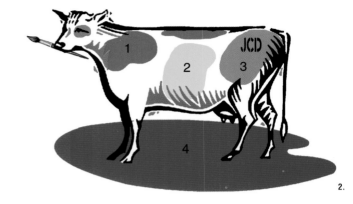

2.

3.

4.

5.

Tautron

6.

7.

1, 5, 7
Design Firm **Knoth & Meads**
2
Design Firm **Jerry Cowart Designers**
3, 4
Design Firm **Phillips Ramsey**
6
Design Firm **Cole Design Group**

1.
Client *McMillin Homes*
Designers José Serrano, Tracy Sabin
Illustrator Tracy Sabin

2.
Client *Jerry Cowart Designers*
Designers Jerry Cowart, Barbara Ward, Gary Socomon

3.
Client *San Diego Wild Animal Park*
Designer Kevin Stout
Illustrator Tracy Sabin

4.
Client *The San Diego Zoo*
Designers Kevin Stout, Tracy Sabin
Illustrator Tracy Sabin

5.
Client *McMillin Homes*
Designers José Serrano, Tracy Sabin
Illlustrator Tracy Sabin

6.
Client *General Signal Networks Tautron*
Designer Jason Berry

7.
Client *McMillin Communities*
Art Director José Serrano
Designer, Illustrator
    Tracy Sabin

(opposite)
Client *Zonk, Inc.*
Design Firm **Tracy Sabin Graphic Design**
Art Director Greg Sabin
Designer, Illustrator
    Tracy Sabin

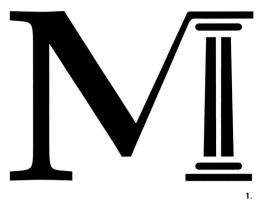

3.

7.

1.

5.

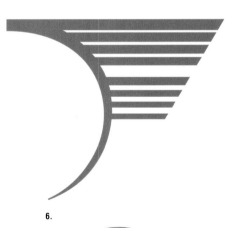

2.

8.

4.

6.

9.

10.

11.

12.

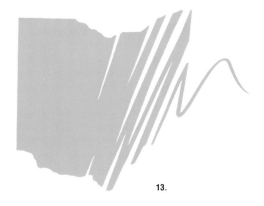

13.

ARROW

14.

15.

231

UB Networks

1.

ONESERVER™

2.

3.

4.

5.

scient™

6.

7.

8.

SUPERIOR PACIFIC™

INSURANCE GROUP

9.

QUALITY

CLASSICS

10.

COURY
ENTERPRISES
11. CONTRACTORS

12.

The REPUBLIC of TEA

13.

Hartwood Construction

14.

pillar

15.

1, 2, 4-6, 13, 15
Design Firm **Studio Archetype**
3, 8-12, 14
Design Firm **McNulty & Co.**
7
Design Firm **Fresh Squeezed Design**
1.
  Client   *UB Networks*
  Designers Josh Distler, Jennifer Anderson
2.
  Client   *One Server*
  Designers Jennifer Anderson,
             Samantha Fuetsch
3.
  Client   *First Interstate Tower*
  Art Director, Designer
             Jennifer McNulty
4.
  Client   *Mirage*
  Designer Clement Mok
5.
  Client   *Studio Archetype Design*
             (formerly Clement Mok Designs)
  Designer Clement Mok
6.
  Client   *Scient*
  Designers Matt Carlson, Jack Herr
7.
  Client   *Fresh Squeezed Design*
  Designers Paige Keiser-Rezac, Steven Rezac

8.
  Client   *Property Prep*
  Art Director, Designer
             Dan McNulty
9.
  Client   *Superior Pacific*
  Art Director Dan McNulty
  Designer Mark Luscombe
10.
  Client   *Quality Classics*
  Art Director Dan McNulty
  Designer Patrick Auyoung
11.
  Client   *Coury Enterprises*
  Art Director Mark Luscombe
  Designer Kristin Koch
12.
  Client   *Savage*
  Art Director, Designer
             Dan McNulty
13.
  Client   *Republic of Tea*
  Designer Clement Mok, Nancy Bauch
14.
  Client   *Hartwood Construction*
  Art Director, Designer
             Dan McNulty
15.
  Client   *Pillar*
  Designer Clement Mok

1.

2.

3.

REMEDIATION RESOURCES, INC.

4.

5.

6.

7.

RAPAX

8.

Page One

Business Productions, L.L.C.

9.

10.

ShokT

11.

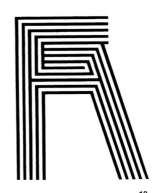

12.

13.

14.

15.

1, 4, 8, 9, 11, 14
Design Firm **30sixty design, Inc.**
2, 3, 5-7, 10, 12, 13, 15
Design Firm **Sommese Design**

1.
Client   *30sixty design, Inc.*
Designers   Pär Larsson, Henry Vizcarra

2.
Client   *Dantes Restaurants Inc.*
Designer   Lanny Sommese

3.
Client   *Ralph Licastro C.P.A.*
Designer   Lanny Sommese

4.
Client   *Remediation Resources, Inc.*
Designer   Pär Larsson

5.
Client   *Aquatics & Exotics*
Designer   Lanny Sommese

6.
Client   *Penn State Summer Fest Theatre*
Designer   Lanny Sommese

7.
Client   *Dante's Restaurants Inc.*
Designer   Lanny Sommese

8.
Client   *RAPAX*
Designer   Henry Vizcarra

9.
Client   *Page One Business Productions, L.L.C.*
Designer   Pär Larsson

10.
Client   *Remodelers Workshop*
Designers   Lanny Sommese, Kristin Sommese

11.
Client   *Shokt*
Designer   Rickard Olsson

12.
Client   *Fitness America*
Designer   Lanny Sommese

13.
Client   *Hoag's Catering*
Designer   Lanny Sommese

14.
Client   *30sixty design, Inc.*
Designer   Pär Larsson

15.
Client   *Women's Awareness Group, Penn State University*
Designer   Kristin Sommese

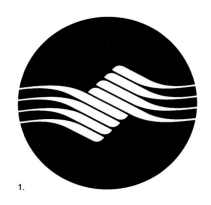

1.

2.

SCOTT STOLL

PHOTOGRAPHY

3.

4.

IW LAHTI DESIGN, WEST

5.

SUNDOWN

SAFARI

6.

7.

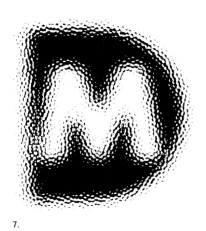

8.

236

9.

10.

B E L Y E A
D E S I G N
A L L I A N C E

11.

GLOBAL CAPITAL SECURITIES, INC.

12.

13.

Salty Dog Productions, Inc.

14.

15.

1, 4, 7, 10, 13, 15
  Design Firm **Sommese Design**
2, 5, 14
  Design Firm **Lahti Design West**
3, 11, 12
  Design Firm **Belyea Design Alliance**
6
  Design Firm **Vince Rini Design**
8, 9
  Design Firm **Phillips Design**

1.
  Client   *Midstate Banking*
  Designer   Lanny Sommese
2.
  Client   *Yoshiki Yamanchi*
  Designer   A. Lahti
3.
  Client   *Scott Stoll Photography*
  Designer   Christian Salas
4.
  Client   *"The Park"*
  Designers   Lanny Sommese, Kristin Sommese
5.
  Client   *Lahti*
  Designer   A. Lahti
6.
  Client   *Los Angeles Zoo*
  Designer   Vince Rini

7.
  Client   *Design Mirage*
  Designer   Lanny Sommese
8.
  Client   *American College of Physician Executives*
  Designer   Michael V. Phillips
9.
  Client   *Phillips Design*
  Designer   Michael V. Phillips
10.
  Client   *Central Pennsylvania Festival of the Arts*
  Designer   Lanny Sommese
11.
  Client   *Belyea Design Alliance*
  Designers   Samantha Hunt, Adrianna Jumping Eagle, Brian O'Neill, Jani Drewfs
12.
  Client   *Global Capital Securities*
  Designer   Patricia Belyea
13.
  Client   *Penn State Theatre Dept.*
  Designer   Lanny Sommese
14.
  Client   *Salty Dog Production, Inc.*
  Designer   A. Lahti
15.
  Client   *Children's Day-Care Center*
  Designer   Lanny Sommese

1.

2. **i!** **impact** U N L I M I T E D

THE Jewish Center FOR
Community Services
3. OF EASTERN FAIRFIELD COUNTY

THE EDUCATORS NETWORK®
4. Linking Consultants and Trainers with Industry and Government

5. **jumbo** entertainment

6.

ISP·TV

7.

8.

THE SNORING INSTITUTE

9.

10.

WOLFROM HOMES

11.

HERITAGE GREEN
AT HOBBIT'S GLEN

12.

13.

Search Alliance

14.

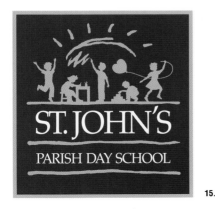

1, 3-6, 8, 10, 13
Design Firm **Dart Design**

2
Design Firm **AERIAL**

7, 9, 11, 12, 14, 15
Design Firm **Cornerstone**

1.
Client — Parrot Greens
Designer — Linda Anderson

2.
Client — Impact Unlimited
Designer — Tracy Moon

3.
Client — Jewish Community Center
Designers — David Anderson, Linda Anderson

4.
Client — The Educators Network
Designer — David Anderson

5.
Client — Jumbo Entertainment
Designer — David Anderson

6.
Client — Touch Fitness
Designer — David Anderson

7.
Client — DIGEX
Designer — Jack Hovey

8.
Client — Connecticut Association of Production Professionals
Designers — David Anderson, Linda Anderson

9.
Client — Weiss, McCorkle & Mashburn
Designer — Jack Hovey

10.
Client — Great River Golf Course
Designers — David Anderson, Linda Anderson

11.
Client — Wolfrom Homes
Designer — Jennifer Kozak

12.
Client — Columbia Builders
Designer — Jennifer Kozak

13.
Client — Take The Lead, Inc.
Designers — David Anderson, Linda Anderson

14.
Client — Search Alliance
Designer — Jack Hovey

15.
Client — St. John's
Designer — Jack Hovey

15.

American Airlines

1.

BANKERS TRUST

2.

SKY CHEFS

3.

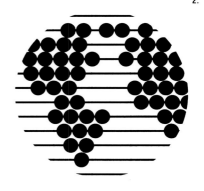

4.

PRATT & WHITNEY

5.

Raritan

6.

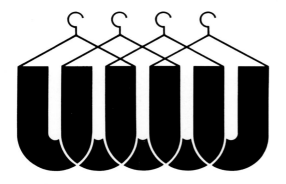

7.

1-3, 5, 6
Design Firm **Henry Dreyfuss Associates**
4
Design Firm **Capt Flynn Advertising**
7
Design Firm **Tri-Arts Studio**
1.
Client *American Airlines*
2.
Client *Bankers Trust*
3.
Client *Sky Chefs*
4.
Client *International Institute for Literacy*
Designer Tom Rigsby

5.
Client *Pratt & Whitney*
6.
Client *Raritan*
7.
Client *Uniforms Unlimited*
Designer Tom Rigsby
Artist Richard Vartian
(opposite)
Client *Deere & Company*
Design Firm **Henry Dreyfuss Associates**

1.

2.

3.

4.

5.

6.

7.

8.

9.

10.

NEW YORK
Marketing
Services

11.

12.

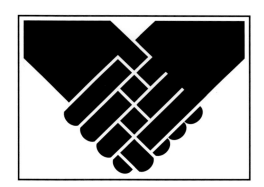

13.

14.

15.

(all)

Design Firm	**Mike Quon/Designation Inc.**	
Designer	**Mike Quon**	
1.		
Client	*American Express*	
2.		
Client	*Dream Makers/Japan*	
3.		
Client	*Mike Quon Design Office*	
4.		
Client	*American Express*	
5.		
Client	*American Express*	
6.		
Client	*British Airways*	
7.		
Client	*British Airways*	
8.		
Client	*Bell Atlantic*	
9.		
Client	*Intergold*	
10.		
Client	*Philip Morris*	
11.		
Client	*American Express*	
12.		
Client	*American Express*	
13.		
Client	*Center for Public Resources*	
14.		
Client	*British Airways*	
15.		
Client	*Good Times Home Video*	

1.

MATRIX PHARMACEUTICAL, INC.

2.

3.

4.

5.

MEAN JEAN
PRODUCTIONS

6.

7.

8.

ARTEMIS®

9.

10.

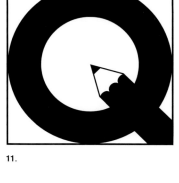

11.

12.

13.

SINO(GEN

14.

15.

1, 4, 8, 10, 12, 13
  Design Firm **Malowany.Chiocchi.Inc.**
2, 7, 9, 14
  Design Firm **ARTEMIS**
3, 11
  Design Firm **Mike Quon/Designation Inc.**
5, 6
  Design Firm **Janet Scabrini Design Inc.**
15
  Design Firm **Designation Inc.**

1.
  Client   *Panda Group International*
  Designers   Tim Fisher, Gene Malowany
2.
  Client   *Matrix Pharmaceutical, Inc.*
  Designers   Pam Van Orden, Betsy Palay
3.
  Client   *The Spot*
  Designer   Mike Quon
4.
  Client   *Freeborn & Peters*
  Designers   Jennifer Davis, Gene Malowany
5.
  Client   *Silvester Tafuro Design Inc.*
  Designer   Janet Scabrini
6.
  Client   *Mean Jean Productions*
  Designer   Janet Scabrini

7.
  Client   *Synergy Partners*
  Designers   Wes Aoki, Gary Nusinow, Ian Smith,
               Betsy Palay
8.
  Client   *Transcontinental Properties*
  Designers   William C. Boyd, Gene Malowany
9.
  Client   *Artemis*
  Designers   Pam Van Orden, Betsy Palay
10.
  Client   *Scottsdale Film Festival*
  Designers   William C. Boyd, Gene Malowany
11.
  Client   *Mike Quon Design Office*
  Designer   Mike Quon
12.
  Client   *American Village Development*
  Designer   Gene Malowany
13.
  Client   *Cactus Sales & Leasing*
  Designer   Gene Malowany
14.
  Client   *Sinogen*
  Designers   Wes Aoki, Gary Nusinow,
               Betsy Palay
15.
  Client   *American Express*
  Designer   Mike Quon

1.

Investment Horizons

2.

3.

Perfect Sense

P R O D U C T S

4.

EVERGREENE
CONSTRUCTION

5.

ROYALTY
CRUISE LINE

6.

Skip a Trip
month

7.

8.

P E H P

HEALTHY UTAH
The Art of Fitness

9.

10.

OWL RIDGE
VINEYARD

11.

12.

13.

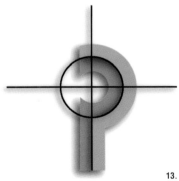

14.

FARMINGTON
PRESERVE

15.

NEWQUEST

1.

2.

3.

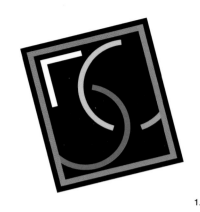

4.

5.

6.

7.

8.

THE
UNIVERSITY
OF UTAH

9.

10.

11.

MICRO
BREW

12.

B

BONNEVILLE
M A C H I N E

13.

14.

NETWORK™
MULTIMEDIA

15.

249

(all)
Design Firm **Richard & Swensen, Inc.**

1.
Client   *Utah Symphony*
Designer   William Swensen

2.
Client   *Dunn Communications*
Designer   Louis Johnson

3.
Client   *Public Employees Health Program*
Designer   William Swensen

4.
Client   *Salt Lake Acting Co.*
Designers   Micheal Richards, William Swensen

5.
Client   *I.N.V.U.*
Designer   Micheal Richards

6.
Client   *Oasis Academy*
Designer   Micheal Richards

7.
Client   *KUED Channel 7*
Designers   Micheal Richards, Alan Loyborg

8.
Client   *Dunn Communications*
Designer   William Swensen

9.
Client   *University of Utah*
Designers   Micheal Richards, William Swensen

10.
Client   *U.S. Figure Skating Assoc.*
Designers   Micheal Richards, William Swensen

11.
Client   *U.S. Figure Skating Assoc.*
Designers   Micheal Richards, William Swensen

12.
Client   *Network Multimedia*
Designer   William Swensen

13.
Client   *Bonneville Machine*
Designers   Micheal Richards,
Connie Christensen

14.
Client   *Redman Moving & Storage*
Designer   Michael Richards

15.
Client   *Network Multimedia*
Designers   William Swensen, Michael Low

1.

2.

3.

4.

GRAPHIC ARTS CENTER

5.

6.

7.

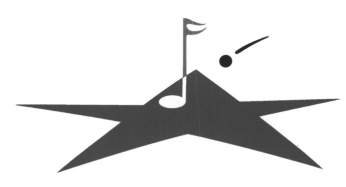

8.

9.

10.

celestial

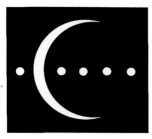

harmonies

11.

12.

13.

COTTONWOOD PROPERTIES

14.

15.

1-4, 6-15		**7.**	
Design Firm	**Boelts Bros. Associates**	Client	Men's 20/30 Club of Tucson
Designers	Eric Boelts, Jackson Boelts, Kerry Stratford	**8.**	
		Client	Ringo Starr/Sierra Tucson Foundation
5		**9.**	
Design Firm	**The DuPuis Group**	Client	Epic Café
1.		**10.**	
Client	Acid Rain	Client	University of Arizona
2.		**11.**	
Client	Peccary King Productions	Client	Celestial Harmonies
3.		**12.**	
Client	Southwest School of Music	Client	River Road Brewery
4.		**13.**	
Client	Tucson Art Expo	Client	Estabon Apodaca
5.		**14.**	
Client	GAC (Graphic Art Center)	Client	Cottonwood Properties
Designer	Hasyun Ruettgers	**15.**	
6.		Client	Men's 20/30 Club of Tucson
Client	Southwest Traditions		

KEYTECH
ASSOCIATES

1.

2.

the**KEYS**

3.

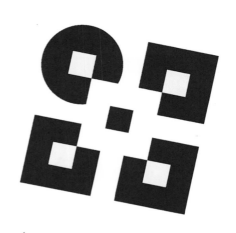

4.

SOUND
ADVICE

5.

PHARMACEUTICAL TECHNOLOGIES, INC.

6.

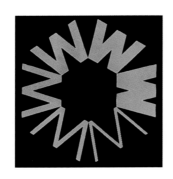

7.

DAYSPRING

8.

9.

10.

Wharton

11.

TERRAFIRMA
CONSULTING

12.

the creative center

13.

WEARHOUSE
ALTERNATIVE CLOTHING OUTFITTERS

14.

15.

1, 3, 12, 14
Design Firm **Georgopulos**
2, 5, 6, 8, 9, 13
Design Firm **Dotzler Creative Arts**
4, 7, 15
Design Firm **Katz Wheeler**
10
Design Firm **Premier Solutions**
11
Design Firm **Joel Katz Design Associates**

1.
Client *Key Tech Associates*
Designer Jonathan Georgopulos
2.
Client *River View Golf Course*
3.
Client *The Keys (rep. Mario Carsollo)*
Designer Jonathan Georgopulos
4.
Client *Center City District*
Designer Katz Wheeler
5.
Client *Sound Advice*

6.
Client *Pharmaceutical Technologies, Inc.*
7.
Client *The Winchester Group*
Designer Katz Wheeler
8.
Client *Day Spring*
9.
Client *Dove*
10.
Client *SunGard AMS*
Designer Jonathan Georgopulos
11.
Client *The Wharton School*
University of Pennsylvania
Designer Joel Katz Design Associates
12.
Client *Terra Firma Consulting*
Designer Jonathan Georgopulos
13.
Client *The Creative Center*
14.
Client *Wearhouse ltd.*
Designer Jonathan Georgoulos
15.
Client *Penn's Landing*
Designer Katz Wheeler

CAPRI
HEART & LUNG INSTITUTE

1.

HARRISON

2.

3.

ECLIPSE

4.

KINGS HILL

5.

GRACIÉS

6.

7.

1-3, 6
Design Firm **Snodgrass Design Associates**
4, 5
Design Firm **John Langdon Design**
7
Design Firm **TLG**
1.
Client *Capri-Heart & Lung Institute*
Designer Leslie Snodgrass
2.
Client *Harrison Hospital*
Designer Leslie Snodgrass
3.
Client *St. Helens Sparkling Mountain Water*
Designer Leslie Snodgrass

4.
Client *Oberheim*
Designer John Langdon
5.
Client *Willard Rouse Developers*
Designer John Langdon
6.
Client *Gracie's Restaurant*
Designer Leslie Snodgrass
7.
Client *Vernell's Candy Company*
Designer Leslie Snodgrass
(opposite)
Client *Gais Bakery*
Design Firm **TLG**
Designer Leslie Snodgrass

1.

2.

3.

4. **HAWKINS** CONSTRUCTION COMPANY

5.

6.

7.

TANNENBAUM'S

OLD MARKET FLORIST

8.

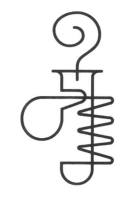

9.

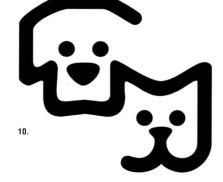

10.

11.

12.

13.

14.

15.

1, 2, 6, 9, 10, 12
Design Firm **Design Center**
3-5, 8, 11, 14
Design Firm **Dotzler Creative Arts**
7, 13, 15
Design Firm **Mod 3 Design**

1.
Client   *Riverside Medical Center*
Designers   John Reger, Dan Olson
2.
Client   *Business Week Magazine*
Designers   John Reger, Dan Olson
3.
Client   *Dotz Digital Pre Press*
4.
Client   *Hawkins Construction Company*
5.
Client   *Bill Drake*
6.
Client   *Biesse Networks*
Designers   John Reger, Bill Philsen

7.
Client   *Fox FX Cable*
Designer   Mod 3 & John DiMinnico
8.
Client   *Tannenbaum's Old Market Florist*
9.
Client   *McGinly & Associates*
Designers   John Reger, Sherwin Schwartz Rock
10.
Client   *Ramsey County Humane Society*
Designers   John Reger, Dick Stanley
11.
Client   *Casa De Oro Foods*
12.
Client   *Fourth Shift Users Group*
Designers   John Reger, Jon Erickson
13.
Client   *Mod 3 Design*
Designer   Jim Breazeale
14.
Client   *Condo Link*
15.
Client   *NFL Properties N.Y.*
Designers   Jim Breazeale, Bruce Burke,
         Kurt Osaki

Oridion

1.

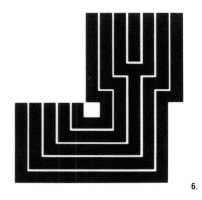

2.

3.

beans

4.

NetScout

5.

6.

Northern Light

7.

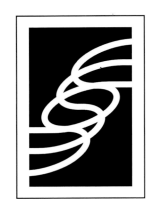

The Park School Wonder Dog

8.

9.

10.

11.

Coffee

12.

13.

LUCY'S LACES

14.

A B A C O

15.

(all)		
Design Firm	**Gill Fishman Associates, Inc.**	

1.
Client — *Oridion Medical*
Designer — Michael Persons

2.
Client — *Standard Uniform*
Designers — Fred Odlinko, Gill Fishman

3.
Client — *Symbiotics*
Designers — Condee Freeman, Gill Fishman

4.
Client — *Beans Coffees*
Designers — Gill Fishman, Anne Alvarez

5.
Client — *Netscout Software*
Designers — Alicia Ozyjowski, Gill Fishman

6.
Client — *Editions Judaica*
Designer — Gill Fishman

7.
Client — *Northern Light*
Designers — Michael Persons, Alicia Ozyjowski, Gill Fishman

8.
Client — *The Park School*
Designer — Gill Fishman

9.
Client — *Digital Delivery*
Designer — Michael Persons

10.
Client — *Inso Corp.*
Designers — Gill Fishman, Condee Freeman

11.
Client — *Queen of Clean*
Designers — Nora Higgins, Gill Fishman

12.
Client — *Haagen Dazs*
Designers — Michael Persons, Gill Fishman

13.
Client — *Rainbowworld*
Designer — Gill Fishman

14.
Client — *Lucy's Laces*
Designers — Gill Fishman, Ann Casady

15.
Client — *Abaco*
Designer — Michael Persons

259

1.

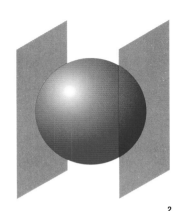

Keyfile

3.

2.

4.

5.

6.

Prominet

7.

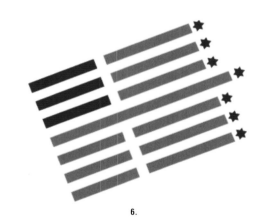
SecurityDynamics

8.

9.

10.

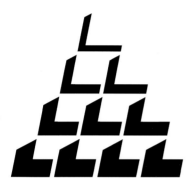

11.

TELE SALES

12.

13.

Rendition

14.

Saber

15.

IMAGERY
S O F T W A R E

1.

Kurzweil
Educational
Systems

2.

C·R·E·S·T

3.

VIS

4.

PACIFIC
OCEAN
GROUP
INC.

5.

6.

BIG GREEN

7.

DEL ORO
REGIONAL RESOUCE CENTER

8.

ROMANOW

CONTAINER

9.

UNITED STATES
POSTAL SERVICE

OFFICIAL OLYMPIC SPONSOR

10.

11.

DANNON®

12.

13.

Eastern Casualty

14.

CELEBRATION OF

COURAGE

15.

263

1, 2, 4, 9, 14
  Design Firm **Gill Fishman Associates, Inc.**
3, 5
  Design Firm **Diane Kuntz Design**
6
  Design Firm **Canetti Design Group Inc.**
7, 8, 15
  Design Firm **Wiley Design**
10 - 12
  Design Firm **Yasumura Assoc./**
              Muts & Joy & Design
13
  Design Firm **Lincoln Design**

1.
  Client   *Imagery Software/Kodak*
  Designers Condee Freeman, Gill Fishman
2.
  Client   *Kurzweil Educational*
  Designers Alicia Ozyjowski, Gill Fishman
3.
  Client   *Santa Monica/Malibu School District*
  Designer Diane Kuntz
4.
  Client   *VIS*
  Designer Gill Fishman

5.
  Client   *Pacific Ocean Group, Inc.*
  Designer Diane Kuntz
6.
  Client   *Kenya Tourist Office*
  Designer Nicolai Canetti
8.
  Client   *Del Oro Regional Resource Center*
  Designer Jean Wiley
9.
  Client   *Romanow Container*
  Designers Gill Fishman, Nora Higgins
10.
  Client   *USPS Olympic*
  Designer Gisele Sangiovanni
11.
  Client   *USA Today*
  Designer Joy Greene
12.
  Client   *Dannon Co.*
  Designers Belinda H., Muts
13.
  Client   *Tom Lincoln Inc.*
  Designer Thomas Lincoln
14.
  Client   *Eastern Casualty*
  Designer Michael Persons
15.
  Client   *American Cancer Society*
  Designer Katie Richardson

1.

Kelly's
Coffee & Fudge Factory

2.

RANDALL
MUSEUM

3.

Café
Coté

4.

BAUER

5.

WHITE OAK

6.

NIMAN

7.

RANCH

8.

9.

10.

11.

12.

planet U

13.

computersAmerica™

14.

15.

1, 4, 5, 7, 9, 15
Design Firm **Pinkhaus Design**
2
Design Firm **Joe Advertising**
3, 6, 8, 10-14
Design Firm **CookSherman**
1.
 Client   *Mercury Restaurant*
 Designer   Todd Houser
2.
 Client   *Kelly's Coffee*
 Designer   Sharon Occhipinti
3.
 Client   *Randall Museum Friends*
 Designers   Ken Cook, Inica Mucia
4.
 Client   *Café Cofé Restaurant*
 Designers   Todd Houser, Joel Fuller
5.
 Client   *Nike—Bauer In-Line Skates*
 Designer   John Norman
6.
 Client   *Boisseau Evans & Associates
             White Oak*
 Designer   C. Randall Sherman

7.
 Client   *Garment Corporation of America*
 Designers   Joel Fuller, Laura Latham
8.
 Client   *Niman Ranch*
 Designer   Ken Cook
9.
 Client   *Daniel Williams, Architect*
 Designer   Joel Fuller
10.
 Client   *Digital Imaging Group*
 Designers   Ken Cook, I-Hua Chen
11.
 Client   *Calyx & Corolla Flower*
 Designer   Ken Cook
12.
 Client   *Andromedia*
 Designers   Ken Cook, Louisa Louie
13.
 Client   *Planet U*
 Designers   Ken Cook, I-Hua Chen
14.
 Client   *Kallen Computer Products*
 Designers   Ken Cook, I-Hua Chen
15.
 Client   *Pepsi Stuff*
 Designers   John Norman, Mark Cantor,
             Todd Houser

1.

2.

3.

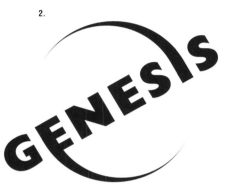

4.

5.

6.

7.

1-3, 6, 7
Design Firm **Hornall Anderson Design Works**
4, 5
Design Firm **Internal Creative Department, CheckFree Corporation**

1.
Client *The Summit at Snoqualmie*
Designers Jack Anderson, David Bates, Sonja Max

2.
Client *XactData Corporation*
Designers Jack Anderson, Lisa Cerveny, Jana Wilson, Julie Keenan

3.
Client *Bruce Clark Productions*
Designers Jack Anderson, Heidi Favour, Mary Hermes

4.
Client *CheckFree Corporation*
Designer Michael Higgins

5.
Client *CheckFree Corporation*
Designer Michael Higgins

6.
Client *Food Services of America*
Designers Jack Anderson, Cliff Chung, Scott Eggers, Leo Raymundo, Bruce Branson-Meyer

7.
Client *Food Services of America*
Designer Jack Anderson

(opposite)
Client *CW Gourmet/Mondeo*
Design Firm **Hornall Anderson Design Works**
Designers Jack Anderson, David Bates, Sonja Max

if **you**
will it
it is no
dream
אם תרצו

C O R B I S
1.

2.

L·A·

JAVA

GOURMET COFFEE

3.

PACIFIC
PLACE

4.

5.

StahDesign

6.

Country Marketplace

7.

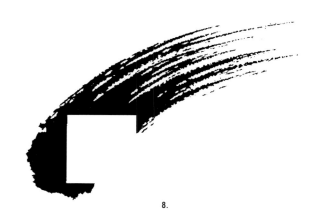

8.

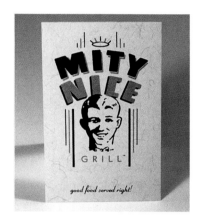

9.

10.

11.

12.

ALTA

13.

POWER PARTNERS

14.

Domestic Abuse Does Not Discriminate

15.

1, 4, 5, 8, 9, 12, 13
Design Firm **Hornall Anderson Design Works**
2, 10, 15
Design Firm **Hadassah Creative Services**
3, 7
Design Firm **Marcia Herrmann Design**
6, 14
Design Firm **Stahl Design Inc.**
11
Design Firm **True Ideas, Inc.**

1.
Client — *Corbis Corporation*
Designers — Jack Anderson, John Anicker, David Bates
2.
Client — *Hadassah Convention Department*
Designer — Michael Cohen
Illustrator — Michelle Lui
3.
Client — *L.A. Java*
Designer — Marcia Herrmann
4.
Client — *Pacific Place*
Designers — Jack Anderson, Heidi Favour, Bruce Branson-Meyer, David Bates
5.
Client — *Internation Corporation*
Designers — Jack Anderson, Leo Raymundo, Julia Lapine
6.
Client — *Stahl Design Inc.*
Designer — David Stahl
7.
Client — *Country Marketplace*
Designer — Marcia Herrmann

8.
Client — *Mahlum & Nordfors McKinley Gordon*
Designers — Jack Anderson, Scott Eggers, Leo Raymundo
9.
Client — *Teledesic Corporation*
Designers — Jack Anderson, Leo Raymundo, Jana Nishi, Julie Keenan
10.
Client — *Hadassah Convention Department*
Designer — Michael Cohen
11.
Client — *Lettuce Entertain You Enterprises, Inc.*
Designers — Cynthia Kerby, Ignatius Aloysius
12.
Client — *Rod Ralston Photography*
Designers — Jack Anderson, Leo Raymundo, Julie Keenan
13.
Client — *Alta Beverage Company*
Designers — Jack Anderson, Larry Anderson, Julie Keenan
14.
Client — *Waukesha/Dresser*
Designer — David Stahl
15.
Client — *Hadassah American Affairs Department*
Art Director — Michael Cohen
Designer — Jennifer Eisenfeld Norton

1.

2.

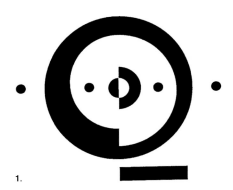

Digital Island®
www.digisle.net

3.

4.

5.

Jim **SPORTS** Kelly

6.

7.

1, 4, 5
Design Firm **Hornall Anderson Design Works**
2, 6, 7
Design Firm **Gold & Associates**
3
Design Firm **Max Graphics**
1.
Client   *Quebecor Integrated Media*
Designers   Jack Anderson, Heidi Favour,
           Mary Hermes, Mary Chin
           Hutchinson, Julia LaPine
2.
Client   *Harcourt Brace*
Designers   Keith Gold, Joseph Vavra
3.
Client   *Digital Island*
Designers   Bob Schonfisch, Ron Higgins

4.
Client   *Jamba Juice*
Designers   Jack Anderson, Lisa Cerveny,
           Suzanne Haddon
5.
Client   *Hornall Anderson Design Works*
Designers   Jack Anderson, David Bates
6.
Client   *Jim Kelly*
Designers   Keith Gold, Raul Febles
7.
Client   *Time Life Music*
Designers   Keith Gold, Joseph Vavra
(opposite)
Client   *Best Cellars*
Design Firm **Hornall Anderson Design Works**
Designers   Jack Anderson, Lisa Cerveny,
           Jana Wilson

3.

1.

2.

4.

5.

6.

7.

8.

Lily's Alterations

9.

SOUTH UMPQUA
B · A · N · K

10.

Fifth Ward Pediatrics

11.

rendition

12.

C-CUBE

13.

The Children's Doctors

14.

15.

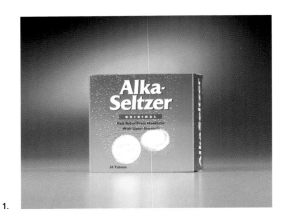

1.

2.

3.

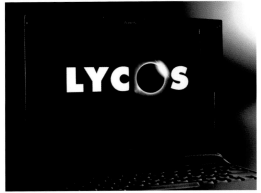

4.

5.

6.

(all)
Design Firm **Wallace Church Assoc., Inc.**

1.
Client   *Bayer*
Designers   Stan Church, Derek Samuel

2.
Client   *Ultrafem Inc.*
Designers   Stan Church, Wendy Church,
                 Derek Samuel

3.
Client   *Lycos*
Designers   Stan Church, Craig Swanson

4.
Client   *Spalding Sports Worldwide*
Designers   Stan Church, John Waski,
                 David Ceradini

5.
Client   *Frito Lay*
Designers   Stan Church, Phyllis Chan-Carr

6.
Client   *Smith Kline Beecham*
Designers   Stan Church, Phyllis Chan-Carr

(opposite)
Client   *Dunlop Maxfli Sports Corp.*
Design Firm **Wallace Church Assoc., Inc.**
Designers   Stan Church, Bob Russell, John
                 Waski, Derek Samuel

1.

2.

3.

4.

5.

6.

7.

8.

9.

WORLD

WATCH

10.

11.

12.

13.

FULL CIRCLE MUSIC
THE ECLIPSE OF MUSIC & TECHNOLOGY

14.

LORÁN
COLOR GROUP & DAY SPA
LORÁN

15.

(all)
Design Firm **Mark Palmer Design**

1.
Client   *Java Springs*
    Marriott's Desert Springs Resort
Designer   Mark Palmer

2.
Client   *Tahquitz Creek*
Designer   Mark Palmer

3.
Client   *Blue Angel Bar & Grille*
Designer   Mark Palmer

4.
Client   *Provident*
Designer   Mark Palmer

5.
Client   *AG Heinze*
Designer   Mark Palmer

6.
Client   *At The Beach*
Designer   Mark Palmer

7.
Client   *Desert Icicles*
Designer   Mark Palmer

8.
Client   *Cactus Cafe*
Designer   Mark Palmer

9.
Client   *Java The Hut*
Designer   Mark Palmer

10.
Client   *World Watch*
Designer   Mark Palmer

11.
Client   *Design Guidance*
Designers   Mark Palmer, Pat Kellogg

12.
Client   *Coachella Valley Wild Bird Center*
Designers   Mark Palmer, Pat Kellogg

13.
Client   *Dove Printing*
Designers   Mark Palmer, Stephen Brogdon

14.
Client   *Full Circle Music*
Designer   Mark Palmer

15.
Client   *Lorán Lorán*
Designers   Mark Palmer, Paul Hanson

1.

2.

3.

4.

5.

6.

7.

8.

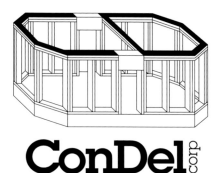

ConDel corp

9.

PETTIT
CONSTRUCTION, LLC ™

10.

BUILDING BRIDGES & BEYOND
SOUTHWEST COMMUNITY CHURCH

11.

STARTER

12.

The Westin | Mission Hills

13.

MASTER POOLS ™

14.

DESIGN
DEVELOPMENT ■
Innovative Architecture

15.

279

1, 3, 10, 12
Design Firm **Silverman Group, Inc.**
2, 4-9, 11, 13-15
Design Firm **Mark Palmer Design**
1.
  Client *Bridgeport Bluefish*
  Designer Bill Silverman
2.
  Client *Guthy-Renker*
  Designer Mark Palmer
3.
  Client *Electrical Contractors*
  Designer Dick Brassil
4.
  Client *Surgery Centers of the Desert*
  Designer Mark Palmer
5.
  Client *Hoth Fine & Company*
  Designers Mark Palmer, Pat Kellogg
6.
  Client *Our Savior's Community*
  Designer Mark Palmer

7.
  Client *Chaney Enterprises*
  Designer Mark Palmer
8.
  Client *The Diamond Collection*
  Designer Mark Palmer
9.
  Client *ConDel*
  Designer Mark Palmer
10.
  Client *Pettit Construction*
  Designer Bill Kavanaugh
11.
  Client *Building Bridges & Beyond*
  Designers Mark Palmer, Pat Kellogg
12.
  Client *Starter Corporation*
  Designers Dick Brassil, Marissa Taddei
13.
  Client *The Westin Mission Hills*
  Designer Mark Palmer
14.
  Client *Master Pools*
  Designer Mark Palmer
15.
  Client *Design Development*
  Designer Mark Palmer

ATHERTON

1.

synergy

2.

TURNSTONE

3.

4.

BALBOA

5.

6.

DANCING DESERT PRESS

7.

8.

ViroLogic

9.

10.

11.

EMPART

12.

13.

INTER**A**CTIVE

14.

15.

1, 3, 9, 12
Design Firm **RKD, Inc.**
2, 4-8, 10, 11, 13, 14
Design Firm **Vaughn/Wedeen Creative**
15
Design Firm **Hallmark Cards, Inc.**
1.
    Client   *Atherton Group*
    Designer Rick Klein
2.
    Client   *Synergy*
    Designer Steve Wedeen
3.
    Client   *Turnstone Systems Inc.*
    Designer Jim Curl
4.
    Designer Steve Wedeen
5.
    Client   *Balboa Travel*
    Designer Dan Flynn
6.
    Client   *Sandia Imaging*
    Designer Dan Flynn

7.
    Client   *Dancing Desert Press*
    Designer Rick Vaughn
8.
    Client   *Aids Walk New Mexico*
    Designers Steve Wedeen, Adabel Kaskeweicz
9.
    Client   *ViroLogic*
    Designers Jim Curl, Mike Mescal
10.
    Client   *Horizon Healthcare*
    Designer Dan Flynn
11.
    Client   *Summitt Construction*
    Designer Rick Vaughn
12.
    Client   *Empart*
    Designer Jim Curl
13.
    Client   *Concert Connection*
    Designer Rick Vaughn
14.
    Client   *Interactive*
    Designer Steve Wedeen
15.
    Designer Barb Mizik

MERCY MAGIC

October 4, 1997

Goes Under
the Sea

1.

2.

IBEX

3.

4.

BLUE RAVEN
EXPEDITIONS

5.

6.

STATES
INDUSTRIES

7.

8.

9.

10.

11.

Biocycle

12.

13.

Towson
ORTHOPAEDIC
ASSOCIATES

Est. 1927

14.

ARISTA
Advertising & Design

15.

1, 2, 6, 10, 11, 14, 15
Design Firm **Arista Advertising, Inc.**
3
Design Firm **Platinum Design, Inc.**
4, 9
Design Firm **Zeewy Design**
5, 7, 8, 12, 13
Design Firm **Funk & Associates, Inc.**
1.
Client *Mercy Medical Center*
Designers Joe Ferraro, III, Fanny Chakedis
2.
Client *Mercy Medical Center*
Designers Amy Mallick, Fanny Chakedis
3.
Client *United Auto Group*
Designer Kelly Hogg
4.
Client *Rittenhouse Optical*
Designers Lia Cautoun, Orly Zeewy
5.
Client *Blue Raven Expeditions*
Designer David Funk
6.
Client *Sweet Magnolia Lingerie*
Designers Patti Gerding, Fanny Chakedis

7.
Client *States Industries*
Designers David Funk, Chris Berner
8.
Client *Commercial Equipment Lease*
Designer Chris Berner
9.
Client *Gocial and Company*
Designers Jeremy Holmes, Orly Zeewy
10.
Client *Orville & Wilbur Publishing*
Designers Pattie Gerding, Joe Ferraro, III
11.
Client *Produccion Dinamica*
Designer Fanny Chakedis
12.
Client *Biocycle*
Designer Beverly Soasey
13.
Client *N-ION Corp.*
Designer David Funk
14.
Client *Towson Orthopaedic Associates*
Designer Fanny Chakedis
15.
Client *Arista Advertising, Inc.*
Designers Amelea Krieger, Fanny Chakedis

PRECISION COLOR

Innovative Imaging

1.

LITTLE HARBOR

2.

Golden Neo-Life

3.

SUN GRAPHIX

4.

DIVERSITY

5.

Sailors' Secret™

6.

ECLIPSE

7.

Mild and Natural™

MOUNTAIN TOP
Heavy Equipment Repair & Service, Inc.

1.

CARMEL MARINA CORPORATION

2.

SUNSET
TENNIS
CLASSIC

3.

4.

THE RACER'S GROUP

5.

blue fin
CAFE & BILLIARDS

6.

UNIVERSAL
INTERNET

7.

MORGAN
WINERY

8.

9.

10.

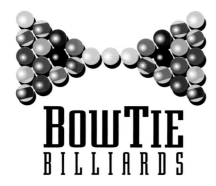

11.

12.

14.

13.

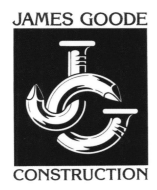

15.

287

1-3, 5-13
Design Firm **The Wecker Group**
4, 14, 15
Design Firm **Horvath Design**
1.
Client *Mountain Top Repair*
Designer Robert J. Wecker
2.
Client *Carmel Marina Corporation*
Designer Robert J. Wecker
3.
Client *Sunset Tennis Classic*
Designer Robert J. Wecker
4.
Client *Dr. Art Weisman*
Designer Kevin Horvath
5.
Client *The Racer's Group*
Designers Robert J. Wecker, Matt Gnibus
6.
Client *Blue Fin Billiards*
Designer Robert J. Wecker

7.
Client *Universal Internet*
Designer Robert J. Wecker
8.
Client *Morgan Winery*
Designer Robert J. Wecker
9.
Client *Navecom*
Designer Robert J. Wecker
10.
Client *Aquafuture*
Designer Robert J. Wecker
11.
Client *Bow Tie Billiards*
Designers Robert J. Wecker, Matt Gnibus
12.
Client *Falling Sun Publications*
Designer Robert J. Wecker
13.
Client *McAbee Beach Cafe*
Designers Robert J. Wecker, James Kyllo
14.
Client *Investment Securities*
Designer Kevin Horvath
15.
Client *James Goode Construction*
Designer Kevin Horvath

1895 1995
GLEN RIDGE
CENTENNIAL

1.

2.

Trent ™

3.

INSTRUCTORS INC

4.

5.

6.

7.

8.

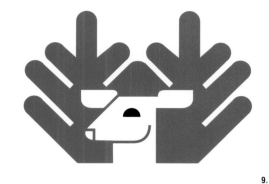

9.

10.

11.

12.

Bellin Heartwatch Plus:
New Ideas
for Healthy Living

13.

WOMEN'S
HEALTH CENTER
AT CLARA MAASS

14.

15.

1-9, 11, 14
Design Firm **The Design Shop**
10, 13, 15
Design Firm **Bellin Hospital Marketing/
Communications Dept.**
12
Design Firm **Dan Meehan Design**
1.
Client   *Glen Ridge Historical Society*
Designer   Bill Wood
2.
Client   *Glen Ridge Congregational Church*
Designer   Bill Wood
3.
Client   *Trent Corporation*
Designer   Bill Wood
4.
Client   *Life Instructors Inc.*
Designer   Bill Wood
5.
Client   *Bell Atlantic*
Designer   Bill Wood
6.
Client   *Borough of Glen Ridge NJ*
Designer   Bill Wood

7.
Client   *National Exchange Carrier Assoc.*
Designer   Bill Wood
8.
Client   *Sigma Software Inc.*
Designer   Bill Wood
9.
Client   *Rockland Corporation*
Designer   Bill Wood
10.
Client   *Bellin Hospital/Cardiac
          Emergency Network*
Designer   Daniel Green
11.
Client   *Computer Power Inc.*
Designer   Bill Wood
12.
Client   *Precision Mowing & Lawn
          Maintenance*
Designer   Dan Meehan
13.
Client   *Bellin Heartwatch Plus*
Designer   Daniel Green
14.
Client   *Clara Maass Medical Center*
Designer   Bill Wood
15.
Client   *Bellin Hospital*
Designer   Daniel Green

1.

2.

3.

4.

5.

6.

7.

8.

9.

10.

11.

12.

13.

COLORADO MASSAGE

C E N T E R

14.

15.

(all)
Design Firm **Robert W. Taylor Design, Inc.**

1.
Client   *Boulder Philharmonic Orchestra*
Designer   Clyde Mason

2.
Client   *Colorado Christian Home*
Designer   Robert W. Taylor

3.
Client   *Symbion, Inc.*
Designer   Laura Schnell

4.
Client   *Colorado Special Olympics*
Designers   Robert W. Taylor, David Schenk,
René Bobo

5.
Client   *ERIC Group, Inc.*
Designers   Robert W. Taylor, Kathleen Stier,
Anne Deister

6.
Client   *Aeronautics Leasing, Inc.*
Designer   Robert W. Taylor,
Karey Christ-Janer

7.
Client   *Rocky Mountain Translators*
Designer   Anne Deister

8.
Client   *Vail Valley Foundation*
Designer   Anne Deister

9.
Client   *Longmont Foods Company, Inc.*
Designers   Robert W. Taylor, Tim Stortz

10.
Client   *The Community Foundation
Serving Boulder County*
Designers   Robert W. Taylor, Susan Davis

11.
Client   *Monfort of Colorado, Inc.*
Designer   Chuck Arndt

12.
Client   *City and County of Denver*
Designers   Robert W. Taylor, Clyde Mason,
Kathleen Stier

13.
Client   *Vail Valley Foundation*
Designer   Kathleen Stier

14.
Client   *Colorado Massage Center*
Designer   Neil Quiddington

15.
Client   *Geode Consulting, LLC*
Designers   Robert W. Taylor, Lorisa Neff,
Alan Hesker

1.

SOUTHEASTERN
WISCONSIN REGIONAL

cancer
center

2.

3.

4.

PROMOTIONS

5.

6.

7.

8.

AMERICAN WAY GOURMET

9.

US TRUCK BODY

10.

Caffé á Roma™

11.

RACINE RAIDERS FOOTBALL

12.

HARBOR FEST
RACINE WISCONSIN

13.

NAVCONTROL
MARINE ELECTRONICS

14.

15.

1, 5, 7, 14, 15
Design Firm **Callery & Company**
2-4, 8, 9, 11-13
Design Firm **The Weber Group Inc.**
6
Design Firm **Robert W. Taylor Design, Inc.**
10
Design Firm **Madison Avenue East**

1.
Client *East End Food Co-Op*
Designer Kelley Callery
2.
Client *Southeastern Wisconsin Regional Cancer Center*
Designer Anthony Weber
3.
Client *Milwaukee County Parks*
Designer Anthony Weber
4.
Client *Silver Creek Industries*
Designer Anthony Weber
5.
Client *Promotions Specialties*
Designer Kelley Callery

6.
Client *Saint Francis Interfaith Center*
Designers Robert W. Taylor, Jose Aguayo
7.
Client *Empire Entertainment Productions*
Designer Kelley Callery
8.
Client *Wisconsin Mutual Insurance Corporation*
Designer Anthony Weber
9.
Client *Yuppie Gourmet*
Designer Anthony Weber
10.
Client *US Truck Body*
Designer Kelley Callery
11.
Client *Caffé á Roma*
Designer Jeff Tischer
12.
Client *Racine Raiders Football*
Designer Anthony Weber
13.
Client *HarborFest*
Designer Eric Groetenhuis
14.
Client *Navcontrol Marine Electronic*
Designer Kelley Callery
15.
Client *Fleets Cove Seafood*
Designer Kelley Callery

1.

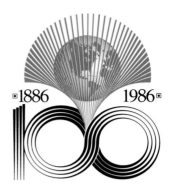

2.

3.

4.

5.

6.

7.

8.

9.

10.

omni
OFFICE SYSTEMS

11.

12.

13.

14.

15.

1-3, 6, 9, 12, 13		
Design Firm	**The Weber Group Inc.**	
4, 7, 8, 10, 11		
Design Firm	**Callery & Company**	
14		
Design Firm	**Summit Advertising**	
15		
Design Firm	**Madison Avenue East**	
1.		
Client	*J.C. Pendergast*	
Designer	Jeff Tischer	
2.		
Client	*S.C. Johnson & Son, Inc.*	
Designer	Anthony Weber	
3.		
Client	*Access Outreach Services*	
Designer	Anthony Weber	
4.		
Client	*LI Philharmonic*	
Designer	Kelley Callery	
5.		
Client	*FFTA (Flexsys)*	
Designer	Kelley Callery	

6.		
Client	*The Docks*	
Designer	Anthony Weber	
7.		
Client	*Peconic Electronic*	
Designer	Kelley Callery	
8.		
Client	*LN Marketing*	
Designer	Kelley Callery	
9.		
Client	*S.C. Johnson & Son, Inc.*	
Designer	Anthony Weber	
10.		
Client	*NJ Cougars*	
Designer	Kelley Callery	
11.		
Client	*Omni Office Systems*	
Designer	Kelley Callery	
12.		
Client	*Tapawingo National Golf Club*	
Designer	Anthony Weber	
13.		
Client	*S.C. Johnson & Son, Inc.*	
Designer	Anthony Weber	
14.		
Client	*Summit Advertising*	
Designer	Kelley Callery	
15.		
Client	*North Fork Bank*	
Designer	Kelley Callery	

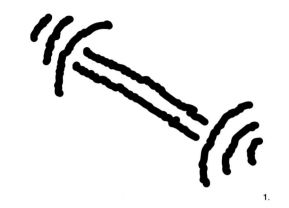

1.

COZY COUNTRYSIDE
COUNSELING

2.

3.

E-B

4.

SIMANTEL | GROUP

5.

Tuneshare

6.

HANSON
CLEANERS

7.

8.

9.

10.

Truckin' Time

11.

CONCLAVE™

12.

13.

INSTANT HEALTH LINE

14.

AFTER THE
FLOOD

15.

297

1-7, 9-15		
Design Firm	**Simantel Group**	
8		
Design Firm	**The Weber Group Inc.**	
1.		
Client	*Jim's Gym*	
Designer	Wendy Behrens	
2.		
Client	*Debbie Krause*	
Designer	Wendy Behrens	
3.		
Client	*Roehm Renovations*	
Designer	Becky Krohe	
4.		
Client	*Eric Behrens - Photojournalist*	
Designer	Wendy Behrens	
5.		
Client	*Simantel Group*	
Designer	Chris Moehn	
6.		
Client	*Tuneshare*	
Designer	Becky Krohe	

7.	
Client	*Hanson Cleaners*
Designer	Wendy Behrens
8.	
Client	*S.C. Johnson & Sons, Inc.*
Designer	Anthony Weber
9.	
Client	*CEFCU*
Designer	Wendy Behrens
10.	
Client	*Mad Cow Farms*
Designer	Lisa Lucas
11.	
Client	*Caterpillar Inc.*
Designer	Wendy Behrens
12.	
Client	*Internet Dynamics, Inc.*
Designer	Lisa Lucas
13.	
Client	*Mitsubishi Motors LPGA Charity Pro-Am*
Designer	Molly Vonachen
14.	
Client	*SVI Inc.*
Designer	Chris Moehn
15.	
Client	*Peoria Journal Star*
Designer	Wendy Behrens

1.

2.

GOTHAM
Bar and Grill

3.

MANHATTAN
COUNTRY CLUB

4.

Roger Ball Photography

5.

Creative
Underground

6.

PRIDE

7.

earlyears
International Playthings

8.

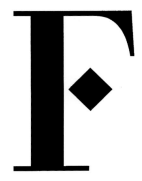

9.

10.

GLEN

11.

12.

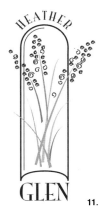

CROSSROADS

14.

13.

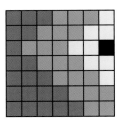

KITCHEN LOGIC

15.

1
Design Firm **The Jefferies Association**
2, 3, 8, 9, 12
Design Firm **Donovan and Green**
4
Design Firm **Continental Graphics**
5, 10, 13, 15
Design Firm **Mervil Paylor Design**
6, 7, 11, 14
Design Firm **Simantel Group**

1.
Client — Keck Graduate Institute of Applied Life Sciences
Designers — Donna Gedeon, Hauchee Chung
2.
Client — Brandt Resources
Designer — Vanessa Ryan
3.
Client — Gotham Bar and Grill
Designer — Julie Riefler
4.
Client — Manhattan Country Club
Designers — Bryan Friel, Colin Bedding
5.
Client — Roger Ball Photography
Designer — Mervil M. Paylor
6.
Client — Creative Underground
Designer — Wendy Behrens

7.
Client — Peoria Riverfront Investors for Development and Expantion
Designer — Chris Moehn
8.
Client — International Playthings' Earlyears brand
Designer — Rafael Weil
9.
Client — Fenway Partners
Designer — Vanessa Ryan
10.
Client — Warner Development
Designer — Mervil M. Paylor
11.
Client — McCarthy Bush Real Estate/ Judy Steil
Designers — Molly Vonachen, Wendy Behrens
12.
Client — Thomas J. Lipton Co.
Designer — Vanessa Ryan
13.
Client — Brain Injury Association, Inc.
Designer — Mervil M. Paylor
14.
Client — Crossroads Global Crafts
Designer — Becky Krohe
15.
Client — Kitchen Logic
Designer — Mervil M. Paylor

1.

Kalpana

2.

PG&E

Datascope

3.

DANIELA VEO

4.

Beach House

5.

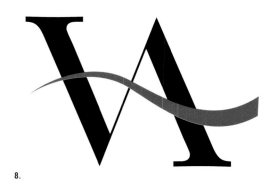

LUCILE SALTER PACKARD
CHILDREN'S HOSPITAL AT STANFORD

6.

REFLECT 15
SUNSCREEN

7.

VA

8.

SūmmaCāre

9.

Compact Devices

10.

PhoenixNetwork.

11.

SM
IMAGING

12.

GENESYS

13.

JOGA CHIROPRACTIC CENTER

14.

salusmedia

15.

B.E.S.T.
PROGRAM

BREAST EXAMINATION
SELF-TEACHING

16.

1, 10, 13
Design Firm **Howry Design Associates**
2, 6
Design Firm **S & O Consultants**
3-5, 7, 9, 11, 12, 15
Design Firm **AERIAL**
8, 14
Design Firm **Kristin Odermatt Design**
16
Design Firm **Diane Kuntz Design**

1.
Client *Kalpana*
Designer & Art Director
 Jill Howry

2.
Client *PG&E*
Designers Tracy Moon, Tony Hyun

3.
Client *Datascope Corp.*
Designer Tracy Moon

4.
Client *DFS Group Limited*
Designer Tracy Moon

5.
Client *Pacific Beach House, Inc.*
Designer Tracy Moon

6.
Client *Lucile Salter Packard Children's
 Hospital at Stanford*
Designer Tracy Moon

7.
Client *Reflect Inc.*
Designer Tracy Moon

8.
Client *Veneklasen Associates*
Designers Kristin Odermatt, Deanna McClure

9.
Client *Sūmma Cāre/Collagen Corp.*
Designer Tracy Moon

10.
Client *Compact Devices*
Art Director Jill Howry
Designer Craig Forsdick

11.
Client *Phoenix Network*
Designer Tracy Moon

12.
Client *Calypso Imaging*
Designer Tracy Moon

13.
Client *Genesys*
Art Director Jill Howry
Designer Michael Mescall

14.
Client *Joga Chiropractic Center*
Designer Kristin Odermatt

15.
Client *Salus Media*
Designers Tracy Moon, Amy Gustincic

16.
Client *Cedars-Sinai Medical Center*
Designers Diane Kuntz, Sherry Caris

1.

COLOR-TEX
INTERNATIONAL

2.

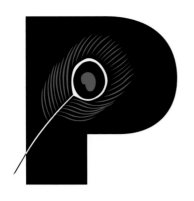

BESTFOODS

3.

4.

KEMPER FUNDS

5.

Beyond
Boxes

6.

7.

CONSECO

8.

FISK

9.

10.

11.

OBJECTWARE

12.

Hilton

13.

LOCKHEED MARTIN ✦

14.

Spectrum HoloByte

15.

1, 2, 4, 7, 10
Design Firm **Doerr Associates**
3, 5, 8, 13, 14
Design Firm **Enterprise IG**
6, 9, 12, 15
Design Firm **Triad, Inc.**
11
Design Firm **360 Design Assoc.**

1.
Client — *Peacock Products*
Designer — Priscilla White Sturges
2.
Client — *Color-Tex International*
Designer — Priscilla White Sturges
3.
Client — *Bestfoods*
Design Director
— Eugene J. Grossman
Designer — Steve Cazlan
4.
Client — *Insight Partners Inc.*
Designer — Priscilla White Sturges
5.
Client — *Kemper Funds*
Creative Director
— William Ayres
Designer — Wendy Squires
6.
Client — *DSC Communications*
Designer — Michael Dambrowski,
Carol Hoover

7.
Client — *Righter Corporation*
Designer — Priscilla White Sturges
8.
Client — *Conseco*
Director — William Ayres
Designer — Sally Hwang
9.
Client — *Fisk Communications*
Designer — Michael Dambrowski
10.
Client — *York Spiral Stairs*
Designer — Priscilla White Sturges
11.
Client — *D.L. White Builders*
Designers — Howard Sturges,
Priscilla White Sturges
12.
Client — *ObjectWare*
Designer — Michael Hinshaw
13.
Client — *Hilton Hotels*
Creative Director
— Gene Grossman
Designer — Aere Cazlau
14.
Client — *Lockheed Martin*
Creative Director
— Gene Grossman
Designer — Bob Wily
15.
Client — *Spectrum HoloByte*
Designers — Richard Wilson, Carol Hoover

1.

2.

3.

4.

Hertz
Claim Management

5.

OPTIMUM GROUP
Marketing & Visual Communications Solutions

6.

7.

8.

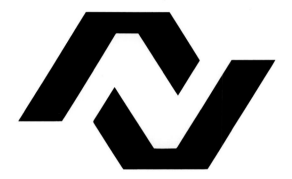

9.

10.

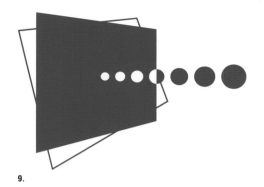

11.

O N E
PENN
PLAZA

14.

13.

15.

1.

2.

FRANCISCAN
INSTITUTE

3.

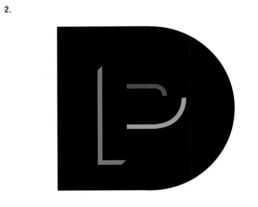

4.

Reaching
out,
one
to another

5.

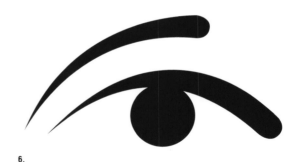

6.

7.

Buffalo Arts Studio

8.

9.

10.

helena pentathlon

11.

12.

International Filler Corporation

14.

13.

15.

1.

ATTICUS

2.

The Davis Academy

3.

4.

5.

6.

7.

8.

BUCKHEAD
PLAZA

9.

10.

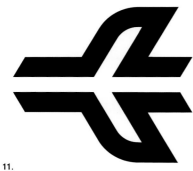

11.

Community
Savings

12.

13.

14.

15.

(all)
Design Firm **Rousso+Associates, Inc.**
Designer Steven B. Rousso

1.			**8.**	
	Client	*Brownlee Jewelers*		Client	*Circle 75 Office Park*
2.			**9.**	
	Client	*The Atticus Group*		Client	*Taylor Mathis*
3.			**10.**	
	Client	*The Davis Academy*		Client	*David's Ltd.*
4.			**11.**	
	Client	*Demand Products*		Client	*Atlanta International Airport*
5.			**12.**	
	Client	*Buffington & Lloyd*		Client	*Community Savings*
6.			**13.**	
	Client	*Centennial American Properties, Ltd.*		Client	*Digital Controls*
7.			**14.**	
	Client	*Georgia Power Company*		Client	*Corporate Resource Development*
			15.	
				Client	*Software Solutions*

1.

2.

3.

Lighting
Services℠
Georgia Power

4.

5.

6.

7.

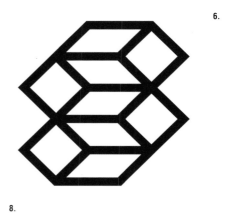

8.

9.

10.

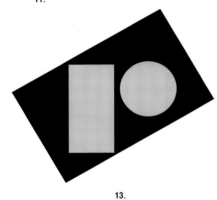

11.

12.

13.

14.

15.

(all)
Design Firm **Rousso+Associates, Inc.**
Designer Steven B. Rousso

1.
Client *Childress Klein Properties*

2.
Client *Harbinger Corporation*

3.
Client *Ferguson Enterprises*

4.
Client *Georgia Power Company*

5.
Client *Digital Glue*

6.
Client *The Metro Companies*

7.
Client *Callaway Carpet Co.*

8.
Client *Southern Engineering Company*

9.
Client *Lotus Carpets*

10.
Client *The Metro Companies*

11.
Client *OmniOffices*

12.
Client *International Banking Technologies*

13.
Client *Rousso+Associates, Inc.*

14.
Client *VIDA*

15.
Client *The West Corporation*

1.

2.

3.

4.

5.

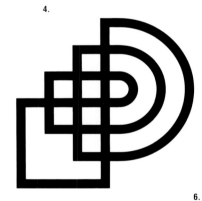

6.

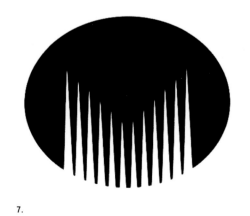

7.

8.

9.

10.

11.

12.

13.

TELEGUITE

14.

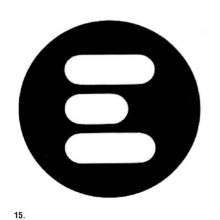

15.

313

1, 6, 10, 13
Design Firm **Rousso+Associates, Inc.**
Designer Steven B. Rousso
2, 3, 7-9, 11, 12, 15
Design Firm **RBMM/The Richards Group**
4
Design Firm **3G Design & Illustration**
5, 14
Design Firm **Design Forum**
1.
Client *Airtouch Cellular*
2.
Client *Summerfield*
Designer RBMM
3.
Client *Hill*
Designer D.C. Stipp
4.
Client *3G Design & Illustration*
Designer Grant Guinouard
5.
Client *Genuardi's Family Markets*
Designer Carolyn Wiedeman
6.
Client *Peterson Properties*

7.
Client *Metrocel*
Designer Steve Miller
8.
Client *Dallas Zoo*
Designer Dick Mitchell
9.
Client *Stoneridge*
Designer RBMM
10.
Client *Jordan Properties*
11.
Client *Bear Creek Wood Works*
Designer Jackson Wang
12.
Client *MIxon Enterprises &*
Mixon Investments
Designer RBMM
13.
Client *Locations South*
14.
Client *Telesuite*
Senior Graphic Designer
Amy McCombs
Designer Ken Cheney
15.
Client *Execucom*
Designer Brian Boyd

1.

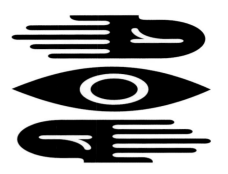

2.

3.

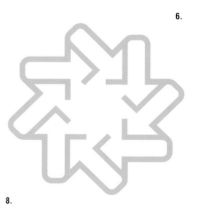

4.

5.

COFFEEHOUSE 98

6.

7.

8.

9.

10.

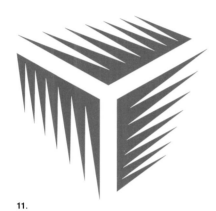

11.

12.

13.

14.

15.

1.

GREAT AMERICAN

PHOTOGRAPHY WEEKEND

2.

3.

4.

CITYPLACE

5.

THE LIBRARY

6.

7.

8.

9.

10.

11.

12.

13.

14.

15.

317

1.

2.

3.

4.

Dallas Public Schools

5.

6.

7.

8.

9.

10.

11.

12.

13.

Adopt An Olympic Brick

14.

15.

(all)		
Design Firm	**RBMM/The Richards Group**	
1.		
Client	*Team Mad Dog*	
Designer	RBMM	
2.		
Client	*The Family Place*	
Designer	Brian Boyd	
3.		
Client	*Norris*	
Designer	RBMM	
4.		
Client	*Dr. Saretsky*	
Designer	Luis Ascevedo	
5.		
Client	*Dallas Public Schools*	
Designer	Dick Mitchell	
6.		
Client	*Mobility*	
Designer	Steve Miller	
7.		
Client	*Hearts & Hammers*	
Designer	Dick Mitchell	

8.	
Client	*The Dallas Symphony Orchestra*
Designer	Horacio Cobos
9.	
Client	*Amerifest*
Designer	Horacio Cobos
10.	
Client	*Central American*
Designer	Horacio Cobos
11.	
Client	*Facial Aesthetic Systems*
Designer	Luis Ascevedo
12.	
Client	*Head Golf*
Designer	Horacio Cobos
13.	
Client	*Film Casters*
Designer	Dick Mitchell
14.	
Client	*Home Depot*
Designer	Kenny Garrison
15.	
Client	*Lewisville Humane Society*
Designer	Luis Ascevedo

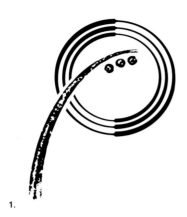

1.

2.

KPT
Kentucky Physical Therapy

3.

4.

DECADE

5.

6.

THE CENTER
For Rural Development

7.

8.

Harald Sund/photographer

9.

10.

11.

McCLOREY
LAW OFFICES

12.

ANDE MAC DESIGN

13.

amon's

14.

15.

1.

2.

3.

4.

5.

6.

7.

8.

TRITON

11.

12.

13.

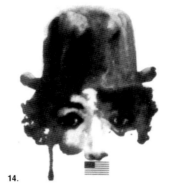

14.

TRUESOUPS

15.

EARTHGRAINS

17.

16.

18.

1-8, 11, 13, 14, 16, 17
Design Firm **RBMM/The Richards Group**
9, 10, 18
Design Firm **Diane Kuntz Design**
12, 15
Design Firm **Walsh & Associates, Inc**

1.
Client   *Bell Winery*
Designer   Horacio Cobos
2.
Client   *Candle Ridge*
Designer   RBMM
3.
Client   *El Paso Chile Co.*
Designer   Luis Ascevedo
4.
Client   *Riverside*
Designer   RBMM
5.
Client   *Victim's Outreach*
Designer   RBMM
6.
Client   *Casa Rosa*
Designer   RBMM
7.
Client   *Rivery*
Designer   Dick Mitchell
8.
Client   *Rumble*
Designer   Luis Ascevedo

9.
Client   *California Hospital Medical Center*
Designer   Diane Kuntz
10.
Client   *Grand Hope Neonatology Group*
Designers   Diane Kuntz, Linda Eberle
11.
Client   *Triton*
Designer   Steve Miller
12.
Client   *Chukar Cherry Company*
Designer   Miram Lisco
Illustrator Jim Hays
13.
Client   *Monarch Paper*
Designer   Ed Brock
14.
Client   *USA Film Festival (1972)*
Designer   RBMM
15.
Client   *Truesoups*
Designer   Miriam Lisco
16.
Client   *Airborne Connectors*
Designer   RBMM
17.
Client   *Earth Grains*
Designer   RBMM
18.
Client   *Pacific Cardiothoracic Surgery Group, Inc.*
Designer   Diane Kuntz

1.

2.

3.

4.

5.

6.

7.

8.

9.

10.

326

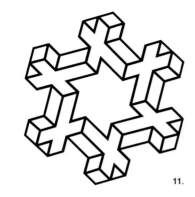

11.

12.

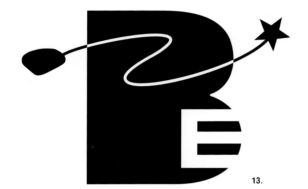

13.

14.

15.

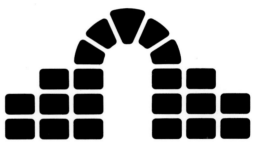

16.

NEXTEK

17.

1-3, 5, 7, 8, 10
Design Firm **Lipson • Alport • Glass & Associates**

4
Design Firm **The Chesapeake Group, Inc.**

6, 17
Design Firm **Burnett Group**

9
Design Firm **Elliot Van Deutsch**

11, 12, 14, 16
Design Firm **RBMM/The Richards Group**

13
Design Firm **Waterman Design**

15
Design Firm **Kirby Stephens Design, Inc.**

1.
Client *Marriott Corporation*
Designer Keith Shupe

2.
Client *Morton International*
Designer Lipson • Alport • Glass & Associates

3.
Client *Courtyard By Marriott*
Designer Lipson • Alport • Glass & Associates

4.
Client *T. Marzetti Company*
Designer John C. Sullivan

5.
Client *Frasier Paper Company (Mosaic)*
Designer Keith Shupe

6.
Client *JNANA Technologies Company*
Designer Lee Miller

7.
Client *Coregis*
Designer Keith Shupe

8.
Client *Medcor*
Designer Lipson • Alport • Glass & Associates

9.
Client *Vredenburg*
Designers Blake Stenning, Rachel Deutsch

10.
Client *Allegiance*
Designers Keith Shupe, Katherine Holderied

11.
Client *United Christian Congregation*
Designer Jackson Wang

12.
Client *The Oasis*
Designer Dick Mitchell

13.
Client *Bidder's Edge*
Designer Priscilla White Sturges

14.
Client *African American Museum*
Designer Luis Ascevedo

15.
Client *H + M Electric*
Designer Bill Jones

16.
Client *Stonegate*
Designer RBMM

17.
Client *Nextek*
Designer Lee Miller

1.

2.

GARMONG
Design/Build Construction

3.

JOCKEY
Classic
ZONE

4.

MAXWELL HOUSE
Coffee
Good to the last drop

5.

ALLIANCE
FOR GROWTH AND PROGRESS

6.

Glade®

7.

1, 2, 4, 5, 7
Design Firm **Lipson • Alport • Glass & Associates**
3, 6
Design Firm **Miller & White Advertising**
1.
Client — *Tyndar House Publishers (New Living Translation)*
Designer — Lipson • Alport • Glass & Associates
2.
Client — *Lipson • Alport • Glass & Associates*
Designers — Tracy Bacilek, Sam Ciuus
3.
Client — *Garmong Design/ Build Construction*
Designer — Bill White

4.
Client — *Jockey*
Designers — Tracy Bacilek, Carol Davis, Amy Russell
5.
Client — *Kraft Foods, Inc. (Maxwell House)*
Designer — Lipson • Alport • Glass & Associates
6.
Client — *Alliance for Growth & Progress*
Designer — Scott Lee
7.
Client — *S.C. Johnson & Sons*
Designer — Lipson • Alport • Glass & Associates
(opposite)
Client — *Scott Paper Company*
Design Firm — **Lipson • Alport • Glass & Associates**
Designer — Lori Cerwin

1.

5.

8.

4.

2.

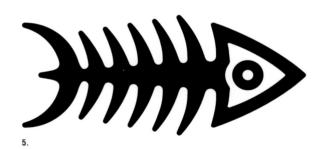

6.

3.

7.

330

9.

10.

11.

12.

13.

14.

15.

(all)
Design Firm **Insight Design Communications**
1, 2, 4, 8, 11, 14, 15
  Art Directors Sherrie & Tracy Holdeman
  Designer Chris Parks
3, 6, 9, 10, 12, 13
  Art Directors Sherrie & Tracy Holdeman
  Designers Sherrie & Tracy Holdeman
1.
  Client *ICE Fastpitch Softball CD-Rom*
2.
  Client *Conductor Energy Systems Management*
3.
  Client *Mixology*
4.
  Client *Kansas Department of Health and Environment*
5.
  Client *Big Fish*
  Art Director & Designer *Chris Parks*

6.
  Client *Wichita Collegiate School*
7.
  Client *Newer Technology, Inc.*
  Art Directors Sherrie & Tracy Holdeman
  Designers Chris Parks & Tracy Holdeman
8.
  Client *Sports Solutions*
9.
  Client *Rock Island Studios*
10.
  Client *Riffels Coffee Company*
11.
  Client *Kansas Department of Health and Environment*
12.
  Client *The Hayes Co., Inc.*
13.
  Client *Wichita Collegiate School*
14.
  Client *Botanica Lawn & Garden*
15.
  Client *Dream Mission-Jackson Foundation*

331

1.

DAWN OF THE
NEW CENTURY

2.

MILLENNIUM
DESIGN

3.

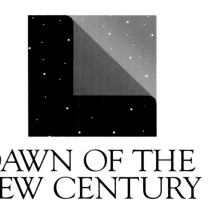

4.

5.

SWAN BROTHERS
DAIRY INC.

6.

7.

NAIAD
TECHNOLOGIES, INC.

8.

9.

10.

11.

14.

13.

15.

1.

2.

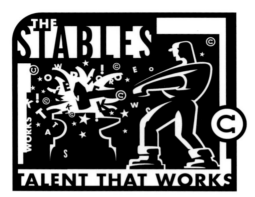

3.

4.

5.

6.

7.

8.

9.

10.

11.

12.

13.

14.

15.

335

1, 4, 5, 8, 10, 11, 14
Design Firm **Bartels & Company, Inc.**
2, 3, 6, 7, 9, 12, 13, 15
Design Firm **Insight Design Communications**
Art Directors Sherrie & Tracy Holdeman
1.
　　Client　　*Javaworks*
　　Designer　David Bartels
2.
　　Client　　*McMinimy Photography*
　　Designers　Sherrie & Tracy Holdeman
3.
　　Client　　*The Stables*
　　Designers　Sherrie & Tracy Holdeman
4.
　　Client　　*The Genesis Institute*
　　Designers　Ron Rodemacher, David Bartels
5.
　　Client　　*Fair St. Louis Organization*
　　Designers　Bob Thomas, David Bartels
6.
　　Client　　*20/20 Solutions*
　　Designers　Sherrie & Tracy Holdeman

7.
　　Client　　*Solid Solutions*
　　Designers　Sherrie & Tracy Holdeman
8.
　　Client　　*ERA GSM*
　　Designers　David Bartels, Brian Barclay
9.
　　Client　　*Big Dog Custom Motorcycles Inc.*
　　Designers　Sherrie & Tracy Holdeman
10.
　　Client　　*Deltalog*
　　Designers　Brian Barclay, David Bartels
11.
　　Designer　David Bartels, Brian Barclay
12.
　　Client　　*Association of Blockbuster
　　　　　　　Franchisees*
　　Designer　Chris Parks
13.
　　Client　　*WouArts
　　　　　　　(Women of Untraditional Arts)*
　　Designers　Sherrie & Tracy Holdeman
14.
　　Client　　*Quantitative Capital Partners*
　　Designers　David Bartels, Ron Rodemacher
15.
　　Client　　*Newer Technology, Inc.*
　　Designers　Chris Parks, Tracy Holdeman

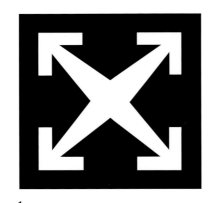

1.

2.

3.

4.

5.

6.

7.

8.

9.

10.

11.

12.

QuadraSeps

13.

14.

15.

1, 4, 5, 7, 10, 11, 14, 15
  Design Firm **Insight Design Communications**
  Art Directors & Designers
      Sherrie & Tracy Holdeman
2, 3, 6, 8, 9, 12, 13
  Design Firm **Shields Design**
1.
  Client   *Interex*
2.
  Client   *Maxim Mortgage Corporation*
  Designer Charles Shields
3.
  Client   *The Ken Roberts Company*
  Designer Charles Shields
  Illustrator Doug Hansen
4.
  Client   *Fresh Paint*
5.
  Client   *Kicks*
6.
  Client   *Keiser Sports*
  Designer Charles Shields

7.
  Client   *Twin Valley*
8.
  Client   *The Ken Roberts Company*
  Designer Charles Shields
  Illustrator Doug Hansen
9.
  Client   *Revell & Associates*
  Designer Charles Shields
10.
  Client   *Network Interface Corporation*
11.
  Client   *Hastings Filters Inc.*
12.
  Client   *Great Pacific Trading Company*
  Designer Charles Shields
  Illustrator Doug Hansen
13.
  Client   *QuadraSeps*
  Art Director Charles Shields
  Designer Juan Vega
14.
  Client   *Timberline Steakhouse & Grill*
15.
  Client   *Tortilla Factory*

1.

ALISTAR
INSURANCE, INC.

2.

3.

4.

KÁRA

5.

6.

7.

8.

ATTiTUDE
ONLINE

9.

10.

11.

MAIN STREET
TRADING COMPANY

12.

13.

14.

CROWN

PRINTING

15.

1.

2.

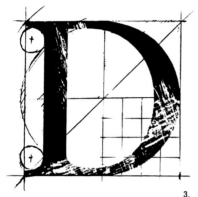

3.

4.

5.

6.

7.

8.

ValliWide Bank℠

9.

10.

11.

THE **PURPLE** MOON
D A N C E   P R O J E C T

12.

topo

13.

Phil ____ Rudy

Photography

14.

SPORT SLING

15.

1
Design Firm **Big Fish Design**
2, 7, 9, 10, 14
Design Firm **Shields Design**
3, 5, 15
Design Firm **Laura Coe Design Associates**
Designers Laura Coe Wright,
 Ryoichi Yotsumoto
4, 11
Design Firm **Zenn Graphic Design**
Designer Zengo Yoshida
6, 8
Design Firm **Bob Rankin Design**
Designer Bob Rankin
12
Design Firm **Hunt Weber Clark Associates**
13
Design Firm **Performance, Inc. (Internal)**
1.
 Client *Big Fish Design*
 Designer Paul Ocepek
2.
 Client *HealthComp Inc.*
 Designer Charles Shields
3.
 Client *Laura Coe Design Associates*
4.
 Client *John Mung-Whitfield
 Commemorative Center for
 International (Grassroots)
 Exchange*

5.
 Client *Salzman International*
6.
 Client *ICEX*
7.
 Client *Camerad Inc.*
 Designer Charles Shields
8.
 Client *Aspen Creek Apts.*
9.
 Client *Valliwide Bank*
 Art Director Charles Shields
 Designer Juan Vega
10.
 Client *Shields Design*
 Designer Charles Shields
11.
 Client *Zenn Graphic Design*
12.
 Client *Purple Moon Dance Project*
 Designers Christine Chung, Nancy Hunt-Weber
13.
 Client *Performance, Inc.*
 Art Director Bill Teague
 Designer Elliot Strunk
14.
 Client *Phil Rudy Photography*
 Designer Charles Shields
 Photographer
 Phil Rudy
15.
 Client *Sport Sling*

1.

2.

3.

4.

TIG

5.

6.

7.

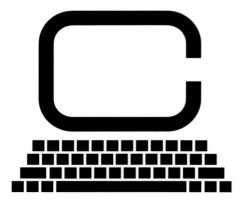

8.

342

9.

10.

The Shubert Organization

11.

12.

13.

14.

INDIES
RESTAURANT & BAR

15.

343

1, 7, 10, 15
Design Firm **Jeff Fisher LogoMotives**
2, 6, 9, 13
Design Firm **Insight Design Communications**
Art Directors Sherrie & Tracy Holdeman
3, 5, 8, 12, 14
Design Firm **Taylor & Ives Incorporated**
4, 11
Design Firm **Fujita Design, Inc.**

1.
Client — Samuels Yoelin Kantor Seymour & Spinrad LLP
Designer — Jeff Fisher
2.
Client — Raytheon Corporation
Designers — Sherrie & Tracy Holdeman
3.
Client — Bankers Trust Company/ Globe Set
Designer — Alisa Zamir
4.
Client — Vanguard Fruit Company
Designer — Alisa Zamir
5.
Client — TIG Holdings, Inc.
Designer — Alisa Zamir

6.
Client — Cityarts
Designer — Chris Parks
7.
Client — Ed Cunningham
Designer — Jeff Fisher
8.
Client — New York Stock Exchange
Designer — Alisa Zamir
9.
Client — Love Box Company
Designers — Sherrie & Tracy Holdeman
10.
Client — Samuels & Nudelman
Designer — Jeff Fisher
11.
Client — The Shubert Organization
Designer — Alisa Zamir
12.
Client — NaPro BioTherapeutics, Inc.
Designers — Alisa Zamir, Martin Fujita
13.
Client — Massco
Designer — Chris Parks
14.
Client — Somerset
Designer — Alisa Zamir
15.
Client — Indies Restaurant & Bar
Designer — Jeff Fisher

1.

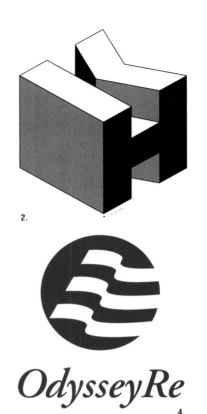

2.

3.

OdysseyRe

4.

StARS

5.

6.

BROCK

7.

**U.G.L.Y.
BARTENDER
CONTEST**

8.

9.

10.

double entendre

11.

12.

13.

14.

EVENTX

15.

THERMOLASE
C O R P O R A T I O N

1.

2.

3.

TG**R** TOLL GATE
RADIOLOGY INC.

4.

INSTIN:::T

5.

6.

7.

8.

9.

10.

eagle eye   11.

IntelliGenetics   12.

GRAND AIRE EXPRESS   13.

COFFEE KIDS™

GROUNDS FOR HOPE   14.

15.

J O B P R O

FLEXIBLE STAFFING SOLUTIONS   17.

16.

18.

1
Design Firm **Maddocks & Company**
2, 13
Design Firm **Schlatter Design**
3, 4, 8, 10, 14-17
Design Firm **Creative Vision Design Co.**
Designer   Gregory Gonsalves
5, 6
Design Firm **Yuguchi Group, Inc.**
7
Design Firm **Emphasis Seven Communications, Inc.**
9
Design Firm **RMI, Inc.**
11, 12
Design Firm **Philip Quinn & Partners**
Designer   Philip Quinn
16
Design Firm **Diane Kuntz Design**

1.
Client   *Thermolase Corporation*
Creative Director   Mary Scott
Designers   Camille Favilli, Carrie Dobbel
2.
Client   *Axiom Communications*
Designers   Richard Schlatter, Frederick DeRuiter
3.
Client   *Little Kids, Inc.*
4.
Client   *Toll Gate Radiology*

5.
Client   *Instinet*
Designer   Clifford Yuguchi
6.
Client   *Rockwell*
7.
Client   *KMC Telecom*
Designer   Debra Nemeth
8.
Client   *Ecotrition Foods*
9.
Client   *Saab Cars USA, Inc.*
Designer   Lee Einhorn
10.
Client   *Lepre Physical Therapy*
11.
Client   *Eagle Eye*
12.
Client   *IntelliGenetics, Inc.*
13.
Client   *Grand Aire Express*
Designer   Richard Schlatter
14.
Client   *Coffee Kids*
15.
Client   *Rick Sippel/Sippel Photography*
16.
Client   *Hidden Valley Ranch*
Designers   Diane Kuntz, Marneu Jameson
17.
Client   *Jobpro*
18.
Client   *Pizzeria Uno*

1.

2.

3.

4.

5.

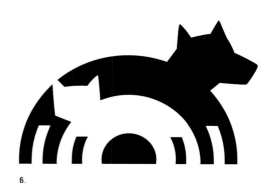

6.

7.

1
Design Firm **DeMartino Design**
2, 3, 6, 7
Design Firm **Graphic Design Continuum**
4, 5
Design Firm **Dennis S. Juett &
Associates Inc.**

1.
Client *Haynes Security Inc.*
Designer Erick DeMartino
2.
Client *Paradigm*
Designer John Emery
3.
Client *New Futures of Dayton*
Designer John Emery
4.
Client *TransWorld Video Lab, Inc.*
Designers Jeffrey Lawson, Dennis S. Juett

5.
Client *The Graphics Shop*
Designer Dennis Scott Juett
6.
Client *Humane Society of Greater Dayton*
Designer Danielle Dumont
7.
Client *Victoria Theatre Association
(Camp Victoria)*
Designer Danielle Dumont
(opposite)
Client *FAO Schwarz*
Design Firm **Walker Group/CNI**
Designers Sandra Hagashi, Edwin Sierra

348

 F·A·O SCHWARZ
FIFTH AVENUE

1.

2.

3.

4.

5.

6.

7.

8.

350

Huntington Hospital

9.

10.

OXFORD
CLINIC

11.

JULIAN HARO

12.

ALPINE PRESS
INCORPORATED

13.

ARTS

14.

AVIALL

15.

Midtown
Pointe

1.

2.

3.

ALLIANCE FOR HEALTH

4.

5.

DesignPartnership

6.

7.

8.

9.

MacIlwinen
Development, Inc.
10.

Crisp
Hughes
Evans
LLP
11.

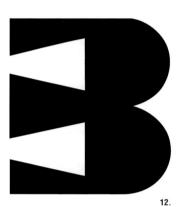

12.

LEADERSHIP GREER

13.

14.

15.

1, 5-8, 10, 11, 13-15
Design Firm **Westhouse Design**
2, 3, 4, 9, 12
Design Firm **Graphic Design Continuum**

1.
Client *City of Greenville*
Designers Jack DelGado, Daniel Jones

2.
Client *Lexis Nexis (Cultural Diversity Program)*
Designer Dwayne Swormstedt

3.
Client *Sinclair Community College*
Designer Dwayne Swormstedt

4.
Client *Alliance for Health*
Designer Dwayne Swormstedt

5.
Client *Bistro Europa*
Designers Jack DelGado, Daniel Jones

6.
Client *Design Partnership, Inc.*
Designers Jack DelGado, Daniel Jones

7.
Client *Rocky Creek Bakehouse*
Designers Jack DelGado, Daniel Jones

8.
Client *Corner Pocket Steaks, Ribs & Spirits*
Designers Jack DelGado, Daniel Jones

9.
Client *Victoria Theatre Association (International Children's Festival)*
Designer John Emery

10.
Client *MacIlwinen Development, Inc.*
Designers Jack DelGado, Daniel Jones

11.
Client *Crisp Hughes Evans LLP*
Designers Jack DelGado, Daniel Jones

12.
Client *Benchmark*
Designers Dwayne Swormstedt, John Emery

13.
Client *Greater Greer Chamber of Commerce*
Designers Jack DelGado, Daniel Jones

14.
Client *DigiTech, Inc.*
Designers Jack DelGado, Daniel Jones

15.
Client *Langston Black Real Estate, Inc.*
Designers Jack DelGado, Daniel Jones

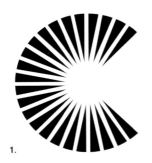

1.

2.

3.

MaguirePhotographics

4.

5.

6.

7.

Greater Greer Development Corporation

8.

9.

10.

354

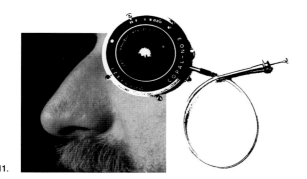

11.

12.

GSPAIRPORT
INTERNATIONAL

13.

14.

hands on
greenville

15.

16.

17.

1-3, 5, 6, 11
Design Firm **Graphic Design Continuum**
4
Design Firm **Denise Kemper Design**
7
Design Firm **Wes Garlatz Graphic Design**
8, 13, 15
Design Firm **Westhouse Design**
10, 16
Design Firm **Liska & Associates**
14
Design Firm **Hanson Associates, Inc.**
17
Design Firm **DeMartino Design**

1.
Client   *Careview*
Designers Dwayne Swormstedt,
           Cindy Welsh
2.
Client   *Shafor Johnson Architects*
Designer   John Emery
3.
Client   *Vanguard Management, Inc.*
Designer   John Emery
4.
Client   *Maguire Photographics*
Designer   Denise Stratton Kemper
5.
Client   *First Light*
Designer   Dwayne Swormstedt
6.
Client   *Zellerbach*
Designers John Emery, Dwayne Swormstedt

7.
Client   *Functional Solutions Group*
Designer   Wes Garlatz
8.
Client   *Greater Greer Development Corp.*
Designers Jack DelGado, Daniel Jones
9.
Client   *Golf Dome*
Designer   Todd Nickel
10.
Client   *Spiegel, Inc.*
Designer   Holle Andersen
11.
Client   *BBS Images*
Designer   John Emery
12.
Client   *Green Dreams*
Designer   Todd Nickel
13.
Client   *Greenville - Spartanburg
           International Airport*
Designers Jack DelGado, Daniel Jones
14.
Client   *Arroyo Grille*
Designer   Tobin Beck
15.
Client   *Hands On Greenville*
Designers Jack DelGado, Daniel Jones
16.
Client   *AccuColor*
Designers Staff
17.
Client   *BoBoLinks*
Designer   Eric DeMartino

1. SELECTS

2.  RED PEPPA™

3.  SKYLINE ENTERPRISES

4.  WESTHOUSE DESIGN

5. DigiTech *Software Duplication*

6.  GATEWAY INTERNATIONAL BUSINESS CENTER

7.  Pediatric HealthCare

8.  TIGER TRANSPORT

9.  HITO 熱點

10.  Fueltrimmer

OHIO MADE FILMS

11.

MARTIN ROGERS

12.

MEASURE

13.

14.

De Colores

16.

THE PILLAR OF SUPPORT CAMPAIGN

17.

15.

1, 10-12, 14, 15
Design Firm **Liska & Associates**

2
Design Firm **Hanson Associates, Inc.**

3-6, 8
Design Firm **Westhouse Design**
Designers Jack DelGado, Daniel Jones

7
Design Firm **Denise Kemper Design**

9
Design Firm **David Brewster Design & Denise Kemper Design**

13, 17
Design Firm **Alphawave Designs**
Designer Douglas Dunbebin

16
Design Firm **Rick Johnson & Company**

1.
Client *Benson & Hedges*
Designers Staff

2.
Client *Pillsbury*
Designer Tobin Beck

3.
Client *Skyline Enterprises, Inc.*

4.
Client *Westhouse Design*

5.
Client *DigiTech, Inc.*

6.
Client *Gateway International Business Center*

7.
Client *Pediatric Health Care*
Designer Denise Stratton Kemper

8.
Client *Tiger Transport Services*

9.
Client *Circle K- Taiwan "Hito"*
Designers Denise Stratton Kemper, David Brewster

10.
Client *Grainger*
Designers Staff

11.
Client *Ohio Made Films*
Designer Maria Cunningham

12.
Client *Martin Rogers*
Designer Steve Liska

13.
Client *Population Reference Bureau MEASURE program*

14.
Client *Loret Carbone*
Designer Steve Liska

15.
Client *Geldermann*
Designers Staff

16.
Client *De Colores*
Designer Tim McGrath

17.
Client *Washington Adventist Hospital Foundation*

1.

2.

3.

4.

5.

The Wexan Group, Ltd.

6.

QuickCat

7.

8.

9.

THE BLACK BOOK

10.

358

11. MATTALIANO

PLACE

12.

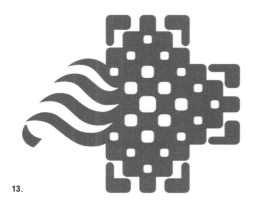

13.

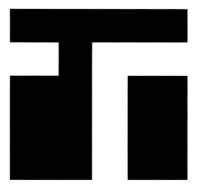

14.

Angotti/McHugh

15.

AFOP

16.

17.

1, 4, 5, 8, 12, 13, 16
Design Firm **Alphawave Designs**
2, 3, 6, 7, 9, 10, 11, 14, 15, 17
Design Firm **Liska & Associates**

1.
Client *Division of Clinical Sciences, NCI*
Designer Douglas Dunbebin

2.
Client *Spiegel, Inc.*
Designers Staff

3.
Client *Frommer & Goldstein*
Designers Staff

4.
Client *World Kids Inc.*
Designer Douglas Dunbebin

5.
Client *Bonin & Associates*
Designer Douglas Dunbebin

6.
Client *The Wexan Group, Ltd.*
Designers Staff

7.
Client *Grainger*
Designers Staff

8.
Client *Alphawave Designs*
Designer Douglas Dunbebin

9.
Client *Elizabeth Zeschin Studio*
Designer Staff

10.
Client *Black Book*
Designer Steve Liska

11.
Client *Mattaliano*
Designer Marcos Chavez

12.
Client *N. E. Place/*
Matthews Media Group, Inc.
Designer Douglas Dunbebin

13.
Client *National Hispanic Health Coalition*
Designer Douglas Dunbebin

14.
Client *Torchia Associates*
Designer Nancy Blackwell

15.
Client *Angotti/McHugh*
Designer Steve Liska

16.
Client *Association of Farmworker*
Opportunity Programs
Designer Douglas Dunbebin

17.
Client *Chicago Mercantile Exchange*
Designer Steve Liska

1.

2.

INOCHI

3.

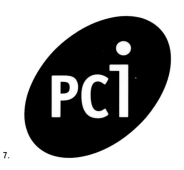

4.

5.

6.

7.

8.

9.

10.

Maryland
Biotechnology
11. Institute

Fun in the Sun   12.

AcuStaf
13. C O R P O R A T I O N

14.

15.

16.

17.

1.

HealthLink 2.

PETROCAP

3.

4.

GARDENSCAPES

5.

6.

IREM

7.

8.

9.

JOE LUNARDI
ELECTRIC
INCORPORATED

10.

362

John Buck Company 11.

 12.

 13.

VIRTUEM
ENTERTAINMENT 14.

A M E R I C A N

CREW

15.

 16.

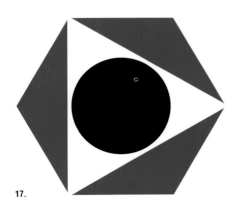

17.

1, 4, 5, 12, 13, 16, 17
Design Firm **Ikola designs…**
Designer   Gale William Ikola
2, 3, 6-8, 11, 14, 15
Design Firm **Liska & Associates**
9, 10
Design Firm **Horjus Design**
Designer   Peter Horjus
1.
  Client   Airtronic
2.
  Client   HealthLink
  Designers   Staff
3.
  Client   Petro Cap
  Designer   Steve Liska
4.
  Client   Brunswick United
              Methodist Church
5.
  Client   Gardenscapes
6.
  Client   The Inter Exchange Group
  Designers   Staff

7.
  Client   Institute of Real Estate
              Management
  Designer   Valerie Cote
8.
  Client   Reptile Artists Agent
  Designer   Holle Andersen
9.
  Client   Point Loma College
10.
  Client   Joe Lunardi Electric
11.
  Client   John Buck Company
  Designer   Steve Liska
12.
  Client   Charlene & Robert Burningham
13.
  Client   Beulow Architects
14.
  Client   Virtuem Entertainment
  Designer   Nancy Blackwell
15.
  Client   American Crew
  Designer   Marcos Chavez
16.
  Client   Digital Excellence
17.
  Client   Hoerner Waldorf Corporation

1.

2.

3.

4.

5.

6.

7.

8.

9.

10.

11.

12.

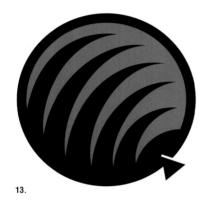

13.

14.

15.

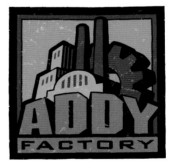

16.

17.

1, 2, 8, 9, 10
Design Firm **Liska & Associates**
3, 11
Design Firm **Ikola designs…**
Designer Gale William Ikola
4
Design Firm **Nick Kaars & Associates**
5
Design Firm **Cube Advertising & Design**
6, 7
Design Firm **Jasper & Bridge**
12
Design Firm **Scott Brown Design**
13, 14, 16
Design Firm **Dot Zero Design**
15, 17
Design Firm **ZGraphics, Ltd.**
Designer Gregg Rojewski
1.
Client *Learning Curve*
Designer Holle Anderson
2.
Client *Terra International*
Designer Steve Liska
3.
Client *Centennial Lakes Dental Group*
4.
Client *Territorial Savings*
Designers Nick Kaars & Fallon Lee
5.
Client *Nabanco, Inc.*
Designer David Chiow

6.
Client *Unitas*
Designer Andy Thorington
7.
Client *Volk Packaging Corporation*
Designers Alexander Bridge & Dan Howard
8.
Client *Oman*
Designer Steve Liska
9.
Client *Van Kampen Merritt*
Designer Steve Liska
10.
Client *Horticulture Design*
Designers Staff
11.
Client *Northern States Power Company*
12.
Designers Scott Brown, Janis Wong
13.
Client *Pioneer Balloon*
Designer Jon Wippich
14.
Client *Pioneer Balloon*
Designers Jon Wippich, Karen Wippich
15.
Client *Dundee Mainstreet*
16.
Client *Advertising Federation*
Designers Jon Wippich, Karen Wippich
17.
Client *Allen and Sons*

1.

2.

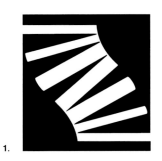

Welch Hydraulix

A PDR Company

3.

The BEAUMONT

inn

4.

5.

6.

MAMA

RECORDS

7.

8.

BROADCAST VIDEO RENTALS, LTD.

9.

10.

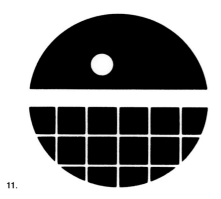

11.

12.

13.

OUTRIGGER
Hotels Hawaii

14.

15.

16.

17.

1, 4, 8, 15
Design Firm **CWA, Inc.**
2, 6
Design Firm **Cube Advertising & Design**
3, 16
Design Firm **South & Hickory Concept & Design**
5, 7, 12, 13, 17
Design Firm **Vrontikis Design Office**
9, 10
Design Firm **Spencer Zahn & Associates**
Designer Spencer Zahn
11, 14
Design Firm **Nick Kaars & Associates**

1.
Client *Hyspan*
Designers Susan Merritt, Calvin Woo
2.
Client *Wildwood Developer, Inc.*
Designer David Chiow
3.
Client *WELCH Hydraulix*
Creative Director
Richard Poole
Designer Jodi Myers
4.
Client *Beaumont Inn*
Designers Calvin Woo, Sylvie Puig
5.
Client *Jackson's Restaurant*
Art Director Petrula Vrontikis
Designer Kim Sage
6.
Client *Architect Randall Comfort*
Designer David Chiow
7.
Art Director Petrula Vrontikis
Designer Victor Corpuz

8.
Client *UPAC, Union of Pan Asian Communities*
Designers Calvin Woo, Mary Castignolla, Debra Lee, Mark Boydston, Sylvie Puig
9.
Client *BVR*
10.
Client *Art Deco Hotels*
11.
Client *Oahu Racquet Club*
Designer Nick Kaars
12.
Client *Avery Dennison*
Art Director Petrula Vrontikis
Designer Christina Hsiao
13.
Client *Global-Dining, Inc.—Tokyo*
Art Director Petrula Vrontikis
Designer Christina Hsiao
14.
Client *Outrigger Hotels Hawaii*
Designers Nick Kaars & Fallon Lee
15.
Client *Asian Business Association*
Designers Calvin Woo, Sylvie Puig
16.
Client *Vaccinex LP*
Creative Director
Richard Poole
Designer Kevin Willi
17.
Client *CBS Radio—KFWB*
Art Director Petrula Vrontikis
Designers Susan Carter, Petrula Vrontikis

1.

THE SPORTS CLUB/LA

2.

ALPHA
FURNITURE
RESTORATION

3.

SUNSET

DECKS

4.

Ocean Pool

Bar & Grill

5.

[i]e design

6.

7.

five

visual communication
&design

8.

Financial Advisory Services

Providing Solutions

9.

Network World

World Class

10.

11.

SNEAKER SISTERS ™

12.

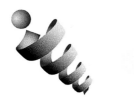

R E L E A S E

13.

S O F T W A R E

14.

C / L / B

F R A N C E S C A   F R E E D M A N

15.

S A N   F R A N C I S C O

16.

17.

1
    Design Firm **RTKL Associates Inc.**
2
    Design Firm **Cozad & Associates**
3, 4
    Design Firm **Kowalski Designworks, Inc.**
5, 13, 16, 17
    Design Firm **Arias Associates**
6
    Design Firm **IE Design**
7, 8
    Design Firm **Five Visual Communication
                  & Design**
9
    Design Firm **Communique**
10
    Design Firm **Horjus Design**
11
    Design Firm **Telesis**
12
    Design Firm **Diane Kuntz Design**
14, 15
    Design Firm **Susan Meshberg Graphic Design**

1.
    Client   *Burford Trocadero plc.*
    Designer   Glyn Rees
2.
    Client   *The Sports Club/LA*
    Designers   Bryan Friel, Bob Cozad
3.
    Client   *Alpha Furniture Restoration*
    Designers   Christine McFarren,
                Stephen Kowalski
4.
    Client   *Sunset Decks*
    Designers   Camille Sauvé, Stephen Kowalski
5.
    Client   *Ocean Pool Bar & Grill,
                Four Seasons Aviara*
    Designers   Mauricio Arias, Marcie Wilson
6.
    Client   *IE Design*
    Designer   Marcie Carson

7.
    Client   Mt. Auburn United Methodist Church
    Designers   Rondi Tschopp, Danielle Fagan
8.
    Client   *Five Visual Communication
                & Design*
    Designers   Rondi Tschopp, Danielle Fagan
9.
    Client   *Sciarabba & Walker*
    Designer   Tim Youngs
10.
    Client   *Network World*
    Designer   Peter Horjus
11.
    Client   *The Lacrosse Foundation*
    Designer   Frederick Kail
12.
    Client   *Sneaker Sisters*
    Designer   Diane Kuntz
13.
    Client   *Release Software*
    Designers   Mauricio Arias, Steve Mortensen,
                Stephanie Yee
14.
    Client   *Bel Canto Fancy Foods Ltd.*
    Creative Director, Designer
                Susan Meshberg
15.
    Client   *Chateau Los Boldos (Chile)*
    Art Director, Designer
                Susan Meshberg
    Computer Artists
                Elaine MacFarlane, Jia Hwang
16.
    Client   *Francesca Freedman*
    Designers   Mauricio Arias, Steve Mortensen,
                Vahn Phan
17.
    Client   *Apple Multimedia*
    Designer   Mauricio Arias

1.

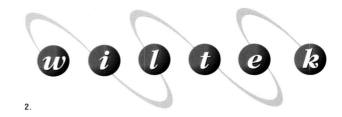

2.

CliniNet

3.

4.

5.

PNN

6.

7.

Strategic
Environmental
Management

8.

9.

Independent Weatherproofing Consultants, LLC

10.

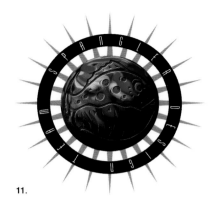

11.

12.

M I N N E S O T A
TECHNOLOGY AWARDS

13.

CLOE

CENTER FOR
LEARNING AND
ORGANIZATIONAL
EXCELLENCE

14.

 Scientific
 Visions Inc.

15.

16.

17.

1
  Design Firm **Steven Guarnaccia**
2, 14
  Design Firm **The Wyant Simboli Group, Inc.**
3-6, 16, 17
  Design Firm **Paganucci Design, Inc.**
8
  Design Firm **Foth & Van Dyke**
9, 12
  Design Firm **Arias Associates**
  Designer Mauricio Arias
10
  Design Firm **Allen Graphic Design**
11, 13, 15
  Design Firm **The Spangler Design Team**
1.
  Client *Steven Guarnaccia*
  Designer Steven Guarnaccia
2.
  Client *Wiltek Inc.*
  Art Director Julia Wyant
  Designers Ruth Teitlebaum, Kim Okosky,
  Julia Wyant
3.
  Client *Sandoz/Novartis*
  Designer Bob Paganucci
4.
  Client *The Child Care Company*
  Designers Bob Paganucci, Frank Paganucci
5.
  Client *Mikasa*
  Designer Bob Paganucci
6.
  Client *Physicians News Network*
  Designer Bob Paganucci
7.
  Client *Waters Corporation*
  Designer Theresa O'Toole

8.
  Client *Foth & Van Dyke*
  Designer Daniel Green
9.
  Client *Z Typography*
10.
  Client *Independent Weatherproofing
  Consultants, LLC*
  Designer Stephen Allen
11.
  Client *The Spangler Design Team*
  Creative Director
  Mark Spangler
  Artist Jeff Spry
12.
  Client *Pottery Barn*
13.
  Client *Minnesota Technology, Inc.*
  Creative Director
  Mark Spangler
  Designer Jeff Spry
14.
  Client *GE Capital*
  Art Director Julia Wyant
  Designers Kristin Kiger, Deborah Davis
15.
  Client *NuAire*
  Creative Director
  Mark Spangler
  Artist Laura Bartley
16.
  Client *Tech-Pro Inc.*
  Designer Bob Paganucci
17.
  Client *IBM*
  Designer Bob Paganucci

2.

3.

4.

5.

6.

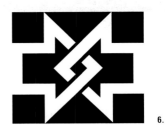

7.

8.

9.

10.

11.

12.

13.

14.

15.

16.

17.

1, 2, 4, 6, 8, 11, 12-15
Design Firm **Paganucci Design, Inc.**
Designer Bob Paganucci
3, 7
Design Firm **By Design**
5
Design Firm **Image Design**
9, 10
Design Firm **Horjus Design**
Designer Peter Horjus
16
Design Firm **Witherspoon Design**
17
Design Firm **Icon Graphics, Inc.**
1.
Client   *IBM*
2.
Client   *IBM*
3.
Client   *D. Chabbott, Inc.*
Designer John Hnath
4.
Client   *Geigy Novartis*
5.
Client   *Masonry Institute/
          Houston-Galveston*
Designer Randy Lynn Witherspoon

6.
Client   *Bell Atlantic*
7.
Client   *Hyde Athletic Industries, Inc.*
Designers John Hnath, Lisa Caputo,
          Elka Raedish
8.
Client   *IBM*
9.
Client   *Byron Pepper*
10.
Client   *The Preference Group*
11.
Client   *ADP*
12.
Client   *Del-Ran*
13.
Client   *Kanes Ltd.*
14.
Client   *SUNY*
15.
Client   *Mikasa*
16.
Client   *O'Connor Company Inc.*
Designer Randi Lynn Witherspoon
17.
Client   *Veritas Technology Inc.*

greenville avenue
Bar and Grill
DALLAS, TEXAS
EST. 1935

1.

OMNIMEDIA
Opening Minds Everywhere

2.

Alka-Seltzer
ANTACID MEDICINE
FAST RELIEF

3.

WARNER
MUSIC
GROUP

4.

Matson

5.

ASSOCIATION FOR ASIAN STUDIES
SOUTHEAST REGIONAL CONFERENCE

6.

7.

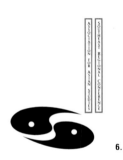

NACCA & COMPANY
CERTIFIED PUBLIC ACCOUNTANTS

8.

9.

10.

11.

ONTARIO
LAMINATED PRODUCTS

12.

THE REALTY GROUP

13.

Polaroid
Pop Shots
instant one-time use camera

14.

N

NORTH AMERICAN
BANKING COMPANY

15.

INFORM   INSPIRE   EXPLORE   REALIZE   16.

17.

1.

2.

STRAWBERRY
LAKE

3.

4.

5.

6.

SITES

7.

THE
FOUNDATION
CENTER

8.

376

9.

ANDERSEN
& ASSOCIATES

10.

11.

BullsEye
DATABASE MARKETING

12.

STARSTREAM
COMMUNICATIONS

14.

365
murad

13.

INFINITI.
UNIVERSITY
TOTAL | OWNERSHIP EXPERIENCE

15.

1.

2.

3.

4.

5.

6.

7.

8.

9.

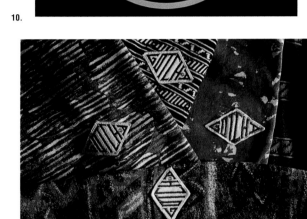

10.

11.

12.

MILD LAGER

KIRIN BREWERY COMPANY, LIMITED

13.

RAIDERS of the LOST ARK™

14.

15.

1.

2.

3.

4.

5.

6.

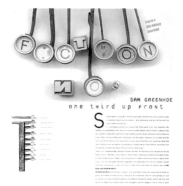

7.

8.

1-3			5.	
Design Firm	arismendi KNOX, Ltd.		Client	Harry's Bar
Designers	Susan K. Hodges, Rafael A. Holguín		Designer	Mike Salisbury
4-8			6.	
Design Firm	Mike Salisbury Communications		Client	Universal Pictures
1.			Designer	Mike Salisbury
Client	Calidad A Tiempo S. A.		7.	
2.			Client	Frances Coppolu
Client	Patchouli Esencias Naturales		Designers	Mike Salisbury,
3.				Mary Evelyn McGoush
Client	Paloma Promotions & Advertising		8.	
4.			Client	Paramount Pictures
Client	Universal Pictures		Designers	Mike Salisbury, Dave Parmley
Designers	Mike Salisbury, Terry Lamb			

INDEX

Design Firm

A

A-Hill Design 87
Ace Design 113
Addis Group 161
Adducci Design 375
Adkins/Balchunas 67
AERIAL 239, 301
After Hours Creative 375, 377
After Hours Design & Advertising 74
Agnew Moyer Smith 129
aire design company 106
AKA Design, Inc. 132
Albert•Bogner Design Communications 201
Allan Miller & Associates 122
Allen Graphic Design 371
Alphawave Designs 357, 359, 361
Andersen & Associates 375, 377
Angela Jackson 183
Apex Technology 91
Arias Associates 369, 371
arismendi KNOX, Ltd. 213, 380
Arista Advertising, Inc. 283
Art 270, inc. 18, 34
ARTEMIS 245
Arthur Andersen, LLP 74
Augusta Design Group 71
Axion Design Inc. 146, 149
Axis Communications 131

B

B.D. Fox & Friends, Advertising 195, 199, 200, 203
Back Yard Design 73
Bailey Design Group, Inc. 82
Ban Advertising 377
Bartels & Company, Inc. 335
Becca Smidt 77
Becker Design 361
Beggs Design 54, 61
Bellin Hospital Marketing/Communications Dep 289
Belyea Design Alliance 85, 237
Berni Design 41
Berry Design, inc 73
Big Fish Design 341
Blevins Design 81
Bob Rankin Design 10, 341
Boelts Bros. Associates 251
bonatodesign 187
Bonnell Design Associates 333
Brandt Resources 299
Bremmer & Goris Communications 91
Brookfield Zoo Design Department 88
Bruce Yelaska Design 149, 171
Burnett Group 327
Burson Marstellar 153
Business Graphics Group 118
By Design 373

C

Cadmus Com 196
Calidad A Tiempo S. A. 380
California Design International 93
Callery & Company 293, 295
Canetti Design Group Inc. 263
Capt Flynn Advertising 240
Cathey Associates, Inc. 135
Cawrse + Effect 77
Chapman and Partners 97
CheckFree Corp, Internal Creative Department 266
Cisneros Design 131
Cleminshaw Design Group 127
Commerce 125
Cole Design Group 137, 228
Coleman Design Group, Inc. 38, 231
Communication Arts Company 185
Communique 369
Conflux Design 223
Congdon & Company LLC 118
Congdon Macdonald Inc. 114
Continental Graphics 299
CookSherman 265
Cornerstone 239
Corporate Visuals 227
Cozad & Associates 369
Creative Dynamics Inc. 127
Creative Link Studio, Inc. 37
Creative Underground 299
Creative Vision Design Co. 347
Crimm Design 37
Crocker Inc. 211
Crouch & Naegli 190
Crowley Webb And Associates 307
CSUS Foundation, Marketing Services 183
Cube Advertising & Design 365, 367
CWA, Inc. 62, 67, 367

D

D4 Creative Group 185
Dan Meehan Design 289
Dart Design 239
David Brewster Design 357
David Brodsky Graphic Design 175, 187
David Lemley Design 65, 101
David Morris Creative, Inc. 227
Dean Corbitt Studio 81
Debra Lamfers Design 127
DeMartino Design 348, 355, 157
Denise Kemper Design 355, 357
Dennis S. Juett & Associates Inc. 348, 351
Desgrippes Gobé & Associates 57
Design Associates, Inc. 159
Design Center 257
Design Forum 313
Design Moves, Ltd. 189
Design North 187
Design Ranch 78
Design/Joe Sonderman 204
Designation Inc. 245
DesignCentre 97
DesignLab 30
Dever Designs 137, 361
Diane Kuntz Design 263, 301, 325, 347, 369
DiBaggio Design 165
Dixon & Parcels Associates, Inc. 94, 97
DLS Design 345, 377
Doerr Associates 303
DogStar 45
Donaldson, Lufkin & Jenrette 122
Donaldson Makoski Inc 127
Donovan and Green 299
Dot Zero Design 365
Dotzler Creative Arts 253, 257
Double Entendre 345
Doublespace 141
Drive Communications 93
DSI/LA 208

E

E. Christopher Klumb Associates, Inc. 131
EAT Advertising & Design 125
Ed Mantels-Seeker 179, 180, 183
Edward Walter Design 305, 307
Eisenkramer Associates 179
Elliot Van Deutsch 327
Ellis Pratt Design 150
Emphasis Seven Communications, Inc. 224, 347
Enock 135
Enterprise IG 303
Ervin Marketing Creative Communications 305
Eskil Ohlsson Associates Inc. 145
Essex Two / Chicago 213

F

Faine/Oller Productions 273
Fairly Painless Advertising 71
Fenway Partners 299
Five Visual Communication & Design 369
Fleury Design 88
FMG Design 132
Foley Sackett 139
Ford & Earl Associates 78
Forma Ltd. 91
Forward Design 78
Foth & Van Dyke 371
Frank D'Astolfo Design 38
FRCH Design Worldwide (Cincinnati) 10, 14, 18, 46, 54, 26, 30
Fresh Squeezed Design 233
Fujita Design, Inc. 343
Fuller Designs, Inc. 167, 169
Funk & Associates, Inc. 283

G

Gable Design Group 165
Gams Chicago, Inc. 110, 121
Gardner Design 42, 46, 49, 50, 53, 57
Gauger & Silva 67
Gee + Chung Design 57
George Tscherny, Inc. 101
Georgopulos 253
Gill Fishman Associates, Inc. 259, 261, 263
Glyphix Studio 26, 29
Gold & Associates 270
Gotham Bar and Grill 299
Grafik Communications, Ltd. 85, 149
Graphic Design Continuum 348, 353, 355
Graphica, Inc. 176, 207
Gregory Group 377
Griego Design 131
Griffith Phillips Creative 231
Gunnar Swanson Design Office 143

H

Hadassah Creative Services 269
Hal Apple Design 42
Halleck Design Group 137
Hallmark Cards, Inc. 77, 281
Hans Flink Design Inc. 69, 71
Hansen Design Company 207
Hanson Associates, Inc. 355, 357
HDS Marcomm 307
Heather Brook Graef 62
Heckler Associates 149
Hedstrom/Blessing, Inc. 361
Henry Dreyfuss Associates 240
Herip Design Associates 153
Hershey Associates 50
Hess Design, Inc. 159
Horjus Design 363, 369, 373, 375
Hornall Anderson Design Works 266, 269, 270, 273
Horvath Design 287
Howard Blonder & Associates 127
Howry Design Associates 171, 301
Hunt Weber Clark Associates 131, 341

I

Icon Graphics, Inc. 102, 373
Icon Imagery 172
ID, Incorporated 93
ID8 (RTKL Associates Inc.) 223
Identity Center 345
IE Design 88, 369
Ikola designs... 363, 365
Image Design 373
Imtech Communications 74
In House Graphic Design, Inc. 13
Inc 3 110
Inklings Design 196
Insight Design Communications 331, 333, 335, 337, 339, 343
International Playthings' Earlyears brand 299

J

J. Robert Faulkner 58
J.J. Sedelmaier Productions, Inc. 223
Jack Nadel, Inc. 50
Janet Scabrini Design Inc. 245
Jasper & Bridge 365
Jeff Fisher LogoMotives 343
Jefrey Gunion Illustration & Design 189
Jerry Cowart Designers 228
Joe Advertising 265
Joe Miller's Company 153
JOED Design Inc. 215
Joel Katz Design Associates 253
John Langdon Design 254
John Stribiak & Assoc. 231, 375
John Walker Graphic Design 58
Joseph Rattan Design 25
Julia Tam Design 135
Julie Johnson Design 93

K

Karen Skunta & Company 196
Katun Corporation 91
Katz Wheeler 253
Kelleher Design 91
Kiku Obata & Company 14, 17, 22, 179, 180, 183
Kim Baer Design 110
King Casey Inc. 71
Kirby Stephens Design, Inc. 315, 317, 321, 327
Klundt + Hosmer Design Assoc. 211
Knoth & Meads 193, 228
Kollberg/Johnson Associates 67, 377
Kor Group 273
Kowalski Designworks, Inc. 369
Kristin Odermatt Design 301

L

LaFond Design 85
Lahti Design West 237
Lambert Design Studio 179
Lance Anderson Design 139
Larsen Design + Interactive 38, 50, 102, 106, 110
Laura Coe Design Associates 341
Laura Kay Design 175
Laura Medeiros —Graphic Design 125
Lauren Smith Design 26
Lebowitz/Gould/Design, Inc. 305
Lee Communications, Inc. 113
Leslie Evans Design 187
Levine and Associates 82
Lighthouse Advertising & Design, Inc. 183
Lightspeed Commercial Arts 13
Lincoln Design 41, 263, 351
Lippincott & Margulies, Inc. 5, 7, 9, 10, 114
Lipson • Alport • Glass & Associates 327, 328
Liska & Associates 355, 357, 359, 361, 363, 365
Little & Company 175, 179
LMImage 78
LMPM 73
Lomangino Studio, Inc. 189
Lorna Stovall Design 73
Lotas Minard Patton McIver 71
Louis London 21
Louisa Sugar Design 284
Love Packaging Group 21
Lumina Studios 42

M

MacVicar Design & Communications 159
Maddocks & Company 195, 215, 347, 377
Madison Avenue East 293, 295
Malowany.Chiocchi.Inc. 245
Manhattan Country Club 299
Marcia Herrmann Design 269
Maritz 377
Mark Palmer Design 277, 279
Marshall Marketing & Graphic Design 284
Matrix International Assoc., Ltd. 155, 157
Matsumoto Incorporated 172
Matthew Huberty Design 377
Maureen Erbe Design 224
Max Graphics 270
McCarthy Bush Real Estate/Judy Steil 299
McDermott Design 129, 201
McElveney & Palozzi Design Group, Inc. 375
McGaughy Design 139
McGrath Design 377
McKenzie & Associates 106
McNulty & Co. 233
MediaConcepts Corporation 165, 171
Mervil Paylor Design 169, 299
Michael Doret Graphic Design 77
Michael Lee Advertising & Design, Inc. 30
Michael Orr + Associates, Inc. 58, 204
Mickelson Design & Assoc. 13
Mike Quon/Designation Inc. 243, 245
Mike Salisbury Communications 379, 380
Millennium Design 333
Miller & White Advertising 328
Minx Design 315
Mires Design, Inc. 150, 190, 217, 219, 220, 223
Miriello Grafico 190
Misha Design Studio 169
Mobilnet Management Services, Inc. 13
Mod 3 Design 257
Mortensen Design 273
Musikar Design 73
Muts & Joy & Design 105, 118, 122, 127, 132, 196, 208, 263

N

Nassar Design 73
NDW Communications 143
Nealy Wilson Nealy, Inc. 73
Nesnadny + Schwartz 17
Nestor•Stermole Visual Communication Group 37
Nick Kaars & Associates 365, 367, 377
Niedermeier Design 351
Nova Creative Group, Inc. 171
Nuts and Bolts Design 351

O

O & J Design, Inc. 85
Oakley Design Studios 139
Olver Dunlop Associates 67
1-earth GRAPHICS 82
Optimum Group 305

P

Paganucci Design, Inc. 371, 373
Parachute, Inc. 187
Pat Jenkins Design 46
Patt Mann Berry Design 187
Pavone Fite Fulwiler 85
Pedersen Gesk 223
Peg Faimon Design 351
Pentagram Design, Inc. 10, 17, 21
Peoria Riverfront Investors for Development 299
Perceive, LLC 81
Performance, Inc. (Internal) 341
Philip Quinn & Partners 347
Phillips Design 74, 237
Phillips Ramsey 228
Phoenix Creative, St. Louis 180, 183
Pink Coyote Design, Inc. 161
Pinkhaus Design 265
Pirman Communications 203
Pisarkiewicz Mazur & Co, Inc. 375
Pittard Sullivan 73, 74, 78
Planet Design Company 61, 62
Platinum Design, Inc. 283
Point Zero Design 87
Polloni Design 215, 217
Premier Solutions 253
Price Learman Associates 175

R

R&R Advertising 247
R. Morris Design 149
Ramsden Design 273
Rapp Collins Communications 17, 34
Rappy & Company, Inc. 305
RBMM/The Richards Group 313, 315, 317, 319, 321, 323, 325, 327
Richard & Swensen, Inc. 247, 249
Richard Danne & Associates 87
Rick Elber Design (RED), RVT Inc. 121
Rick Johnson & Company 357
Rickabaugh Graphics 121
RKD, Inc. 281
RKS Design, Inc. 165
RMI, Inc. 347
Robert Meyers CommunicationDesign & Planning 247
Robert Meyers Design 247
Robert W. Taylor Design, Inc. 291, 293
Roger Ball Photography 299
Ron Bartels Design 377
Ronald Emmerling Design, Inc. 93
Ross West Design 172
Rousso+Associates, Inc. 309, 311, 313
RTKL Associates Inc. 369
Russell Leong Design 215
RVI Corporation 345
RVT Inc. 121

S

S & O Consultants 301
Sacks Design Group 42
Sayles Graphic Design 169
SBG Enterprise 49, 53, 58, 62, 114
Schlatter Design 347
Scott Brown Design 102, 365
Seasonal Specialties In House Design Group 135
Segura Inc 122
Selbert Perkins Design Collaborative 141
Seran Design 375
Shields Design 337, 339, 341
Shimokochi/Reeves 162, 165
Sibley/Peteet Design 67, 109, 169, 183, 220
Signal Communications 203
Silverman Group, Inc. 279
Simantel Group 297, 299
Simple Green Design 190, 203
Skeggs Design 87
Smart Design Inc. 223
Snodgrass Design Associates 254
Sommese Design 235, 237
Sorrell Co. 81
South & Hickory Concept & Design 367
Spencer Zahn & Associates 367
Squires & Company 223
Stahl Design Inc. 269
Stan Gellman Graphic Design 41
Steel Wool Design 87
Stein & Company 141
Stephanie Cunningham 171
Stephen Loges Graphic Design 171
Sterling Group 375
Steve Thomas Marketing Communications 149
Steven Guarnaccia 371
Stewart Monderer 91
Stoorza, Zeigas & Metzger 190
Straightline International 91
Studio Archetype 77, 233
Studio Ilan Hagari Tel Aviv, Israel 41
Summit Advertising 295
Susan Bercu Design Studio 81
Susan Meshberg Graphic Design 369
Swieter Design U.S. 99, 117

T

T+T Design 213
Takigawa Design 77
Taylor & Ives Incorporated 343, 345
Ted DeCagna Graphic Design 9
Telesis 369
TGD Communications, Inc. 9
The Brothers Bogusky 33
The Chesapeake Group, Inc. 327
The Creative DepARTment 377
The Design Shop 289
The DuPuis Group 251
The Flowers Group 190
The Focus Group 87
The Graphic Expression, Inc. 26
The Invisions Group 109, 110
The Jefferies Association 299
The Leonhardt Group 21
The Majestic Group, Inc. 122
The Puckett Group 71
The Rittenhouse Group 85
The Robin Shepherd Group 131
The Spangler Design Team 371
The Visual Group 145
The Weber Group Inc. 293, 295, 297
The Wecker Group 287
The Wyant Simboli Group, Inc. 371
Thibault Paolini Design 284
30sixty design, Inc. 235
Thomas J. Lipton Co. 299
360 Design Assoc. 303
3G Design & Illustration 313
Tim Celeski Studios 139
Tim Kenney Design Partners 22
TLG 254
Tom Fowler, Inc. 99
Toni Showalter Design 137
Tracy Sabin Graphic Design 193, 228
Tri-Arts Studio 240
Triad, Inc. 303
True Ideas, Inc. 269
Turner Design 143
Tyler School of Art Graduate Graphic Design 139

U

UniWorld Group, Inc. 85

V

Vance Wright Adams & Associates 213
Vaughn/Wedeen Creative 281
Via Design Inc. 204
Vince Rini Design 237
Visual Marketing Associates 185
Vrontikis Design Office 367

W

Walker Group/CNI 348
Wallace Church Assoc., Inc. 274
Walsh & Associates, Inc. 321, 325, 323
Warner Development 299
Waterman Design 327
Waters Design Associates Inc. 231
Wes Garlatz Graphic Design 355
Westhouse Design 353, 355, 357
Wet Paper Bag Graphic Design 187
Wiley Design 263
Winni Lum Design + 375
Witherspoon Design 373
Wynn Art Direction 223

Y

Yamamoto Moss 195, 199
Yasumura Assoc. 105, 118, 122, 127, 132, 196, 263
Yoe! Studio 21, 223
Young & Martin Design 25
Young & Roehr, Inc. 333
Yuguchi Group, Inc. 101, 224, 347
Yvonne Fitzner Design 85

Z

Zeewy Design 283
Zenn Graphic Design 341
ZGraphics, Ltd. 365
Zoe Graphics 176
Zunda Design Group 227

Client

A

A. J. Tool 375
Abaco 259
Abbott 5
Abington Hospital 34
Aca Joe 18
Acacia Landscape 122
Acapulco Black Film Festival 85
Access Outreach Services 295
AccuColor 355
Accurate Typing Service, Inc. 88
Accusight 135
Acid Rain 251
Acme Premium Supply 179
Active Voice 65, 101
Activerse 99
AcuStaf Corporation 361
Adams Outdoor Advertising 62
Adenak 105
Adgis, Inc. 113
Adler & Shaykin 345
ADP 373
Adpro 159
Advanced Laser Graphics 22
Advantagekbs 227
Advertising Club of St. Louis 129
Advertising Federation 365
Aeronautics Leasing, Inc. 291
Aerotech 81
African American Museum 327
AFS 105
After Hours Design & Advertising 74
AG Heinze 277
AgriSolutions 175
Aids Walk New Mexico 281
AIGA 45
Air Quality Laboratory 215
Airborne Connectors 325
aire design company 106
AirSystems, Inc. 307
Airtouch Cellular 150, 313
Airtronic 363
Alamo.com 37
Alaskan Harvest Seafoods 273
Alberto Culver 69
Alchemy 91
Aldredge Music Supply 317
Aldus 101
Alice's Handweaving 317
Alimenterics Inc. 38
Alistar Insurance, Inc. 339
Alka Seltzer 375
Allegiance 327
Allegro Dallas 315
Allen and Sons 365
Alliance for Growth & Progress 328
Alliance for Health 353
Allied Corporation 5
Alpha Furniture Restoration 369
Alphawave Designs 359
Alpine Press 351
Alpine Shop 183
Alta Beverage Company 269
Altec Lansing Technologies 93
Alteon Networks 102
Alumitech, Inc. 321
AMC, Inc. 25
AmCon Inc. 315
Ameren Corporation 17
American Airlines 240
American Airshow Network 29
American Association of Spinal Cord In 38
American Campus Communities 109
American Cancer Society 263
American College of Physician Execut 237
American Corporate Counsel Association 38
American Crew 363
American Express 243, 245
American Federation of Government Empl 73
American Greetings 5
American Heart Association 215
American Indian Community Center 211
American Institute of Wine & Food 137
American Isuzu Motors Inc. 88
American Jewish Historical Society 261
American Marketing Association Metro 91
American Portfolio Services 183
American Security Mortgage 345
American Village Development 245
American Zoo & Aquarium Association 85, 88
Amerifest 319
AmeriHealth 25
Ameritrust 71
Amon's Bakery 321
Amquest Financial Corp. 155
Amtrak 5
Anacomp 219
Anastasia Marie Cosmetics 42
Ande Mac Design 321
Andersen & Associates 377
Andersen Consulting 74
Anderson Shumaker 81
Andrew Hunt Photography 145
Andrews Paint 57
Andromedia 265
Anergen, Inc. 171
Angotti/McHugh 359
Anheuser-Busch Companies 132
Anika Therapeutics 150
Animated Rsolutions, L.L.C. 97
Anita Paulus, DDS 179
Annuity Buyers, USA 29
Anthem Homes, Inc. 155
Antonio Mercado 220
Anyware Technologies 223
Apple Multimedia 369
Apple Valley International, Inc. 41
Applied Global University 171
Applied Professional Systems 127
Applied Strategic Knowledge Solutions 171
Aquafuture 287
Aquarian Bicycles 125
Aquatic Leisure International 26
Aquatics & Exotics 235
Arachnid Design 171
Arc International Inc. 131
Architect Randall Comfort 367
Ardco, Inc. 121
Argo 323
Argyle Associates, Inc. 113
Arista Advertising, Inc. 283
Arizona International Campus 106
Aronoff Center for the Arts 14
Array Technology 61
Arrow Electronics, Inc. 231
Arroyo Grille 355
Art Center 33
Art Deco Hotels 367
Art Effects 333
Artax 29
Artemis 245
Artisan Films 45
Arturo Designs 165
Ascent Entertainment Group 26
Asian Business Association 367
Aspen Creek Apts. 341
Aspen Home Systems 74
Associated Design Services 231
Association for Women in Communica 284
Association of Blockbuster Franchise 335
Association of Farmworker Opportunit 359
Association of Home Appliance Manufact 189
Association of Universities for Rese 159
Asterisk 34
At The Beach 277
ATCC (American Type Culture Collection 171
ATDC 46
ATEEC Advanced Technology Environme 377
Atherton Group 281
Atlanta International Airport 309
ATMI/Hypernex 118
ATMI/Novasource 118
Attitude Online 339
Aubrey Hair 323
Auto Craft 49
Autodesk Engineering 149
Avante 29
AVASTOR (Digital Equipment Corporation 102
Avenue One 220
Avenue Skin Care 77
AVEO, Inc. 61
Avery Dennison 367
AVIALL 351
Avikan International Academies 106
Axiom Communications 347
Axiom Training, Inc. 189
Axon 315
Azalea Films 196

B

B-Tree 175
B-WILD 65
Back Yard Design 73
Backdoor Delivery 117
Bagel Heaven 88
BAIGlobal Inc. 113
Bailey Design Group, Inc. 82
Balboa Travel 281
Banco De Ponce 105
Bank Atlantic 5
Bankers International Trust 217

Bankers Trust 240
Bankers Trust Company/Globe Set 343
Barclay Towers 157
Barlow Research Associates 195
Barnes West County Hospital 179, 180
Barr Pictures 143
Barry Fishler Direct Response Copywrit 101
Barton Group 261
Baskin Robbins 7
Batrus Hollweg 25
Bayer 274
Bayer Corp. 69
BB - Interactive 77
BBS Images 355
Beacon Hill Club 137
Beans Coffees 259
Bear Creek Wood Works 313
Beaumont Inn 367
Beaver College 18
Beaver Construction 45
Beckley Imports 169
Beecken Petty & Company 67
Bel Canto Fancy Foods Ltd. 369
Bell • Carter Foods 161
Bell Atlantic 243, 289, 373
Bell Winery 325
Bellin Heartwatch Plus 289
Bellin Hospital 289
Belyea Design Alliance 237
Ben & Jerry's Homemade, Inc. 227
Benchmark 353
Benson & Hedges 357
Benton Shipp Golf Tournament 25
Berbee Information Networks Corp. 62
Berkly System 49
Berlex 223
Berlin Packaging "Pinnacle" 169
Berman Marketing Reserve 57
Best Cellars 270
Best Cookies Baking 227
Bestfoods 303
Beulow Architects 363
Bidder's Edge 327
Biesse Networks 257
Big Deahl 150
Big Dog Custom Motorcycles Inc. 335
Big Entertainment 199
Big Fish Design 331, 341
Bill Ballenberg 87
Bill Drake 257
Billy's 45
Biocycle 283
Biodynamics, Inc. 204
Biodyne 351
Birdwell Beach Britches 379
Birm 122
Birmingham Ecoplex 45
Birmingham Metropolitan Arts Council 45
Bistro Europa 353
Black Book 359
Blessed Sacrament School of Alexandr 91
Blood Center 187
Blooming Prairie Natural Foods 78
Blue Angel Bar & Grille 277
Blue Fin Billiards 287
Blue Raven Expeditions 283
Bluefins 14
BMJ Financial Services, Corporation 97
BMW Manufacturing Inc. 93
BoBoLinks 355
Bodyscapes, Inc. 213
Boisseau Evans & Associates White Oak 265
Bonin & Associates 359
Bonneville Machine 248
Bonneville Productions 224
Borden Inc. 94
Borders (Cafe Espresso) 54
Borough of Glen Ridge NJ 289
Botanica Lawn & Garden 331
Boulder Philharmonic Orchestra 291
Boundless Technologies 109
Bow Tie Billiards 287
Brain Injury Association, Inc. 299
Branded Restaurant Group 73
Bridge Medical 87
Bridge To Life 323
Bridgeport Bluefish 279
Bridges International Repertory Theatr 207
Brill Metalworks 175
Brimm's Inc. 307
British Airways 243
Brocato International 208
Brock Software Products 345
Bronn Journey 165
Bronson Brothers Inc. 157
Brookfield Zoo 88
Broudy Printing, Inc. 127
Broughton International 132
Brownlee Jewelers 309
Bruce Clark Productions 266
Brunswick United Methodist Church 363
Buchanan Printing 183
Buffalo Arts Studio 307
Buffington & Lloyd 309
Building B Creations 29
Building Bridges & Beyond 279
Bull's Head Animal Hospital 99
Bullseye 143, 377
Burford Trocadero plc. 369
Business Bank of America 49
Business Week Magazine 257
Button Heaven 57
BVR 367
Byron Pepper 373
C
C-Core 109
C-Cube Microsystems 273
Cabaña Hotel 145
Cactus Cafe 277
Cactus Sales & Leasing 245
Café Cofé Restaurant 265
Cafe Lulu 125
Cafe Paragon 67
Cafe Toma 149
CAFFE A go go 85
Caffé á Roma 293
Calidad A Tiempo S. A. 380
California Beach Co. 193
California Cafe 139
California Center for the Arts 150
California Hospital Medical Center 325
California State Lottery 49
California University of Pennsylvania 129
Callaway Carpet Co. 311
Caltex 5
Calypso Imaging 300
Calyx & Corolla Flower 265
Cambium House, Ltd. 113
Camerad Inc. 341
Camp Blue Ridge, Potomac Conference of 361
Campaign on Clinical Depression 167
Candle Corporation of America 215
Candle Ridge 325
Cantina Laredo 323
Capitol Risk Concepts, Ltd. 113
Capri-Heart & Lung Institute 254
Careview 355
Carman Engineering 99
Carmé, Inc. 284
Carmel Marina Corporation 287
Carol & Kanda 187
Casa De Oro Foods 257
Casa Rosa 325
Casablanca Cafe 91
Cascade Bike Club 139
Cat Hospital of Wichita 42
Caterpillar Inc. 297
Cathey Associates, Inc. 135
Catholic Diocese of Wichita 53
CBI Laboratories, Inc. 195
CBI Packaging 183
cbk:milieu 183
CBS Radio - KFWB 367
CCAN 58
Cedar Rapids Recreation Commission 13
Cedars-Sinai Medical Center 300
CEFCU 297
Celestial Harmonies 250
Centennial American Properties, Ltd. 309
Centennial Lakes Dental Group 365
Center City District 253
Center for Population, Health and Nu 137
Center for Public Resources 243
Central American 319
Central Avenue Pharmacy 215
Central Exchange 125
Central Park Mall 37
Central Park Mall Southwest Gourmet Fo 37
Central Pennsylvania Festival of the A 237
Centria (Smith Steelite) 7
Ceruzzi Properties 351
CFW Communications 196
Chalet Sports Bar and Grill 333
Challenge International 13
Chaney Enterprises 279
Chaos Lures 219, 220
Charlene & Robert Burningham 363
Charlie Maas 157
Charlotte Motor Speedway 204
Charlton Photos Inc. 361
Chateau Los Boldos (Chile) 369
CheckFree Corporation 266
Cherokee Communications 176
Chesapeake Bagel—St. Louis 22
Chesebrough-Pond's 69
Cheskin+Masten/ImageNet 49
Chessboard Café 143
Chic-A-Boom 77
Chicago Mercantile Exchange 359
Chicago Pneumatic Tool Co. 127
Chicago Symphony Orchestra 361
Chicopee 105
Chief Executive Magazine 193
Children's Day-Care Center 237
Childress Klein Properties 311
Chip Desk 375
CHiPS 53
Chiro-Net 125
ChoiceCom 67
Christine's 20th Century Furnishings 169
Chrysalis 71
Chukar Cherry Company 325
Cigar Aficionado Magazine 45
Cincinnati Milacron 85
Cintron Lehner Barrett 25
Circle 75 Office Park 309
Circle K- Taiwan "Hito" 357
Circle Marketing 121
City and County of Denver 291
City of Charlotte 204
City of Greenville 353
City of Spokane 211
City of UTICA 305
City of Wildwood, MO 14
Cityarts 343
Clara Maass Medical Center 289
Clermont Nursing & Convalescent Center 85
Clickcom 143
Cline, Davis & Mann Inc. (Proworx) 145
Clinical Information Consultants, Inc. 215
Clipper Cruise LIne 41
Clorox 146
Clothes The Deal 162
CNS 195
Coachella Valley Wild Bird Center 277
Coaches vs. Cancer 18
Coastal Leasing 73
Coca Cola Co. 114
Coca-Cola Southwest—Splash Down 37
Coffee Kids 347
Coleman Design Group, Inc. 231
Colgate Palmolive 69
College of Education and Psycholog 375
Color-Tex International 303
ColorAd Printers 77
Colorado Christian Home 291
Colorado Massage Center 291
Colorado Special Olympics 291
Colorscan Dallas 183
Columbia Builders 239
Com.plete/GlobeWave, Inc. 113
COMCARE of Sedgwick County 339
Comerica 5
Comforts 146
CommCor, Inc. 143
Commerce Bank 125
Commercial Equipment Lease 283
Commercial Federal Bank, Inc. 155
Communication Concepts, Inc./Servic 81
Community Savings 309
Community State Bank 57
Compact Devices 300
Computer Power Inc. 289
Concentra Medical Centers 155
Concept Information Systems 187
Concert Connection 281
Concord Mall 25
Concord Mortgage 323
Concordia College 199
ConDel 279
Condo Link 257
Conductor Energy Systems Management 331
Connect Computer 50
Connecticut Association of Productio 239
Connectware 117
Conoco "breakplace" 7
Conseco 303
Consensus Health 161
Consolidated Correctional Food Servi 169
Consolidated Hydro 305
Consolite Corporation 193
Continental Airlines 7
Converse Basketball 99
Cool Beans Cafe 183
Coolsville Records 77
Coors Field 14
Cop Ranch 315
Copper Development Assn. 113
Corbis Corporation 269
Coregis 327
Corner Pocket Steaks, Ribs & Spirits 353
Cornerstone Natural Foods 82
Corning Incorporated 58
Corpair 118
Corporate Property Consultants 157
Corporate Resource Development 309
Corrin Produce 77
Corvel Corporation 87
CosMed 180
Cosmetic Associates 69
Cottonwood Properties 250
Country Marketplace 269
Courtyard By Marriott 327
Coury Enterprises 233
Coury Financial Services, Inc. 213
Cowley County Community College 42
Cramer Calligraphy 53
Cranford Street 220
Crescent Foods 321
Crest Graphics, Inc. 29
Crest International 67, 94
Cricket Hill Estate 18
Crimm Design 37
Crisp Hughes Evans LLP 353
Critical Path 161
Cromenco, Inc. 54
Crossroads Global Crafts 299
Crowley Webb And Associates 307
Crown Equipment Corp. 176
Crown Printing 339
Crown Zellerbach 87
Crunch 141
CSUS Foundation, Food Services 183
Culinary Arts & Entertainment 377
Cumberland Travel 315
Current Communications 193
Cutler Travel Marketing 169
CVB Consultants 34
CW Gourmet/Mondeo 266
Cypress Bend 183
D
D. Chabbott, Inc. 373
D.L. White Builders 303
D4 Creative Group 185
Dainana Security 105
Dal Tile 109
Dalbow Internal Medicine 143
Dallas Cowboys Football 99
Dallas Public Schools 319
Dallas Zoo 313
D'Amicao, Metropolitan 175
Dan Mullen Photography 203
Dancing Desert Press 281
Danet 29
Daniel Williams, Architect 265
Daniels & Associates, Inc. 155
Dannon Co. 263
Dante's Restaurants Inc. 235
Darien Arts Center 131
Dark Horse Clothing 65
Darwin Asset Management 113
Data Architects 74
Datascope Corp. 301
David Lemley 101
David's Ltd. 309
Davidson Communities 219
Davol Communications 137
Day Spring 253
Dayton Mall 26
Dayton Vineyard Christian Fellowsh 176
De Colores 357
De Martino Design 157
DEAF 50
Dean Witter Realty 157
Debbie Krause 297
Decatur Celebration, Inc. 187
DeCotiis Erhard Strategic Consulting G 53
Deep 6 33
Deep Cool 179
Deep Ellum Association 223
Deere & Company 240
Del Oro Regional Resource Center 263
Del-Ran 373
Delta Cove Townhomes 351
Deltalog 335
Demand Products 309
Denver Buffalo Co. 155
Denver Zoo 113
Department of Power 203
Desert Icicles 277
Design Associates, Inc. 159
Design Development 279
Design Facets 231
Design Guidance 277
Design Milwaukee 61
Design Mirage 237
Design Partnership, Inc. 353
Design Ranch 78
DesignLab 30
DFS Group Limited 301
Diabetes Research Institute 33
Dial-A-Lunch 315
Diamond Technology Partners 141
Diane Strongwater 54
DIGEX 239
Digital Controls 309
Digital Delivery 259
Digital Excellence 363
Digital Glue 311
Digital Imaging Group 265
Digital Island 270
Digital Media 195
Digital Navigation 141
Digital Textures 223
DigiTech, Inc. 353, 357
Dimon 7
DirecTV 73
Disclosure, Inc. 189
Discount Cleaners 215
Disney 379
Diva Video Shop 261
Dividend 67
Division of Clinical Sciences, NCI 359
Dixon & Parcels Associates, Inc. 97
DMS 227
DNA Plant Technologies 82
DogStar 45
Domain Energy (Tenneco) 7
Donnelley Enterprise Solutions 217
Doosan 7
Dotz Digital Pre Press 257
Double Entendre 345
Doug Baldwin • Writer 139
Dove 253
Dove Printing 277
Dow Jones 305
Downtown Import Service 125
Doylestown Presbyterian Church 18
Dr. Art Weisman 287
Dr. Saretsky 319
Drackett 105
Drake Construction Company 93
Draney Telemarketing 175
Dream Makers/Japan 243
Dream Mission-Jackson Foundation 331
Dreyer's 146
DSC Communications 303
DSI/LA 208
Ducks Unlimited 187
Duluth Playhouse 143
Dundee Mainstreet 365
Dunlop Maxfli Sports Corp. 274
Dunn Communications 247, 248, 249
E
E. Alexander Hair Studio 101
E. Christopher Klumb Associates, Inc. 131
E. Leon Jimenes, C. Por A. 105
Eagle Eye 347
Earth Grains 317, 325
Earth Tech 87
East End Food Co-Op 293
Eastern Casualty 263
Eastern Technology Council 201
Eastman Kodak Company 102
EATON 10
Echo Falls 351
Eclipse Construction 284
Ecofranchising, Inc. 171
Ecolab 187
Ecotrition Foods 347
Ed Cunningham 343
Edinboro University of PA 143
Edison Source 81
Editions Judaica 259
Ektelon 217
El Paso Chile Co. 325
Electrical Contractors 279
Electronic Graphic Artists of Dallas 135
Electronic Melody 135
Eli's Roadhouse 67
Elizabeth Gibb Architect 73
Elizabeth Zeschin Studio 359
Elliott Tool Technologies 171
Eltron 165
Embassy Suites 62
Empart 281
Empire Entertainment Productions 293
Energy Central 109
EnerShop 109
Entyron 207
Environmental Management Group 315
Environmental Protection Agency 82
Envirosep 81
EPI General Contractors 165
Epic Café 250
Episcopal School of Dallas 321
EPTI 25
Equibond 29
ERA GSM 335
ErgoCentrics 17
Eric Behrens - Photojournalist 297
ERIC Group, Inc. 291
Ernst & Young—Stanford Project 106
Esprit 29
Estabon Apodaca 250
Ethyl & The Regulars 143
Eureka Bank 49
Eventx Imagemakers 345
Evergreen Woodworking 78
Evolution Film & Tape 73
Evotech Co. Inc. 145
Execucom 313
Experian (TRW) 10
Experience Music Project 21
Exponential Technologies, Inc. 215
Eye Openers 102
F
F.T. & M. Inc. 145
Fabergé 69
Facial Aesthetic Systems 319
Fair St. Louis Organization 335
Fairhaven Partners Investment Group 110
Falling Sun Publications 287
FAO Schwarz 348
Farmland Mortgage 29
Fat Chance 53
FCB/Honig 49
Federated Department Stores, Inc. 97
Feldman Photography 42
FEMA 91
Fer Export Management, Inc. 189
Ferguson Enterprises 311
FFTA (Flexsys) 295
FIberComm L.LC. 185
Ficht 187
Fifth Ward Pediatrics 273
Film Casters 319
Financial Security Assurance 87
Finova 5
Fire and Clay Pottery 321
Firewheel Automotive 227
First Interstate Tower 233
First Light 355
1st National Bank 49
First Union, Community Reinvestment 169
First Union National Bank 114
First World Communications 150
FirsTier Financial Corp. 155
Fiserv Correspondent Services, Inc. 155
Fisk Communications 303
Fitness America 235
Fitzpatrik Masonry 207
Five Visual Communication & Design 369
Flagstar 10
Flea•For•All Idea Group 77
Fleets Cove Seafood 293
Fleetwood Enterprises Inc. 114
Fleury Design 88
Flower Country USA 315
Fluoroware, Inc. 38
FMC 7
Follett Library Resources 110
Fontaine's 87
Food Services of America 266, 273
Forbes Magazine 157
Formula 5 International Inc. 78
Fortran Printing, Inc. 17
Forward Design 78
Foth & Van Dyke 371
Four Seeds Corporation 99
Fourth Shift Users Group 257
Fox FX Cable 257
Frances Coppolu 109
Francesca Freedman 369
Franchini s.r.l. 91
Franciscan Institute 307
Franzia 149
Fraser Papers 10
Frasier Paper Company (Mosaic) 327
Fred Wilkerson 149
Freeborn & Peters 245
Freightliner Trucks 333
Freightliner Used Trucks 333
Fresh Mark Inc. 82
Fresh Paint 337
Fresh Squeezed Design 233
Friends of Powell Gardens 125
Friends of WRR 25
Frito Lay 274
Frommer & Goldstein 359
Frontline Now! 57
Fuddruckers 77
Full Circle Music 277
Fuller Designs, Inc. 167
Fun Junction 167
Functional Solutions Group 355
Fusion Media 219
Fusion Sports 220
G
Gabbert Hood Photography 196
GAC (Graphic Art Center) 251
Gais Bakery 254
Galleria 187
Gannett Co. 105
Garden Botanika 101
Gardenscapes 363
Gardner Design 49
Gargoyles Eyewear 21
Garment Corporation of America 265
Garmong Design/Build Construction 328
Gateway Insurance Company 26
Gateway International Business Center 357
GE Capital 371
Gegenheimer Group Ltd. 99
Geigy Novartis 373
Geldermann 357
Gellman Growth Partners 41
General Cinema 159
General Signal Networks Tautron 228
Generator Digital Post 73
Genesys 300
Geneva Area Chamber of Commerce 13
Genstar 211
Genuardi's Family Markets 313
Geode Consulting, LLC 291
Georgia Power Company 309, 311
Georgia Southern University 97
Gerber Scientific, Inc. 127
Giant Steps 273
Gillette Children's Hospital 199
Giro 67
Glen Brook Golf Club 377
Glen Ridge Congregational Church 289
Glen Ridge Historical Society 289
Global Cable Consulting Group 22
Global Capital Securities 237
Global Trade Partners 25
Global-Dining, Inc.—Tokyo 367
GLORY 46
Glyphix Studio 29
Gocial and Company 283
Golf Dome 355
Golf Lodging LLC 155
Golfdome 122
Good Times Home Video 243
Gordon & Smith 379
GQC Holdings, Inc. 215
Gracie's Restaurant 254
Grainger 357, 359
Grand Aire Express 347
Grand Hope Neonatology Group 325
Grand Metropolitan 223
Grand/Abacus Business Forms 153
Graphic Artists Guild 77
Graphic Pizza 29
Graphtel 189
GRC International, Inc. 22
Great American Photography Weekend 317
Great Lakes Science Center 14
Great Pacific Trading Company 337
Great River Golf Course 239
Greater Buffalo Convention & Visitor 307
Greater Greer Chamber of Commerce 353
Greater Greer Development Corp. 355
Greater Minneapolis Chamber of Commerc 195
Green Dreams 355
Green Field Paper Company 150
Green Mountain Energy Partners 199
Greening Earth Society 203
Greenville - Spartanburg Internati 355
Greenville Avenue Bar and Grill 375
Greenwich Village Chamber of Commerce 172
Grene Vision Group 339
Grider and Company P.A. 53
Group Gallagher 25
GSH Design 30
GTE 231
GUI Dance Technologies, Inc. 143
Guidant 5
Guthy-Renker 279
H
H + M Electric 327
H. K. Gaspar 305
H.Bernbaum Import Export Co. 215
H2 Oh 315
Haagen Dazs 259
Habitat for Humanity 25
Hackney (Freeway Oil) 114
Hadassah American Affairs Department 269
Hadassah Convention Department 269
Haggar Apparel Company 109
HAIR cuts plus 125
Hallmark Cards, Inc. 87
Halogen Systems 109
Ham On Rye Technologies 179
Hamilton Court 50
Hamilton Kennedy 185
Hanaco 25
Handok 5
Hands On Greenville 355
Hanifen Imhoff, Inc. 155
Hanna Perkins 17
Hannibal's Coffee Company 189
Hanson Cleaners 297
Harald Sund Photographer 321
Harbinger Corporation 311
HarborFest 293
Harcourt Brace 270
Harcourt Brace & Co. 190, 193, 220
Hargrove & Partners 261
Harmony Business Machines 13
Harrah's (Carnaval Court) 10, 30
Harrington Elementary Hawk's Nest P 179
Harris Bank 5
Harrison Hospital 254
Harry's Bar 380
Hartmarx 5
Hartwood Construction 233
Harvard Vanguard 5
Hasbro 379
Hastings Filters Inc. 337
Hawkins Construction Company 257
Haynes Security Inc. 348
Head Golf 319
Health & Fitness Center of Oak Brook H 121
HealthComp Inc. 341
HealthLink 363
Hearts & Hammers 319
Heinen Construction 189
Helena Pentathlon 307
Herip Design Associates 153
Hershey Chocolate U.S.A. 227
Hewlett Packard 49, 273
Hidden Valley Ranch 347
Hilbert Interactive Group 42
Hill 313
Hill Refrigeration 97
Hilton Hotels 303
Hitachi Data Systems 307
Hoag's Catering 235
Hoerner Waldorf Corporation 363
Hofbauer Vienna Ltd. 69
Holdeman's Total Lawn Care Service 339

Holland Brothers 161
Home Depot 319
Homebrew Productions 185
Hope Cottage Adoption Center 323
Horizon Healthcare 281
Hornall Anderson Design Works 270
Horticulture Design 365
Hospice of Lake Cumberland 315
Hot Rod Hell 219
Hoth Fine & Company 279
HResults! 18
Hugh Browne 307
Humana 10
Humane Society of Greater Dayton 348
Huntington Memorial Hospital 351
Hyde Athletic Industries, Inc. 373
Hydrotech 33
Hyland Printing 67
HyperShell, Inc. 187
Hyspan 367

I

I.N.V.U. 249
IBM 371, 373
ICE Fastpitch Softball CD-Rom 331
ICEX 341
Icon Design 149
IE Design 369
IFT 105
Illes Construction Company 153
Imagemaker Salon 139
Imagery Software/Kodak 263
Imation Corporation 50
Impact Engineering Solutions, Inc. 85
Impact Unlimited 239
Imperial Bank 224
In House Graphic Design, Inc. 13
Independent Insurance Agents of Americ 159
Independent Weatherproofing Consulta 371
Indian Creek Farm 153
Indies Restaurant & Bar 343
Industrial Valley Bank 97
Industry Pictures 219
Infiniti 377
Information Advantage 50
Infostar, Inc. 189
InGear 185
Inklings Design 196
Inktomi 93
Inland Entertainment Corporation 150
Inland Paperboard & Packaging, Inc. 73
Innovation, Inc. 139
Innovative Computer Systems, Inc. 143
Inochi 361
Insight Partners Inc. 303
Inso Corp. 259
Instinet 347
Institute for Change Research 13
Institute of Real Estate Management 363
Integral Training Systems 137
Integrated Network Concepts 141
IntelliGenetics, Inc. 347
Intelligent Biocides 179
Intellisystems 162
Interactive 281
Interactive Cable Television 93
Interactive Design 139
Interconnect Systems, Inc. 34
Interex 337
Intergold 243
Interlan Networks 215
Intermation Corporation 269
International Association of Printing 46
International Banking Technologies 311
International Broadcast Systems, Inc. 25
International Depository & Clearing In 345
International Filler 307
International Institute for Literacy 240
International Music Network 179
International Religious Liberty Associ 137
International Resource Center 305
International Society for Performa 167
Internet Dynamics, Inc. 297
Internet Source 215
Interplay 195
Inventa Inc. 61
Investment Horizons ©1998 247
Investment Securities 287
IRSA—International Raquet Sports As 159
ISMS 201
ITCN 171
IVAC Corporation 219
IVS 81
Ivy Technologies 179
IX Labs 375

J

J&D Products, Inc. 187
J. L. Alexander Group 85
J. P. Harkins 41
J.C. Pendergast 295
Jabra Corporation 219
Jackson's Restaurant 367
Jacobs Gardner Office Supply 307
Jamba Juice 270
James Goode Construction 287
JAS Technology 200
Java Joes 169
Java Springs Marriott's Desert Springs 277
Java The Hut 277
Javaworks 335
Jenny Woods Dance 122
Jerry Cowart Designers 228
Jewish Community Center 239
Jim Beam Brands 223
Jim Dickinson 175
Jim Henson Productions 21
Jim Kelly 270
Jimmy Dean 146
Jim's Gym 297
Jitters 339
JKW 227
JM Financial 165
JNANA Technologies Company 327
Jobpro 347
Jockey 328
Joe Lunardi Electric 363
Joga Chiropractic Center 300
John Buck Company 363
John D. May, Jr., Inc. 153
John McClorey 321
John Mung-Whitfield Commemorative Cent 341
John Scherer & Associates 211
John Wilmer Studioworkshop Antique Res 62
Johnson Products, Inc. and the Dr. Mar 213
Johnston Metal Industries 159
Jordan Properties 313
Juice & Joe 17
Juice n' Java Caffé and Restaurant 131
Julian Haro 351
Julian Tours 91
Jumbo Entertainment 239
Junebug Films 102
Junior League of Jackson 185
Junk Jewels 185

K

Kabel 1 78
Kaldi's Coffee Roasting 180
Kallen Computer Products 265
Kalpana 301
Kane Regional Center 129
Kanes Ltd. 373
Kansas City Chamber of
Kansas Department of Health and Enviro 331
Kansas Health Foundation/Leadership 49
Kansas Humane Society 57
Kansas State University 57
Kara 339
Kathryn Beich—division of Nestlé 17
Kathryn Buffum, DDS 139
Kawasaki 224
Kaz Technologies 61
Keck Graduate Institute of Applied L 299
Kehrs Mill Family Dental Care 132
Keiser Sports 337
Keith-Beer Medical Group 50
Kelleher Design 91
Keller Groves Inc. 215
Keller Photography 42
Kelly's Coffee 265
Kemper Funds 303
Kenn Ingalls 17
Kenny G/Artista Records 165
Kentucky Physical Therapy 321
Kenya Tourist Office 263
Kenya's Gourmet Bakery 127
Key Tech Associates 253
Keyfile Corp. 261
Kicks 337
Kidfest 317
Kim Cooper 176
Kimpton Hotel Group 131
King Casey Inc. 71
Kirin Beer 379
Kirk Alford 45
Kirkwood Athletic Assoc. 21
Kitchen Dimensions 87
Kitchen Logic 299
Klein and Hoffman Inc. 345
KMC Telecom 341
Ko-Thi Dance Company 361
Kobrick Cendant Funds 5
Kohler and Sons Printing Company 41
Kollberg/Johnson Associates 67
Komar 141
Kootenai Medical Center 155
Kor Group 273
KPMG 93
Kraft Foods, Inc. (Maxwell House) 328
Kroma Lithographers, Inc. 145
KUED Channel 7 249
Kurzweil Educational 263
KVK Computers 189

L

L.A. Java 269
La Belle Maison 333
La Cabana 85
La Choy Food Products, Inc. 94
La Mop Hair Studio 61
La Pinata 149
Lahti 237
Lake Cumberland Performing Arts 317
Lakemary Center 125
Lamar University 30
Land Expressions 211
Langston Black Real Estate, Inc. 353
Laser & Skin Aesthetics Center 161
Laura Coe Design Associates 341
Laura Medeiros 125
Lawless Packaging & Display 305
Lazy G Ranch 57
LD Supply 333
Leadership Network 321
Learning Curve 365
Leeds Inc. 207
Lehigh University 97
Leisuremaster, Inc. 201
Lemongrass 67
LensCrafters 97
Lepre Physical Therapy 347
Leshner Inc. 208
Lettuce Entertain You Enterprises, I 269
Lewisville Humane Society 319
Lexant 21
Lexington Square 361
Lexis Nexis (Cultural Diversity Progra 353
Lexis-Nexis 207
LI Philharmonic 295
Liberty Printing Company 41
Life Instructors Inc. 289
LifeScan 50
Lightgate, Inc. 61
Lighthouse Advertising 183
Lighthouse for the Blind 94
Lil' Britches 183
Lily's Alterations 273
Lincoln Elementary School PTA, Aileen 129
Linda Creed Breast Cancer Foundation 34
Lindsay Olives Co. 161
Linkon Corporation 127
Linus Pauling Institute 227
Lipson • Alport • Glass & Associates 328
Lithia Automotive 175
Little Harbor, Inc. 284
Little Kids, Inc. 347
LN Marketing 295
Locations South 313
Lockheed 203
Lockheed Martin 303
Loews Ventana Flying V Bar & Grill 106
Loftin & Company 149
Logical Software 261
Logitech, Inc. 61
Long Shot 207
Longmont Foods Company, Inc. 291
Lopresti Bros. Aircraft, Inc. 165
Lorán Lorán 277
Loret Carbone 357
Los Angeles International Airports 141
Los Angeles Times/Starbucks Coffee STA 135
Los Angeles Zoo 237
Lotas Minard Patton McIver 71
Lotus Carpets 311
Louisiana Electric Cooperatives, Inc. 208
Louisiana Health Services, LLC 208
Love Box Company 343
Lucile Salter Packard Children's Hos 301
Lucy's Laces 259
Lumen, Inc. 377
Lutheran Brotherhood 195, 199
Lycos 274
Lyman Realty 261

M

M-Two 99
M.G. Swing Company 217
MacDonald Construction 172
Machado & Associates 77
MacIlwinen Development, Inc. 353
Mad Cow Farms 297
Maguire Photographics 355
Maharam 172
Mahlum & Nordfors McKinley Gordon 269
Main Street Trading Company 339
MainSail Production Services 171
Maitri Aids Hospice 77
Majestic Air Services 247
Major League Soccer Players Associatio 85
Making America Work 46
Manes Space 137
Manor Style 231
Marhoefer Communications 167
MariCulture Systems 207
Mark Industries 127
Mark Watson Building & Renovation 77
Market Sciences 87
Marketing Sciences America 159
Marlo Graphics Inc. 41
Marriott Corporation 327
Mars, Inc. 94, 97
Martin Rogers 357
Mary Kay Cosmetics—Career Essentials 179
Maryland Biotechnology Institute 361
Masonry Institute/Houston-Galveston 373
Massco 343
Master Pools 279
Masters Group 220
Matinee 21
Matra Systems/Wilson Communications 61
Matrix Pharmaceutical, Inc. 245
Matson Navigation Company 375
Mattaliano 359
Matthew A. Weatherbie & Co., Inc. 110
Max Factor 73
Maxim Mortgage Corporation 337
McAbee Beach Cafe 287
McCauley Propellers 171
MCD 379
McGinly & Associates 257
McGraw Hill Home-Interactive 217
MCI/Vnet Card 137
McLean County Prenatal Clinic 58
MCM 379
McMichael Auman Consultants 41
McMillin Communities 228
McMillin Homes 190, 193, 228
McMinimy Photography 335
Mead Products 207
Meadowlark Estates 33
Mean Jean Productions 245
MedChem 78
Medcor 327
Memtek 146
Menards 135
Men's 20/30 Club of Tucson 250, 251
Mental Health Association of Kansas 33
Mercantile Leasing Corp. 145
Mercury 105
Mercury Messenger 117
Mercury Messenger Service 109
Mercury Restaurant 265
Mercury Systems 165
Mercy Medical Center 283
Merrill Lynch 71
Merrill Lynch Realty 105
Merry Mary Fabric 224
Meta•Logic 377
Metaphase/NCR Consulting Design Group 179
Metasys 149
Methodist Hospital Foundation 361
MetLife 118
Metrocel 313
Meyer Projection Systems 139
MGM/UA Home Video 200
Miacord 33
Miami County Recovery Council 82
Miami University School of Fine Arts 351
Miami Valley Women's Center 176
Michael Bondi Metal Design 139
Michael Bonilla Illustration 207
Michael Fox, Inc. 41
Mickey & Co. 21
Microsoft 65
Microtech Co. Inc. 145
Microtouch Systems 261
Midstate Banking 237
Mikasa 371, 373
Mike King Photography 109
Mike Quon Design Office 243, 245
Mike Salisbury Communications 379
Military Benefit Association 231
Millenium Pharmaceuticals 37
Millennium Design 333
Miller Brewing Co. 21
Miller Brewing Company 217, 219
Miller SQA 71
Milwaukee County Parks 293
Mingtai Insurance 165
Minneapolis Institute of Arts 17
Minneapolis Planetarium 106
Minnesota State Arts Board 199
Minnesota Technology, Inc. 371
Minnetonka Center for the Arts 17
Mirage 233
Mirror Mountain Motorcycles 61
Mississippi Museum of Art 185
Misty River Woodworks 61
Mitsubishi Foods 219
Mitsubishi Motors LPGA Charity Pro-Am 297
Mixology 331
MIxon Enterprises & Mixon Investments 313
Mobility 319
Mod 3 Design 257
Monarch Paper 325
Moneta Group Inc. 41
Monfort of Colorado, Inc. 291
Monkey Studios 193
Monrovia 224
Monsanto 41, 377
Monterey Bay Aquarium 113
Montgomery Wards 135
Moore & Associates 220
Morgan Winery 287
Morley Financial Services 13
Morse Diesel 137
Morton International 327
Moss Cairns 139
Mostel 93
Mother Care 361
Motorola, Inc. 213
Mount Mercy Academy 307
Mountain Top Repair 287
Mountaineer Race Track & Resort 213
Move It 10
Mowtown 127
Mr. Gatti's Restaurants 169
Mt. Auburn United Methodist Church 369
Mt. Sinai Children's Center 211
MTM Television Distribution 199
MTV Networks/Nickelodeon 223
Mullikin Medical Transcriptions 127
Municipal Flow Promotions 203
Murad, Inc. 377
Muzak 65, 101

N

N-ION Corp. 283
N. E. Place/Matthews Media Group, Inc. 359
Nabanco, Inc. 365
Nabisco 69
NACCA & Co. 375
Naiad Technologies, Inc. 333
Nanocosm Technologies, Inc. 57
NaPro BioTherapeutics, Inc. 343
Nardelli Associates 88
NASDAQ International Market Initiative 22
National Digital Corporation 307
National Exchange Carrier Assoc. 289
National Hispanic Health Coalition 359
National Physicians Network 81
National Policy & Resource Center on 81
National Sports Center for Disabled 211
National Surgery Centers, Inc. 213
National Telephone Cooperative Associa 38
National Travelers Life "Century Club" 169
Nationwide Insurance 121
Nationwide Transit, Inc. 305
Natural Nylon 62
Navatek Ships 62
Navcontrol Marine Electronic 293
Navecom 287
NBA Properties 77, 121
Neo-Life 284
Nestea 73
Nestlé 69
Net Effects 180
Netscout Software 259
Network Interface Corporation 337
Network Multimedia 248
Network Power & Light 93
Network World 369
New Canaan Madrigal Ensemble 118
New England Transit Authority Corpor 305
New Futures of Dayton 348
New York Stock Exchange 343
New York University School of Contin 85
Newer Technology, Inc. 331, 335
Newquest Technologies 247
NewsHound 187
Newsletter Services, Inc. 159
Nextek 327
NFL Properties N.Y. 257
Niehaus Ryan Group 93
Nike Boyswear 101
Nike, Inc. 150, 217, 223
Nike—Bauer In-Line Skates 265
Nike—Official Brand 101
Niman Ranch 265
Nix Health Care System 165
NJ Cougars 295
No Tomorrow 333
Nomads 203
Norelco 71
Norfleet Press 87
Norris 319
North American Banking Company 375
North Fork Bank 295
Northern Light 259
Northern Possessions 361
Northern States Power Company 365
Northstar Cold Storage 323
Northwest Airlines 195
Nova Marketing Company 132
Novacor 153
Novalis International Limited 201
Novellus Systems 110
NuAire 371
Nuclear Energy Institute 22
Nuts and Bolts Design 351
NYC Economic Development Corporation 305
NYNEX 99
Nynex 7
NYSAIR/NYSEG 58
NYSEG 58

O

Oahu Racquet Club 367
Oak Valley Resort 87
Oasis Academy 249
Oasis Club/Gatehouse Companies 165
Oasys Telecom 118
Oberheim 254
Object Space 25
ObjectWare 303
O'Brien International 65
Ocean Fox Dive Shop 99
Ocean Pool Bar & Grill, Four Seasons A 369
O'Connor Company Inc. 373
Odyssey Reinsurance Corporation 345
Offline Media (Webmark) 345
Ohio Arts Council 231
Ohio Made Films 357
Oil Changers 161
Okinawa Aquarium 172
Old Capitol Mall 46
Old Town Association of Wichita 333
Oman 365
Ominidia, Inc. 99
Omni Office Systems 295
Omnigraphics 137
OmniMedia 375
OmniOffices 311
On-Site Solutions 377
107 Ocean Bistro 67
One Penn Plaza 305
One Reel 101
One Server 233
One World Music 179
One World Software 321
Ontario Laminating 375
OPASTCO 38
Open Market, Inc. 141
OpenCon Systems, Inc. 227
Optimum Group 305
Opus Corporation 50
Oridion Medical 259
Orient Airlines Assn. 121
Origin Software 37
Originalis 77
Oris Technologies 49
Orville & Wilbur Publishing 283
Oryx Energy 317
Our Savior's Community 279
Outrigger Hotels Hawaii 367
Ovarian Cancer Detection & Preventio 81
Overlake Press 101
Overland Trading Co. 42
Overseas Development Council 22
Ovid Technologies 21
Owl Ridge Vineyard 247
Oxford Clinic 351
OXO International 223

P

Paccar Parts 53
Pace Development 307
Pace Entertainment Group 213
Pacific Beach House, Inc. 301
Pacific Cardiothoracic Surgery Group, 325
Pacific Ocean Group, Inc. 263
Pacific Place 269
Pacific World Corporation 165
Pacificare Matters on Maternity 37
Page One Business Productions, L.L.C. 235
Palo Alto Utilities 77
Paloma Promotions & Advertising 380
Pan American Bank 33
Panache Resources & Systems Corp. 97
Panda Group International 245
Pandesic 161
Parachute Press 21
Paradigm 348
Paradigm Communication Group 85
Paragon Capital 211
Paramount Pictures 380
Parrot Greens 239
Parrot Tree Plantation 137
Partnership Ministries Unlimited 97
Pasadena Civic Ballet 227
Paslode, Inc 213
Pasta Pomodoro 131
Pasternak 62
Patchouli Esencias Naturales 380
Paul Allen & Associates ©1988 247
PCEQ 122
PCI Computers Limited 361
Peacock Products 303
Peapod Properties Ltd. 207
Peccary King Productions 251
Peconic Electronic 295
Pediatric Health Care 357
Pegasus Travel 33
Penn State Summer Fest Theatre 235
Penn State Theatre Dept. 237
Penn's Landing 253
Pentamerica Pictures 195
Peoria Journal Star 297
Pepsi Stuff 265
Pepsi-Co Company 223
PepsiCo of Eugene 351
Perfect Sence Products 247
Performance, Inc. 341
Performance Management Associates 127
Personal Care Group 227
Personal Communications Interactiv 78
Personal Library Software 38
Personnel Unlimited 211
Peterson Properties 313
Petro Cap 363
Pettit Construction 279
PG&E 301
Pharmaceutical Technologies, Inc. 253
Pharmavite 146
Phil Rudy Photography 341
Philadelphia Bar Foundation Legal Soci 34
Philadelphia Theatre Company 18
Philip Morris 243
Phillips Design 74, 237
Phoenix Consulting Corporation 185
Phoenix Network 300
Phoenix Ventures 81
Photo Effects 203
Physicians News Network 371
Piccari Press, Inc. 143
PicketFence Community, GeoCities, Inc. 187
Picnic Works 213
Picture Factory 203
Pierce Contracting 99
Pilch, Inc. 204
Pillar 233
Pillsbury 357
Pinewild 323
Pioneer Balloon 365
Pirman Communications 203
Pisarkiewicz Mazur & Co, Inc. 375
Pittsburgh Civic Arena 213
Pittsburgh Dance Council 129
Pittsburgh Department of City Planning 129
Pittsburgh Light Rail Transit System 129
Pittsburgh Penguins 213
Pittsburgh Sports Festival 213
Pittsburgh Zoo 129
Pizza Hut 224
Pizzaz Sports Bar 131
Pizzeria Uno 347
Plan West Inc. 157
Planet U 265
Player's Inc. 85
Players Theatre 121
Plaza Builders Inc. 196
Point Loma College 363
Polaris Venture Partners 207
Polaroid-Popshots 375
Polloni Design 217
Popeyes Chicken & Biscuits 73
Population Reference Bureau MEASURE 357
Port Authority of NY & NJ 157
Port Columbus Executive Park 121
Port of Pittsburgh 129
Portland Public Market 187
Post Tools 58
Pottery Barn 371
Potts Design 273
PR Newswire 157
Prairie Print 333
Pratt & Whitney 240
Praxair 7
Precision Color, Inc. 284
Precision Mowing & Lawn Maintenanc 289
Premier Bank 208
Premier Banks 345
Premise Communication System 141
Premium Distributors 167
Presage 231
Presidio Systems 54
Preview Travel 161
Price Waterhouse LLP 345
Prime Companies, Inc. 127
Primerica 5
PrimeStar Satellite TV 185
Primetech, Inc. 145
Printech 247
Prism Systems 215
Procter & Gamble 69
Procurement & Logistics Dept./Southe 135
Produccion Dinamica 283
Produce One 176
Professional Practice Environments 139
Professional Reclamation Inc. 13
Prominet Corp. (now Lucent) 261
Promotions Specialties 293
Property Prep 233
ProTix, Inc. 61
Provident 277
Public Employees Health Program 247, 249
Public Executions 317
Puerto Rico Tourism & Commerce 105
Pulaski County Public Library 317
Pump Records 110
Pure, Inc. 159
PuriLens, Inc. 113
Purple Moon Dance Project 341

Q

Q101 Radio 122
QuadraSeps 337
Quaker 375
Quaker State Corporation 94
Quality Classics 233
Quantitative Capital Partners 335
Quantum 153
Quebecor Integrated Media 270
Queen of Clean 259
Quester Technology/AL Shultz Advertisi 61

R

R & R Transportation Services 175
R. B., Inc. 284
R.J.R. Foods, Inc. 94
Raccoon River Brewing Company 169
Racine Raiders Football 293
Racotek 195
Radius 273
Rage Magazine 379
Rainbowworld 259
Raintree Homes 33
Ralph Licastro C.P.A. 235
Ramsey County Humane Society 257
Randall Museum Friends 265
RAPAX 235
Raritan 240
Raytheon Corporation 343
RCG Information Technology 345
Reality Technologies, Inc. 159
Red Mountain Park 45
Red Tomato Inc. 215
Redman Moving & Storage 248
Reel City Productions 161
Reflect Inc. 300
Rege Creative 125
Reily Electrical 208
Release Software 369
Rembrent Productions 195
Remediation Resources, Inc. 235
Remodelers Workshop 235
Renaissance Cosmetics Inc. 71
Rendition 273
Rendition Software 261
Reptile Artists Agent 363
Republic of Tea 233
Republic Pictures 199
Resonate 102
Resurrection Health Care 224
Reunion Arena 317
Revell & Associates 337
Ribbit 315
Rice Paper, Inc. 215
Richard Reens 315
Rick Sippel/Sippel Photography 347
Riffels Coffee Company 331
Righter Corporation 303
Ringo Starr/Sierra Tucson Foundation 250
Rite Hite Corporation 361
Rittenhouse Optical 283
River North Association 213
River Road Brewery 250
River View Golf Course 253
Riverfront Park 211
Riverside 325
Riverside Medical Center 257
Riverwalk San Antonio Video 37
Rivery 325
RKS Design, Inc. 165
Roadway "caliber" 5
Robert Reck Photography 87
Robinson Marketing 81
Robinson Racing Products 33
Rock and Roll Hall of Fame and Museum 17
Rock Creek Aluminum 159
Rock Creek Technology 131
Rock Island Studios 331, 333
Rocket Productions 153
Rockland Corporation 289
Rockwell 347
Rocky Creek Bakehouse 353
Rocky Mountain Translators 291
Rod Ralston Photography 269
Roehm Renovations 297
Rollerblade, Inc. (RB) 377
Rolling Stone 379
Romanow Container 263
Ronald Emmerling Design, Inc. 93
Ronald H. Rasmussen Assoc. 153
Roto-Rooter 17
Rousso+Associates, Inc. 311
Route 66/Mirage 131
Rowdy Boards 17
Royal Rack 99
Royalty Cruise Line ©1991 247
RPM Investment 127
Rumble 325
Run for Christ 121
Russian-American Music Association 169
Rutenberg Homes 33
Rutgers University School of Managemen 38
RVP (Recreational Vehicle Products) 49

S

S. Asimakopoulas Cafe 139
S.C. Johnson & Son, Inc. 295, 297, 328
S.M.A.R.T. 106
Saab Cars USA, Inc. 347
Saban 73
Saber Software 261
Saint Francis Interfaith Center 293
Salem State College 141
Salisbury Studios 62
Salon et Soleil 17
Salt Lake Acting Co. 249
Salty Dog Production, Inc. 237
Salus Media 300
Salzman International 341
Samaritan 53
Samsung 5
Samuels & Nudelman 343
Samuels Yoelin Kantor Seymour & Spinrad 343
San Antonio Parks & Recreation JazzSale 37
San Antonio Sports Foundation 37
San Diego Gas & Electric (Coyote Divis 190
San Diego Wild Animal Park 228
San Francisco Clothing 101
San Francisco Food Bank 161
Sandford Color Corporation 135
Sandia Imaging 281
Sandoz/Novartis 57
Santa Monica/Malibu School District 263

Sara Lee 146
Saratoga Semiconductor 61
Savage 233
Sazaby, Inc. 172
Scana 7
Scheaffer Collection Agency 13
Schmid 171
Schoonover 91
Schwan's Sales Ent. 223
Sciarabba & Walker 369
Scient 33
SCIMAT Scientific Machinery, Inc. 69
Scitex Corporation Ltd. 41
Scotland Yards 109
Scott Braman Photography 139
Scott Brown Design 102
Scott Paper Company 328
Scott Stoll Photography 237
Scottsdale Film Festival 245
Screenz 361
Scripps 7
Search Alliance 239
SeaSea Multi-Hulls 30
Seattle Symphony 121
Second Opinion Interiors 135
2nd Swing 187
Security Associates International 81
Security Dynamics 261
Sega of America 199, 203
Sell Track 317
Sentius Corporation 145
Sequoia Technology 204
Serrano Interiors 117
SF Giants 53
SF Symphony 53
Shade 153
Shadow Wood 33
Shadyside Chamber of Commerce 247
Shafor Johnson Architects 355
Shandwick USA/Jewish Federation of St. 180
Shawmut Capital 91
Shear Edge 189
Shears 117
Sheerland Forests 189
Shell Oil Company 21
Sheraton Washington Hotel 189
Sherpa 61
SheWear 305
SHIELD Healthcare Centers 351
Shields Design 2
Shinkosky Remodeling & Design 200
Shoalwater Bay Oyster Co. 323
Shokt 235
Shore Scores 185
Shower Head 117
Sigma Software Inc. 289
Signal Bank 196
Signature Group 167
Silicon Graphics 189
Silver Creek Industries 293
Silvester Tafuro Design Inc. 245
Simantel Group 297
Simco 73
Simon DeBartolo Group 14
Sinclair Community College 353
Sinogen 141
Skaneateles Country Club 127
Skirball Cultural Center 110
Sky Chefs 240
Skyline Enterprises, Inc. 357
SmartShield Sunscreens, LTD. 81
Smith Kline Beecham 274
Smithsonian Institution 85
Sneaker Sisters 369
Software Solutions 309
Solaris Group 161
Solectek 67
Solid Solutions 335
Solutia 41
Solutions Planning Group 22
Somerset 343
Songsmith 26
Sonic 7
Sonics & Materials Inc 137
Sound Advice 253
South Umpqua Bank 273
Southeast Asian Studies Association 375
Southeastern Wisconsin Regional Canc 293
Southern Company 7
Southern Engineering Company 311
Southern Florida Bank/Wilson Communica 54
Southern Oregon Appraisal Services 175
Southern Oregon Hand Rehabilitatio 175
Southland Corporation 317
Southwest School of Music 251
Southwest Traditions 251
Space Age Advertising, Inc. 161
SPACES 91
Spalding Sports Worldwide 274
Spark Holdings 17
Spectrum HoloByte 303
Spiegel, Inc. 213, 355, 359
Splash! Vacation Magazine Amateur Phot 315
Spokane Airport System 211
Spokane Valley Chamber of Commerce 211
Sport Sling 341
Sports Lab 117
Sports Metaskills 114
Sports Office 117
Sports Solutions 331
Springbrook Commons/Gatehouse Cos. 165
Sprint 231
Sprout Group 122
Square D 176, 207
St. Cloud Technical College 361
St. Elizabeth Hospital's Wilton P. H 30
St. Helens Sparkling Mountain Water 254
St. John's 239
St. John's Hospital 175
St. John's Orthopaedic Services 29
St. Louis Blues, NHL 129

St. Louis Public Schools 14
St. Paul's Episcopal Day School 125
Stacks' 149
Stahl Design Inc. 269
Standard Uniform 259
Starbucks Coffee Co. 65, 149
Starland Cafe 203
Starret 305
Starstream Communications 377
Starter Corporation 279
State Street Cafe 34
States Industries 283
Sterling Imaging Radiology & Mammograp 317
Sterner Lighting System Inc. 195
Steuben Child Care Project 204
Steve Marsel Studio 211
Steven Guarnaccia 37
Stone Center/Wellesley Centers for Wom 273
Stonegate 327
Stoneridge 313
Story Time 13
Strategic Focus Consulting 34
Strawberry Lake 377
Street Savage 117
Struct-A-Lite 171
Studio Archetype Design (formerly Clem 233
Studio E / Hok Architects 183
Successmaker Solo 17
Summa Care/Collagen Corp. 300
Summerfield 313
Summit Advertising 295
Summit Consulting Group 159
Summit Entertainment 199
Summit Partners 159
Summit Strategies, Inc. 129
Summitt Construction 281
Sun + Moon 122
Sun Graphix 284
Sun Microsystems 57
SunGard AMS 253
Sunhouse 185
Sunset Decks 369
Sunset Tennis Classic 287
SUNY 373
Superior Battery Mfg. Company 315
Superior Brands, Inc. 94
Superior Pacific 7
Supon Design Group/Intnl logos & TM 3 45
Surgery Centers of the Desert 279
SurLuster 171
Susquehanna Addiction Center 200
SVI Inc. 297
Swan Brothers Dairy, Inc. 333
Sweet Magnolia Lingerie 283
Sylvestre Franc/Hair Salon 169
Symantec Corporation 57
Symbion, Inc. 291
Symbiotics 259
Synergy 281
Synergy Partners 245
Synetics 149
Synteni 179

T

T+T Design 213
T. Marzetti Company 327
T. Rowe Price 145
T.H. Quest 117
Take The Lead, Inc. 239
Tallgrass Prairie Producers 57
Tandem 153
Tangerine 179
Tannenbaum's Old Market Florist 257
Tanya's Soup Kitchen 339
Tapawingo National Golf Club 295
Tapestry International 37
Tara Labs 175
TARGET Greatland 199
Target Stores 361
Tater Knob Pottery & Farm 321
Taxi Service Co. 145
Taylor Guitars 193, 217
Taylor Mathis 309
TBS - Tokyo Broadcasting System 162
Team Mad Dog 319
Tech-Pro Inc. 371
Technology Chambers 149
Technology Source 14
Tee Shirt Company 217, 219
Telcom Insurance Group 137
Telecel 71
Telecellular, Inc. 135
Teledesic Corporation 269
Teledyne 146
Telesales 261
Telesis Health Care 135
Telesuite 313
Televentures 109
Teloquent 261
Telus 7
Temple University 139
Tenneco 7
Tepper Innovations 175
Terra Firma Consulting 253
Terra International 365
Territorial Savings 365
Texas Christian University Graphic Des 187
Texas Office Products 30
Texas Utilities Electric Company 231
Thermolase Corporation 347
30sixty design, Inc. 235
Thomas Hayward 21
Thomas Register 175
3-D Inc. 21
3G Design & Illustration 313
3M 53
Three Rivers Stadium 129
TIAA CREF 99
Tian-Tan Carpets 105
Tickets Now, Inc. 132

The Benedum Center for the Performing Arts 129
The Bon Marché via Leslie Phinney 101
The Boston Plan for Excellence in the 171
The Buffalo Club 109
The Butcher Company 127
The Cat/Northumberland 45
The Center For Rural Development 321
The Child Care Company 371
The Children's Doctors 273
The Children's Hospital 157
The Clorox Company 223
The Coffee Millers 57
The Community Foundation Serving Bould 291
The Container Store 109
The Creative Center 253
The Dallas Symphony Orchestra 319
The Davis Academy 309
The Democratic Cause 169
The Diamond Collection 279
The Docks 295
The Educators Network 239
The Fairchild Corporation 113
The Family Place 319
The Fantastic World of Gourmet Chocola 21
The Foundation Center 377
The Freedom Forum 196
The Fulcrum Network, Inc. 213
The Galbreath Comany 121
The Gauntlett Group 171
The Genesis Institute 335
The Gillette Company 5
The GlobalServe Corporation 17
The Graphics Shop 348
The Great Atlantic and Pacific Tea Com 114
The Greater Dallas Chamber 321
The Gunlocke Company 58
The Hayes Co., Inc. 331
The Hayes Company, Inc. 333, 339
The Hernia Institute 183
The Hertz Corporation 305
The Hilton Head Co. 204
The Hotel Juliana/Kimpton Hotel Group 131
The Iams Company 85
The IBM PC Company 57
The Independent School 49
The Independent School—3 Level Privat 53
The Inter Exchange Group 363
The Investment Properties Group 114
The Invisions Group 110
The Jerde Partnership 141
The Journey to Teams 217
The Ken Roberts Company 337
The Keys (rep. Mario Carsollo) 253
The Kinsey Institute 135
The Kitchen 141
The Kossow Corp. 157
The Lacrosse Foundation 369
The Learning Company 161
The Legacy Group (Estate Planners) 132
The Loop Corporation 207
The Masters Group 190, 220
The Mentoring Institute 183
The Merritt Co. 110
The Metro Companies 311
The Miller Band 193
The Minnesota Zoo 34
The Mutual Life Insurance Company of N 231
The Nasdaq Stock Market 135
The Oasis 327
The Ohio State University 121
The Orchard 185
"The Park" 237
The Park School 259
The Performing Arts League of Philadel 18
The Praedium Group 87
The Preference Group 373
The Print Company 143
The Printing Source 132
The Racer's Group 287
The Realty Group 375
The Richard E. Jacobs Group 153
The Ridge 190
The Riverside Church/Partnerships of H 91
The Sambistas 180
The San Damiano Players 129
The San Diego Zoo 228
The Sci-Fi Channel 195
The Shubert Organization 343
The Spangler Design Team 371
The Sports Club/LA 369
The Spot 245
The St. Paul 7
The Stables 335
The Summit at Snoqualmie 266
The Tai Ping Yang Westin— Shanghai 207
The Trails 323
The University of California 149
The Vein Center 180
The Venetian Hotel & Resort 195
The Visual Group 145
The Weaving Workshop, Inc. 213
The West Corporation 311
The Westin Mission Hills 279
The Wexan Group, Ltd. 359
The Wharton School University of Penns 253
The Winchester Group 253
Theis Doolittle Associates 125
Ther Merit System/Jefferson Co. Person 45
Thermolase Corporation 347

TIG Holdings, Inc. 343
Tiger Transport Services 357
Tigers Success Series 211
Timber Creek 7
Timberland Steakhouse & Grill 337
Time Life Music 270
TimeBridge Technologies 167
Title Nine Sports 81
TNT 74
To The Point 145
Tocqueville Asset Mgmt. 113
Toll Gate Radiology 347
Tom Lincoln Inc. 263
Tom Thumb - Page 317
Torchia Associates 359
Tortilla Factory 337
Tortilla Ventures 67
Toscana Restaurant 110
Touch Fitness 239
Touchscreen Media Group 305
Towson Orthopaedic Associates 283
Tracy Sabin Graphic Design 193
TradeLink America, Inc. 215
Trammell Crow Company 167
TransAmerica 33
Transamerica 53
Transcontinental Properties 245
Transcore 82
Transworld Lubricants, Inc. 74
TransWorld Video Lab, Inc. 348
Travelers Group 7
Treasured Moments 176
Treasures of China 74
Trent Corporation 289
Triangle MLS 215
TriNet Healthcare Systems 167
Triton 325
Troy Systems 149
Truesoups 325
TRUSTEC 351
Tucson Art Expo 251
Tucson Electric Power Co. 106
TumbleDrum 53
Tumi Incorporated 74
Tunes & Tones 13
Tuneshare 297
Turnberry Associates 223
Turner Entertainment 193
Turnstone Systems Inc. 281
20/20 Solutions 335
20th Century Fox 379
Twin County Grocers, Inc. 41
Twin Valley 337
Tyndar House Publishers (New Living Tr 328
Typhoon 45

U

U.S. Department of Energy 91
U.S. Figure Skating Assoc. 248
UB Networks 233
Ultrafem Inc. 274
UNC Charlotte 204
Uniforms Unlimited 240
Unilever HPC, USA 69, 71
Unitas 7
United Airlines 162
United Auto Group 283
United Brands Inc. 105
United Brotherhood of Carpenters 82
United Christian Congregation 327
United States Postal Service 71, 127, 132
United Technologies 7, 231
United Van Lines 114
United Way of America 162
Universal Advisory Services, Inc. 37
Universal Bar 172
Universal Internet 287
Universal Pictures 379, 380
University Chiropractic Clinic 54
University Federal Savings & Loan 33
University Mall 10
University of Arizona 250
University of California, San Diego 190
University of Montevallo Falcons 45
University of Utah 247, 248
UNR Inc. 121
UNUM 5
UPAC, Union of Pan Asian Communiti 367
Upper Deck 219
Uptown Car Wash 193
Uptown Jazz Festival 117
US Air 53
US Employment Service, Dept. of Labor 113
US Tel 29
US Truck Body 293
USA Film Festival (1972) 325
USA Today 263
USPS Olympic 263
Utah Symphony 249

V

Vaccinex LP 367
Vail Associates, Inc. 157
Vail Valley Foundation 291
Valley Fresh Produce 339
Valliwide Bank 341
Van Kampen Merritt 365
Van Romer Chiropractic 13
Vanguard Airlines 155
Vanguard Fruit Company 343
Vanguard Management, Inc. 355
Vanguard OB/GYN 143
Vantive 54
Vaughan Walls, Inc. 351
Vellum Point 117
Veneklasen Associates 300
Ventana Productions 169
Venture Stores 179, 180
Verdi 323
Veritas Techology Inc. 373
Vernell's Candy Company 254

Version X 26
Vetra 167
Viacare, Inc. 87
Viacom, New Media 141
Viant 93
Victim's Outreach 325
Victoria Theatre Association 348, 353
Victory Coffee 172
VIDA 311
Vignette 109
Viking 159
Ville La Reine 33
Vintage Court Hotel/Kimpton Hotel Grou 131
Virginia Integrated Physicians 167
ViroLogic 281
Virtual Celebrity Productions 339
Virtual Vineyards 57
Virtuem Entertainment 363
VIS 263
Vision Service Plan 161
Vista Clara Ranch 131
Vista Control Systems 131
Vitalli 321
Vivo Software 91
VLSI Technology, Inc. 223
Volk Packaging Corporation 365
Vredenburg 327
Vuepoint, Inc. 93

W

Walder Communications, Inc. 315
Walsh Cinematography 208
Warner Bros. 199, 203
Warner Bros. Records 73
Warner Music Group 375
Warp, Inc. 162
Washington Adventist Hospital Foundati 357
Washington Cheese 323
Washington Hand Surgery Center 139
Washington's Landing 129
Water Music, Inc. 261
Water Spirits Music 189
Waters Corporation 37
Waukesha/Dresser 269
WavePath/Information Arts Inc. 54
WCBF—World Children's Baseball Fair 162
Wearhouse ltd. 253
Weiler Brush Company 67
Weiss, McCorkle & Mashburn 239
WELCH Hydraulix 367
Wellington Publishing 323
Wells Fargo Bank 101
Wesli Mancini Fabric Design 25
West Linn Paper Company 93
Western Humidor 81
Western Washington Multiple Sclerosi 345
Westhouse Design 357
Westlake Surgical Center 85
WFAN (New York) 323
White Cypress Lakes 185
Whole Health Management Inc. 196
Wichita Collegiate School 331
Wichita State Uniersity Men's Crew Tea 46
Wichita State University Shocker Crew 46
Wienstroer Painting 305
Wildwood Developer, Inc. 367
Willard Rouse Developers 254
William Morrow & Assoc. 29
Williams Construction 26
Willis Painting 317
Willows Software 93
Wireless Financial Services, Inc. 171
Wisconsin Mutual Insurance Corporati 293
Wizards of the Coast 165
Wolfrom Homes 219
Wolper Sales Agency 37
Women for Women 167
Women's Awareness Group, Penn State Un 235
Woodland Investment Co. 121
Woodstock Idea Factory 219
Working Warrior 131
World Education Center 58
World Fitness, Inc. 339
World Kids Inc. 359
World Watch 277
Worldesign Foundation 172
WouArts (Women of Untraditional Arts) 335
Wrightwood Industries 345

X

X-Century 162
XactData Corporation 266
Xando 21
Xerox Corp. 102
XL Systems 30

Y

Yale New Haven Health 155
YMCA 219
YMCA of the Rockies 157
York Spiral Stairs 303
Yoshiki Yamanchi 237
Young at Art 26
Young Presidents' Organization 117, 231
Youngs Drug Products Corp. 97
Yuppie Gourmet 293
Yury's Piano / Boston 169

Z

Z Typography 371
Zack Fine Art Photography 361
Zaro's Bread Basket 14
Zellerbach 355
Zeneca Pharmaceutical Corp. 143
Zenn Graphic Design 341
Zero G Software 145
Ziezo Modern Clothes 183
Zoë Pan-Asian Café 71
Zoetics Inc. 105
Zonk, Inc. 228
Zoological Society of Houston 17
Zunda Design Group 227